HOWE·LIBRARY

HANOVER
NEW HAMPSHIRE

HOW TO
OVERTHROW
THE
GOVERNMENT

Arianna Huffington

ReganBooks
An Imprint of HarperCollins*Publishers*

HarperCollins books may be purchased for educational, business, or sales promotional use. For information please write: Special Markets Department, HarperCollins Publishers Inc., 10 East 53rd Street, New York, NY 10022-5299.

FIRST EDITION

Designed by William Ruoto

Printed on acid-free paper.

Library of Congress Cataloging-in-Publication Data has been applied for.

ISBN 0-06-039331-9

00 01 02 03 04 ❖/RRD 10 9 8 7 6 5 4 3

To my older daughter, Christina—whose energy and optimism are an endless source of inspiration

CONTENTS

*Power never concedes anything without a demand;
it never has and it never will.*

—Frederick Douglass

Preface

It was a Washington dinner at the home of Boyden Gray, White House counsel to President Bush and a Beltway fixture. The guest list was a conservative who's who, with Mr. and Mrs. Rush Limbaugh as the guests of honor. "Why is she here?" Mrs. Limbaugh asked our hosts as I walked in. Rush's blushing Internet bride apparently was even angrier than her husband that I—who had dared question his compassion in a column—would be allowed to breathe the same air, eat the same food, and drink the same wine as the Brother Teresa of the airwaves. When I was informed of Mrs. Limbaugh's protective rage, I decided simply to make sure we were not within dinner-roll throwing distance (about twenty-five feet, I estimated) of each other for the rest of the evening.

"Is the conservative movement going to be defined by the social Darwinism and carping small-mindedness of Limbaugh, or by the generous civic-mindedness that was central to America's founding?" I had asked in the offending column. I guess the family Limbaugh—Rush, his wife, and his pettiness and vindictiveness (my, how you two have grown!)—was leaning toward the former.

The evening had only just begun, and Boyden's dining room was already looking to me like trouble: a buffet of beefs, gripes, and grudges, hidden discreetly from sight but sure to be revealed as the evening continued. While keeping an eye on the Limbaughs and the exits—two forward, two aft, one over the library wing—I tried to mingle.

In one corner I spotted Dick and Susan Armey. Susan used to have a clothing store in Virginia, and my daughters and I would occasionally stop in on a Saturday. Susan would help my girls, then five and three, play dress-up—allowing their mother to, well, also play dress-up. Her warmth and humor, coupled with the fact that she and I are both over five feet ten and like the same midcalf skirts and long jackets, made me really like Susan Armey.

So there I was, face-to-face with the Armeys for the first time since writing in a column that the House majority leader's "ersatz, insipid and duplicitous style is only bringing him contempt." I had concluded by saying that "the increasingly inescapable conclusion is that Gingrich and Armey, his presumptive heir apparent, need to go together." I didn't say where exactly, but it was clear I didn't mean Disneyland, or its new branch in Times Square. Of course, you couldn't write a political column without having an opinion about the House leadership. And that was mine.

But the repercussions of the opinions I expressed twice weekly in my column—as well as regular verbal tirades against the malign neglect of millions of Americans living in poverty in the middle of our so-called age of prosperity—were playing themselves out in this room. What has happened to Arianna? my conservative friends were asking.

So here's a little history to explain just what *has* happened to me.

For as long as I have been writing about politics—starting in my mid-twenties, while I was still living in London—there have been certain recurring themes in my work: the bankruptcy of political leaders, who work harder each year to refine and perfect the deceptions they perpetrate on the public; the death of idealism and the massive resistance to political reform; and the dangers of focusing on the blessings of prosperity while forgetting about those it leaves behind.

This largely theoretical understanding was given a human face and a new urgency in 1992. When my ex-husband was running for Congress in the idyllic county of Santa Barbara, I was exposed to another world—of homeless shelters, homes for abused children, and festering health problems in the middle of one of the richest communities in America.

I never considered concern for social justice to be the exclusive province of the Left, although many on the Right have abandoned that collective moral imperative in pursuit of a personal morality policed from above. But the closer I got to the workings of the American political system, especially through Michael's 1994 campaign for the U.S. Senate, the more aghast I became. Modern campaigns, I discovered, are so thoroughly dominated by pollsters and consultants that there's no oxygen left for ideas that might challenge the status quo.

Then came the "Republican Revolution," that Gingrich-led moment when the whole scene changed overnight—or at least seemed to. My first contact with Gingrich had come right after the 1992 election. I had given a speech in Washington challenging conservatives to activate their social conscience and bring the Biblical admonition of caring for the least among us to the very heart of public policy.

Gingrich, who happened to catch the speech on C-SPAN, called me. He told me this was precisely the direction in which he wanted to move the party, and he invited me to speak at the Republican Congressional Retreat in Princeton.

So when, during his first speech as Speaker he said that "the balanced budget . . . doesn't, in my mind, have the moral urgency of coming to grips with what's happening to the poorest Americans," I took him at his word. I assumed he meant that dealing with poverty and the breakdown in America's neglected communities would be his priority.

I'll confess, I was completely fooled. My disillusionment was gradual, and began to creep into my columns just months after Gingrich took over. Then I would hear him give a speech—as he did on the night of the Million Man March: "I don't think that any white conservative anywhere in America ought to look at Louis Farrakhan and just condemn him, without asking yourself where were you when the children died, where were you when the schools failed, where were you when they had no hope; and unless we're prepared to roll up our sleeves, reach out and say, 'I'll give you an alternative.'. . . And if the pain is so great that he makes sense then we had better be a lot more daring and a lot bolder insisting on real solutions sooner." And I would come away from the speech thinking, Oh, well, maybe he's on track again.

But by the end of 1995, his abandonment of these issues was sealed by his embracing for president Bob Dole—a backroom operator without a clear vision for the country.

So I started firing shots in my column. After all, in an earlier incarnation, when he was challenging party ortho-doxies, Gingrich himself had said, "We are committed to ideas, not to men or a man. . . . We're with Reagan if he's Teddy Roosevelt, against him if he's William Howard Taft." But his attitude toward what he saw as my defection was Stalinist. In 1998 I published a column criticizing Gingrich, among others, for whining that Washington had lost the war on drugs. "Conservatives who have been saying for years that the government in Washington can never win the war on poverty," I wrote, "are now blaming insufficient government in Washington for losing the war on drugs." I got a handwritten note from him, which I have framed: "Your column is strategically counterproduc-tive." (Not "wrong," you see, but "counterproductive.") "What good does it do to take on your friends two months before the election?"

Some of my friends kept their feelings to themselves. Back at Boyden Gray's dinner, Dick Armey, ever the politician, simply exchanged pleasantries with me, ignor-ing the fact that I had wished him out of a job. But Susan spoke her mind. "Arianna," she said, "how could you do that? How could you say those things about Dick? You were our friend." I mumbled some stock phrases about how it wasn't personal, just a reflection of our different political views, but Susan was hurt rather than angry, and that's always much harder to deal with.

Thankfully, that squirm-inducing moment was inter-rupted by our host urging us on to dinner. Four round tables with calligraphed place cards awaited us. I found my seat between Senator Bill Frist and columnist Tony Snow. I was already deep in conversation with the senator about the Washington school our kids attended when I noticed that Susan had just taken her seat across from me. The Limbaughs, mercifully, were seated at a different table, but I remained very aware of my unfinished conversation with Susan. So when I saw her get up from the table, I followed her. We stood in the hallway for twenty minutes, talking— me trying to explain why it's no use even trying to write about politics if you censor yourself when it comes to your friends, Susan insisting that loyalty to one's friends is a higher principle and that if you can't say something nice . . .

We were completely engaged in our conversation, having missed dessert, when Dick, who despite his flaws as a politician (I'd rather not get started on that) has flawless social graces, came to find out what was going on. We're fine, we both said. After he left, we hugged each other. If we couldn't be allies, we could strike up a détente. Or at least most-favored-nation status.

Of course, loyalty to one's friends is an important principle. But so is writing what you believe—otherwise, why bother to write at all? In any case, it's becoming harder and harder to reconcile the personal and the political, especially given their angry conflation in the Washington Bile-way.

I had further confirmation of this a few months later at a friend's wedding in Washington. It turned out that the best man was campaign consultant Bob Shrum. Oh no, I thought, as I saw him walk down the aisle. I'd just written a column slamming him for his work on Al Checchi's

failed bid for governor of California—a particularly fetid
example of the nasty, small-minded campaigns that are
befouling our political air. The vicious ads he ran had the
effect of making Checchi, who began the campaign looking like Tony Perkins at the start of *Psycho*, look like
Perkins at the end of *Psycho*.

At the lunch following the wedding, Shrum, looking very
elegant—a morning coat and tails can have that effect—had
trouble mustering a smile. It was a clear departure from the
past. Shrum and I had locked horns on many occasions on
Crossfire, but it was always clear that we liked each other. I
had known his wife even before they were married, and—
this was the hardest part—he had been exceptionally nice
helping me with my seven-year-old and my carry-on lug-
gage on a red-eye flight to Washington.

At one point during the lunch, our paths crossed. "If I
had wanted to be critical about you," he said, "I would
have called you and told you on the phone instead of
putting it in a column."

But what would that have accomplished? The fractures
in our political system are too severe for me—or anyone
else—to hold our tongues in the public forum. In any case,
what I was leveling wasn't a personal criticism, it was an
attempt to highlight how consultants and pollsters hijack
the political process and—with the help of their candidates—reduce everything to the lowest common sound
bite–able denominator.

How strongly I feel about the degradation of our politics
is obvious from this book's title: *How to Overthrow the
Government*. What do I mean? If you've been at all engaged

with the political system in the past decade—and especially if you've come to feel disengaged from the system—you already know.

Many of those who regularly read my column know what I mean, and their e-mails over the last few years have confirmed it: "I have been an active Republican for years, but I'm now completely disenchanted with my party." "I have been working for a Democratic congressman for years on the Hill—please do not use my name—but I'm very let down by the direction of the Democrats." "I have given up on both political parties. I don't even vote anymore."

Anyone who's ever held out hope for a new movement or leader on a white horse to come along and shake up the system should also know what I mean—even if you've been let down before. That means you, former Contract with America supporters. That means you, the millions of Americans who voted for Ross Perot in 1992 or 1996, or who were tempted by any of the other outsider candidates who've reared their heads in this decade. That means you, lifelong Democrats who've spent the Clinton years wondering how many millions are being left out of our "unprecedented prosperity." And that means you, too, the thousands of activists who descended on Seattle and shook the Washington establishment down to its complacent core.

What I mean is simple: Our government is no longer serving us.

While it attends to the needs of the few—lucky investors making their fortunes on Wall Street—far too many of our fellow Americans are building houses of cards on Main Street. We now hold more than $1.3 trillion in consumer debt, with credit card debt nearly tripling since 1992; not surprisingly, a record number of us filed for bankruptcy last year.

Our government today is slow, unfair, corrupt, and peopled by politicians living on graft and sinecure. And, most troubling of all, it's become notoriously resistant to reform. Election after election, new candidates step up to the podium, exhorting us to throw the bums out and let them, the reformers, in to clean house. And election after election we watch as they take possession of their predecessors' cushy jobs, take money from glad-handing lobbyists, and slowly but surely become overtaken by the seductive allure of incumbency.

It's this vicious cycle that explains why 35 million Americans are living in poverty and more children are homeless than at any time since the Great Depression; why middle-income Americans are saddled with crippling levels of debt; why our children attend drug-ridden schools where they are not safe and cannot learn.

The fact is, beneath the thin veneer of prosperity our politicians seem so eager to celebrate, America is a fast-ticking time bomb.

It's time to do something about it, before the clock runs out.

It's time to stop patting ourselves on our prosperous backs, and start finding new ways to help the people left out in the cold. It's time to realize that our government is no longer merely "influenced" by corporate contributions—for all practical purposes its every move is predetermined by them. It's time to recognize that politicians have become more responsive to their poll-wielding consultants than to the true needs of the country.

And it's well past time to acknowledge that the two-party system is bankrupt, that the very process by which we elect our leaders has been seriously compromised by the influx of special interest money.

The Clinton era has been dominated by politicians offering small solutions to small problems. But this year that era is coming to an end. What we need in the new century are dramatic solutions and bold leaders. If we want our democracy to survive—if we are to honor the ideals of the leaders who conceived of this system in the first place—we must have the courage to challenge the status quo as they themselves did.

And the first step will be for the American people to take back their country—to overthrow a governmental system that has gone rotten at the core, and replace it with a reinvigorated democracy that serves all the people, all the time.

Let us begin.

1

A TALE OF TWO NATIONS

We live in a democracy universally acknowledged to be the greatest governing system in the world. But a democracy is only as strong as it is responsive to *all* of its citizens. While our current government crows about the endless rain of profit on Wall Street, average Americans are sitting back and wondering, What about me? What about my children? What about their lousy school? What about my retirement, our health care?

And we have no faith in our elected leaders to do anything about it. The economic boom of the '90s has masked a looming national crisis: a corrupt political system that auctions off public policy to the highest bidder, and leaves the overwhelming majority of Americans feeling alienated from their own government.

American politics is broken—under the thumb of a small corporate elite using its financial clout to control both parties' political agendas. The founding democratic principle of "one man, one vote" has been replaced by the new math of special interests: thousands of lobbyists plus multimillions of dollars equal access and influence out of the reach of ordinary citizens.

From 1997 to 1999, according to the Center for Responsive Politics, the number of registered lobbyists in Washington grew by 37 percent, to more than 20,000, while the amount of money they spent reached $1.42 billion. Crunch the numbers: That's roughly 38 lobbyists for each member of Congress. Like a swarm of ravenous termites reducing a house to sawdust, they are making a meal out of the foundations of our democracy.

And what are we ordinary Americans doing about it? Not much—at least not yet.

Almost two out of three Americans didn't even bother to vote in the last election—115 million eligible voters failed to exercise a right for which a few months later people were willing to die in East Timor, where the turnout was 98.6 percent.

Back at home, among the 36 percent who did vote, many held their noses while voting for the candidate they abhorred the least. According to the Committee for the Study of the American Electorate, since the 1960s national voter participation has fallen more than 25 percent, the largest and longest slide in our country's history. Twenty-five million Americans who used to vote now choose not to.

And if a democracy is only as healthy as its voters, then its life expectancy depends on the involvement of its youngest voters. So it's especially troubling that young people, together with poor people, have the lowest turnout and the steepest decline in participation. Only 20 percent of Americans aged eighteen to twenty-four voted in the 1998 elections. Despite the Rock the Vote campaign, and MTV's growing political forays, as of 1996 fewer than half of America's eighteen- to twenty-four-year-olds had even registered to vote.

Even the idealists are getting discouraged—they're pushing a product no one likes. "How do you sell political participation," Rock the Vote director Seth Matlins asked, "when the state of politics is just so repulsive?" The group's founder, Jeff Ayeroff, concurs: "If 1992 was about enlightenment, then we're in the dark ages now."

When turnout among the young shrinks from 50 percent in 1972 to 32 percent in 1996, it's foolish to keep pretending our democratic future is safe. With that rate of decline, in forty years *nobody* will be voting.

It's a stinging repudiation of the rotten spectacle our elections have become that despite a Motor Voter–fueled surge in voter registration—a net increase of 5.5 million from 1994 to 1998—voter turnout declined by 2.5 million. Registration drives have only increased the number of eligible people choosing not to vote.

The American people aren't satisfied by this—and they aren't stupid. Since 1964, the University of Michigan's National Election Studies has regularly asked eligible voters a simple question: whether, in their opinion, the U.S. government is run "for the benefit of all" or "by a few big interests." In 1998, nearly two-thirds—64 percent—answered "a few big interests," a complete reversal of the electorate's opinion in 1964. Sixty-two percent—compared to 36 percent in 1964—agreed with the statement, "Public officials don't care much what people like me think."

The Michigan study also found that attitudes toward government are clearly divided along lines of class and education. The least-educated respondents agreed much more often (58 percent) than the most-educated (24 percent) that people have no say in their government. The same was true in terms of income. About half of all lower-income Americans feels disenfranchised from the political process, compared with only 18 percent of those whose income is in the top 5 percent. And unskilled workers are nearly twice as likely to feel this way as professionals—64 percent to 33 percent.

Shouldn't the opposite be the case? Shouldn't those with the most have the least to expect from our collective efforts, and those with the least have the most to expect? Isn't that what's meant by comforting the afflicted? If the least educated and the poorest among us—those at society's margins—have the lowest expectations of government accountability and responsiveness, what does that say about our society?

Millions of voters are feeling ignored by politicians more concerned with staying in power than with serving the people. And when a candidate wins, it becomes increasingly unlikely that he or she will ever lose. In 1998, House incumbents ended up running unopposed in 95 districts, while in 127 they faced only token opposition. It's no surprise then that a record 98.5 percent of them were reelected, collecting an average of more than 70 percent of the vote. In an ideal world, a people that reelects almost 99 percent of its leaders would seem to be happy with them. But in the real world, you only have to win once to become a permanent fixture in a rotting political establishment.

Of course, our politicians pay plenty of lip service to reform. But in reality, under our current system, actual efforts to overhaul government last about as long as Bill Clinton's and Newt Gingrich's famous handshake in New Hampshire, when they assured the nation that they were ready to enact reform.

Our political world is divided into two camps: those who consider plummeting turnout and high disengagement a serious threat to our democracy, and those who do not. The problem is that almost every elected official and political consultant is in the latter camp. Which isn't so surprising when you consider how many of them owe their jobs to the worst aspects of the system.

More interesting is what's happening in the first camp, where an ad hoc alliance is bringing together such unlikely bedfellows as Democratic power broker Robert Strauss, perennial activist Ralph Nader, Republican presidential candidate John McCain, and conservative Congressman Peter Hoekstra. Strauss has warned his party-mates about the "brutal truth" of an "unprecedented disengagement from politics by the American people," while Nader notes that "citizens are staying away from the polls in droves because of their disgust, distrust, despair and disillusionment with tweedle-dum, tweedle-dee politics." Hoekstra is even bleaker: "Voter satisfaction and participation are at or near all-time lows. Why should a person vote? And what for?

Candidates who prefer smear over substance, money over principle and length of service over tangible action?"

The defenders of the status quo have no problem with disaffected citizens dropping out—it keeps them from making waves. Better that they get out than care enough to stay in and vote against them. In many ways, it is easier to play to, control, and manipulate a smaller audience. The key is to keep giving them no alternatives until they give up. "In general, the public is satisfied," former Rep. Vic Fazio (D-Calif.) has said, "or as satisfied as they will ever be." No candidate who demonstrates such blithe complacency should be allowed to retire comfortably after twenty years in office, as Fazio did in 1998. He should be kicked to the curb at the next election.

So should any candidate who waxes lyrical about our "unprecedented prosperity" without acknowledging that millions are being left out of it. "Xers may well be the first generation whose lifetime earnings will be less than their parents'," writes Ted Halstead, president of the New America Foundation. "Already they have the weakest middle class of any generation born in this century." Adjusted for inflation, the weekly earnings of men aged twenty to thirty-four have fallen by nearly one-third since 1973.

Getting a college education used to be a ticket out of financial insecurity. But no longer. The current crop of college graduates has seen its earnings from 1989 to 1995 fall by nearly 10 percent in relation to the previous generation— the first time that's ever happened.

At the same time, personal debt has skyrocketed. Americans from twenty-two to thirty-three years old have the greatest personal debt level of any age group. This includes over $2,000 per person in credit card debt, which is carried by 62 percent of Xers. They also suffer the greatest anxiety over debt, with nearly half reporting that it "concerns them a lot."

In fact, up to 60 percent of all Americans carry some credit card debt. In what they proudly term the "democratization of credit," credit card companies in 1998 extended over $2.5 trillion in debt. Americans' personal credit card debt level has increased to over half a trillion dollars in 1998. All that personal debt has turned our economy into a ticking bomb. One family in sixty-eight filed for bankruptcy in 1998—more than saw a child graduate from college. Meanwhile, Congress has proposed legislation that would make it much harder for consumers to erase their debt by declaring bankruptcy.

Not only is this era of prosperity built on a house of cards, the crisis goes much deeper than just the immediate concerns of middle class debtors. "Most things are going right for our country," the president has said—but it's a disturbing statement to anyone who's keeping an eye on the other America: nearly 700,000 layoffs in 1998, 56 percent more than the year before; the biggest one-month surge in unemployment claims in six years; and a study of four Northwest states that revealed more than half of the available jobs do not pay a living wage.

While conventional wisdom holds that America is thriving, it's hard to escape the notion that the United States has been torn in two—divided between a moneyed elite getting rich from globalization and an increasing number of citizens left choking on the dust of Wall Street's galloping bulls. Corporate America has never been more robust; in fact, since 1990—the supposed end of the Greed Decade—the pay of CEOs has gone up more than 440 percent. At a time when the wealth is supposedly spreading, income inequality is higher than ever.

In 1964, 36 million Americans lived in poverty. Thirty-five years and a War on Poverty later, 35.6 million remain below the poverty line.

In the spring of 1999, the Casey Foundation's "Kids Count" report identified 9.2 million children "growing up with a collection of disadvantages that are cause for exceptional alarm," and focused on "the persistent exclusion of far too many of our children and families from the full promise of American life." "Kids Count" directly contradicts the rosy data being spun from both ends of Pennsylvania Avenue, drawing attention to the burgeoning number of children—5.6 million—in families of the working poor. Despite the economic boom and an unemployment rate at a twenty-five-year low, the U.S. child poverty rate remains at 21 percent—the highest in the developed world.

Around the same time, the United Way of Los Angeles released its "Tale of Two Cities" report, spotlighting the growing disparities in the richest city in the nation and concluding that "economic conditions for children have not been so precarious since the Great Depression." One out of three children in Los Angeles lives below the poverty level; the number of abused children placed in foster care has risen 86 percent in the past decade; and even with the recent drop in violent crime, homicide is still the largest single cause of death for children under eighteen.

The story isn't much different around the rest of the country. According to officials of thirty major cities surveyed by the U.S. Conference of Mayors "the strong economy has had very little positive impact on hunger and homelessness." Ninety-three percent of those responding expected the demand for emergency shelter to increase further next year. Second Harvest, the biggest national network of food banks, says its clientele is growing by 10 percent a year—a rate not yet rivaling Starbucks, but demonstrating the growing divide.

A flurry of reports last summer further documented the split between the country's rich and poor:

According to the Center on Budget and Policy Priorities, the poorest fifth of single-mother families lost an average of $577 a year in income and benefits between 1995 and 1997. The Center also projected that the poorest fifth of Americans will be left with 9 percent less than they had in 1977 and the richest fifth with 43 percent more—a record level for the after-tax income gap between rich and poor.

A Children's Defense Fund study, meanwhile, showed that in one year—from 1996 to 1997—the number of children living in extreme poverty (that is, making *less than half* of poverty-level income) rose by 26 percent among single-mother families.

According to the Urban Institute, the median annual income of welfare recipients—including those with children—

who left the rolls for jobs between 1995 and 1997 was $13,788. They may have escaped welfare, but they certainly haven't shaken poverty.

During a recent speech at the Congressional Faith and Politics Institute, I was asked what we could do to raise the profile of poverty in this country. "Put a Republican back in the White House," I replied—not because he would do more for the poor, but because it might inspire the champions of the Left to reunite with their estranged consciences and regain their voices.

During the 1980s, Democrats were quick to deride Ronald Reagan's claims of "Morning in America," with New York Governor Mario Cuomo famously, and rightly, chiding the Great Communicator's vision of "a shining city on a hill" by saying, "There is despair, Mr. President, in faces you never see, in the places you never visit in your shining city." But Cuomo, and many of the most vocal Democrats of the '80s, suddenly came down with laryngitis in the '90s, their cries of outrage replaced by cocktail chatter about the soaring NASDAQ. How many of the faces ignored by Reagan have Democratic leaders seen lately? If the answer is more than zero, they've kept it to themselves.

It was the original "compassionate conservative," Teddy Roosevelt, who called the presidency a "bully pulpit." Unfortunately, the president has failed to use that pulpit to rally Americans on behalf of the poor. Overnight hospital stays, car safety belts, and school uniforms have all merited bully pulpit time, but not the poor. Talk about poverty has been replaced by the assertion that, as Clinton put it in a 1999 radio address, "Finally the rising tide of our economy is lifting all boats."

Like one of those single-issue cable networks, the White House has given us the twenty-four-hour Boom Channel—All Prosperity, All The Time (with, of course, lots and lots of commercial sponsors). Prosperity is the theme of Campaign 2000; the candidates are dishing it out like burgers and watermelon at a straw-poll picnic. Listening to them talk, it's as if they're auditioning not for leader of the free world, but for Regis Philbin's gig on *Who Wants to Be a Millionaire?*

In announcing his candidacy last September (candidates are now allotted, apparently by federal law, roughly half a dozen "announcements," which the media obligingly cover), Bill Bradley repeatedly used the P-word. First he said he was running "to guard the economic fundamentals of our prosperity," presumably the way he used to cover players in the NBA. He then called for "a deeper prosperity . . . a prosperity that makes us feel rich inside as well as out."

What that means is anybody's guess, but even as platitude it's notable. Do you remember the days when campaign rhetoric at least tended to reach for the noble, the inspirational? But "making us feel rich inside and out"? That's more Tony Robbins than Bobby Kennedy.

Al Gore wants us to know that he, too, can pander to our love of money. "I want to keep our prosperity going," Gore said in New Hampshire, "and I know how to do it." He even vowed to make America the "world capital of prosperity." Where does he suppose the capital is now? Russia? North Korea?

Not wanting to seem soft on prosperity, George W. Bush has gone on a prosperity jag himself, determined not to cede one inch of the humming economy to his Democratic rivals. "Some in this current administration think they've invented prosperity," he said. "But they didn't invent prosperity any more than they invented the Internet." In his announcement speech (his third, I believe), Bush used the words "prosperous" or "prosperity" fifteen times. To hear him tell it, prosperity is a panacea. "We must be prosperous to keep the peace," he said, suggesting that economic wealth can even protect us from "terror and missiles and madmen." That's some bull market! Maybe by the time the year is out, the market will be healing the sick and infirm. Or turning water into stock options.

Of course, Steve Forbes is the poster child for prosperity—it's his birthright. Yet Forbes has been railing *against* Federal Reserve Chairman Alan Greenspan and "the high priests of finance at the Fed"; apparently, the current prosperity just isn't prosperous enough for Forbes & Co.

While they play drum major in this prosperity parade, our leaders are ignoring some fundamental truths. "History," Greenspan warned last October, "tells us that sharp reversals in confidence occur abruptly, most often with little advance notice. . . . A bursting bubble [is] an event incontrovertibly evident only in retrospect." In other words, when the downturn hits, watch out—it could be fast, furious, and completely unanticipated.

Playing grasshopper to Greenspan's ant, the White House has downplayed any uncertainty, with Treasury

Secretary Lawrence Summers giving officials explicit orders on what they should and shouldn't say to help prop up confidence. Apparently, if Greenspan doesn't have something nice to say about the economy, we don't want to hear anything at all. This financial fable has been so convincing that Americans spent more than they earned in the first half of 1999—often using paper profits from the stock market to fuel this binge. And there is anecdotal evidence that a growing number of people are even using money borrowed on their credit cards to invest in the market—risking money they don't have on the expectation that the market will continue to surge.

It's another example of the "irrational exuberance"—in Greenspan's memorable phrase—that is leading millions of Americans to deny basic financial realities.

So one key assumption of the prosperity parade is that it will last forever. Another is that keeping the good times roaring will lead to everyone enjoying them—without any special effort or shared sacrifice. The language of the marketplace has eclipsed any appeal to higher values. Don't worry, the market-boosters assure us—there's no need to waste time thinking of community and civic responsibility or anything beyond your own direct economic self-interest—and somehow, a nation we can be proud of will materialize.

Indeed, in the summer of 1999, when the president undertook his ninety-six-hour poverty tour—a sort of Poor-A-Palooza—it was conducted not as an appeal to the nation's conscience but as just another profit-making opportunity. "This is not about charity," said Housing and Urban Development Secretary Andrew Cuomo, not wanting to scare anybody, "it's about investment. There's money to be made." And the president's main concern seemed to be not to alarm Wall Street. "Is there a noninflationary way to add more workers?" he asked meekly. "Is there a noninflationary way to raise wages?"

It's instructive to remember that leadership hasn't always been reduced to keeping inflation low for Wall Street titans, that it didn't always answer only to the laws of supply and demand. Thirty-two years ago, when Robert Kennedy launched *his* poverty tour, he shocked the nation's conscience, holding hungry children in his arms and giving the world a set of televised images that were impossible to forget. Kennedy had faith that if the American people knew more about the poverty in their own backyard, they would respond with something greater than self-interest.

"When Robert Kennedy was assassinated, something died in America," civil rights leader Rep. John Lewis (D-Ga.) has said. "Something died in all of us." Whatever it was, Clinton buried it with his flaccid rhetoric, a pale mockery of Kennedy's stirring words. It was like watching a Vegas lounge show where ersatz legends offer up feeble renditions of your all-time favorites. They've got the look, they mimic the moves—what's missing is the soul.

Maybe the most insidious byproduct of politicians' indifference to the plight of the poor has been a drop-off in attention from the media. During the Reagan years, the plight of the homeless was never too far away from the headlines, with the president roundly criticized for his "trickle-down" economy. But during the Clinton years, as

those same trends have continued, the media, now themselves major players in the bull market game, have been
largely silent, giving the president a free pass for his "don't
look down" economy.

Media watchdogs at the *Village Voice* have traced a
nationwide decline in the frequency, prominence, and
sheer number of column inches the press has devoted to
poverty in this decade: "In the fall of 1988, *The New York
Times* devoted 50 stories to the homeless, including five
front-page pieces. This year the *Times* has run only 10
pieces in the same period; none have begun on A-1." With
a warm-and-fuzzy president who feels our pain and par-
rots back what pollsters tell him we want to hear, many
Americans must have felt relieved to be able to avert their
eyes—while the homeless were kicked off the front page,
shuffled out of public spaces, and sealed out of our political discourse.

Call it the New Callousness: the disturbing trend in our
culture toward getting the "love" out of tough love and
turning an indifferent shoulder to anyone—drug addicts,
the homeless, those behind bars—who hasn't had the good
sense to buy shares of Martha Stewart. After all, they're
getting in the way of the Panglossian message that all is
well "in this best of all possible worlds."

The New Callousness is personified by media figures
like Judge Judy Sheindlin, who, according to Australian
Associated Press, told an audience while on a book tour
Down Under that instead of attempting to control AIDS
and hepatitis by providing clean needles to drug addicts,
we should "give them all dirty needles and let them die."

More evidence of this cold spot on the national heart is all around us. In New York, Mayor Rudy (rhymes with Judge Judy) rang in the holiday season by ordering the NYPD to step up its efforts to sweep the city's streets of homeless people by arresting them for so-called "quality-of-life" crimes. Declaring that the city has not been strict enough in rousting people "who don't belong there," Giuliani claimed that the right to sleep on the streets "doesn't exist anywhere. The founding fathers never put that in the Constitution." He doesn't seem too keen on the homeless living in city shelters either: He recently announced that anyone wanting to stay in one would have to work or face expulsion—mental illness or not.

Apparently, he prefers sending them to jail, where mental-health-unit beds cost $91,000 annually. It costs $20,000 for a bed in a shelter and $12,000 for the supervised apartments that remain woefully underfunded, even though they have proven the most effective in dealing with chronic homelessness. "There were times," Mayor Rudy said, "in which we romanticized this to such an extent that we invited people to do it." Ah, yes, the romance of sleeping under the stars in a cardboard box in the dead of winter.

Proving that heartlessness cuts across party lines, Willie Brown, San Francisco's liberal mayor, oversaw his own crackdown on the homeless—just in time for his runoff election last fall against even-more-liberal rival Tom Ammiano. Brown clearly reveled in this rare chance to stake out the "conservative" position in the race—going so far as to arrest homeless advocates for handing out soup and sandwiches to the poor. "Advocate types claim I'm the most hostile" to the homeless, said Brown. "That's not true. I'm not the most generous. I'm not the most hostile. But I am the most firm." Call Tony Bennett, it's time for a rewrite: "I Lost My Heart in San Francisco."

In fact, more and more of our cities are using the police to enforce arcane laws—such as sanitation statutes that make it illegal to leave cardboard boxes in a public place— to get the homeless off the streets, including many homeless veterans who risked their lives for their country.

Ted Hayes, who has devoted his life to working with the homeless, calls the coast-to-coast crackdown "status cleansing." "For us to turn to outlawing our homeless citizens," he told me, "is a betrayal of the promise of America— 'Send these, the homeless, tempest-tossed, to me.' Perhaps the Statue of Liberty should be turned around to face this country."

Transforming human beings into nuisances—problems that must be eradicated—is a dangerous step along the deadly path of dehumanization. It takes very little to end a life that has been stripped of its humanity.

In Los Angeles last May, a fifty-five-year-old mentally ill homeless woman was shot dead by an LAPD officer for brandishing a screwdriver at him while he attempted to confiscate her shopping cart. The shooting was described by Police Chief Bernard Parks as "in policy." And in Denver, seven homeless men were recently bludgeoned to death, two of the victims beheaded.

Is this the logical endgame for a culture so intent on celebrating its "winners" that it has no room left for life's losers?

That's certainly been the case in Washington, where the only major poverty policy of the Clinton years was welfare reform. The 40 percent drop in welfare caseloads since the law was passed in 1996 has conveyed the false impression that although the poor will always be with us, there are no longer enough of them to deserve our attention. But as the available jobs dry up, what will become of the 5 million welfare recipients who left the rolls? "Welfare reform has done better at moving families off the rolls than it has at moving families out of poverty," said Lawrence Aber, director of Columbia University's Center for Children in Poverty. In other words, welfare reform has been great for swelling the ranks of the working poor.

Meanwhile, the real work of helping the poor goes on largely unnoticed.

"The problem cannot be solved from afar with a media campaign, or other safe solutions operating from a distance," says Jeffrey Canada, who runs forty-three children's programs in New York. "The only way we're going to make a difference is by placing well-trained and caring adults in the middle of what can only be called free-fire zones in our poorest communities."

But instead of using his power to lead us to take up the fight, Clinton has been lulling us to sleep, waxing rhapsodic about his successes. "Now you see the signs of the transformation everywhere," he has said. "Mothers collecting their mail with a little more pride because they know they'll see a bank statement, not a welfare check; children going to school with their heads held a little higher."

The Reverend Jim Wallis, who heads the Call to Renewal, a coalition to combat poverty, paints a very different picture from the one drawn by the president and the presidential candidates. "The new icon of poverty," he told me, "is the working mother with children. I think of the woman a colleague of mine saw at a Burger King recently. She was busing tables, but kept going back to a table in the corner where two kids were sitting. She did this several times before it became apparent that she was their mother and was supervising their homework. That woman at the Burger King is supposed to be our success story."

The real battle line of the first presidential election of the new millennium will be drawn between those who answer to their corporate donors and those who speak for that single mother at the Burger King.

Of course, Americans will never give up on the idea of making things better. This sense of hope has been summoned by Doris Haddock, also known as "Granny D," an eighty-nine-year-old grandmother who recently walked from the Pacific to the Atlantic to call attention to the desperate need for political reform. "The thousands of Americans I have met are discouraged," she says, "but they are not defeated. Without exception, they deeply love the idea of America. It is a dream they are willing to sacrifice their lives for. Many of them do. There is no separating this image of democracy from their longing for personal freedom for themselves, their family, their friends. To the extent that our government is not our own, we are not free people. . . . But the spirit of freedom is strong in the

American soul, and it is the source of our optimism and joy." She's banking that one woman walking across the country can do more than hundreds of congressmen and senators running in place.

Clearly the time has come for a new politics—a politics that will challenge the status quo and contest the conventional wisdom, that will restore integrity to government, empower ordinary citizens, and make the political process once again relevant to the lives of Americans.

It's time to remake our system of government, to rid our country of the culture of greed that has infected our politicians, weakened their consciences, and tainted their policies.

It's time to throw a tent over Washington and fumigate.

2

THE RISING TIDE OF DISCONTENT

Voters are abandoning the political process in droves—and our so-called leaders are inspiring the exodus. Our political landscape is so littered with duplicity and deceit, we've actually come to expect our leaders to lie. What once would have shocked us now barely registers. We've become inured to wrongdoing. So politicians mangle the truth—call it "spin"—and the public lets it slide, too numb to care.

Why do we tolerate spinning? I've come to the conclusion that it's because, even though we don't like it, we don't consider it really damaging. I mean, "spinning" sounds cute, almost constructive—something Penelope did while waiting for Ulysses, or Mom did to finish up a load of laundry, or what Julie Andrews did on an Alp in the *The Sound of Music*. Something that should engender indulgent smiles rather than outrage.

If we're going to do something about spinning, maybe we need to give it a slightly less adorable name. "Propaganda" would be much more apt. Joseph Goebbels, the master Nazi propagandist, described it as the "art of simplification, constant recapitulation, appealing to the instinctive and the emotional and simply ignoring unpleasant facts." Sound familiar? If not, just turn on your television on Super Tuesday.

The propagandist succeeds by claiming to be nothing more than the humble mouthpiece of "the people." And it's always a higher cause that he bravely champions—the people's will, which means the polling results from ten minutes ago. The circle is a vicious one: The more the public is duped, the more its deceivers can claim to express the public's will.

It's a perpetual motion machine that has brought our political discourse to a standstill, proving that everything Orwell said rings true today: There's no swifter route to the corruption of thought than through the corruption of language. And things have only gotten doubleplus ungood since then.

Take the campaign finance scandals, which in the end brought us no reform but rather an orgy of euphemism. Politicians, in broad daylight and with no fear of a controlling legal authority, regularly assaulted everyday speech, scornfully tossing aside the actual meanings of words. Humpty Dumpty would have been right at home. "When I use a word," he told Alice, "it means just what I choose it to mean—neither more nor less."

So the White House coffee klatches for wealthy donors were not fund-raisers, President Clinton gamely asserted, but "opportunities for citizens to discuss issues." And that infamous Buddhist temple visit, Vice President Gore protested, was "community outreach." And, according to Sen. Mitch McConnell, corporations contribute generous checks just to "participate in the democratic process"—under the gloriously euphemistic rubric of "soft money," which McConnell defends as "free speech."

At the moment, our political language is so filled with folderol that we don't even hear it anymore. Official doublespeak became notorious during the Vietnam War and Watergate, and continues today, when "legal intervention" is the phrase used to describe being shot by cops. No wonder, then, that when someone comes along who cuts through the gobbledygook, people take notice. Jesse Ventura is a prime example. Ross Perot was another—though with him the problem became that he also was (pardon the euphemism) two slices short of a full loaf.

But the king of the spinners is our president. A classic example was his sudden loss of memory on the topic of executive privilege. On a trip to Africa at the height of the Lewinsky scandal, he was asked by a reporter to justify invoking executive privilege to protect himself from Ken Starr. Without so much as a hint of blushing, he earnestly replied, "All I know is, I saw an article about it in the paper today. I haven't discussed that with the lawyers. I don't know. You should ask someone who knows." And to think he made it through Yale Law School without anyone ever mentioning executive privilege.

For those wondering why there hasn't been more public outrage at the president's deceptions, the answer can be found in the Republican lies about the 1998 budget deal.

Without so much as a by-your-leave, the Republican leaders abandoned their much touted spending caps, and, grinning giddily, explained that the $21 billion in additional spending actually constituted "supplemental spending." So supplemental spending is not spending in the same way that oral sex is not sex. "It's crazy," Sen. Rick Santorum (R-Pa.) told me. "We bust the budget, spend $21 billion of the Social Security trust fund, and everyone is making nice and using all this doublespeak so as not to hurt our chances in November."

But Republican chances *were* hurt in 1998 because in the battle between two deceivers, the more practiced, polished, and passionate one will win. When it comes to the current crop of party leaders, I'm feeling increasingly the way Mary McCarthy felt about Lillian Hellman: "Every word she writes is a lie, including 'and' and 'the.' "

The public seems to consider politicians' abuse of language and the truth to be as inevitable as carbon monoxide emissions. We don't like them, but we can't imagine a world without them. In 1998, House Majority Leader Dick Armey (R-Tex.) told the world that "an internal report at the IMF found that the fund's own activities worsened the Asian crisis. Given this report . . . how can any member of Congress explain a vote to send taxpayer dollars to the IMF?" Well, not too long after this episode of high dudgeon, he voted to send $18 billion of taxpayer dollars—not a penny less than the president requested—to the IMF. And, with a straight face, he called the modest IMF reforms that accompanied the $18 billion "a major step toward a more responsible international economic policy." Whatever. I suppose it depends on what you mean by "responsible" and what you mean by "major" and what you mean by "a."

A new expert in the Washington art of cloaking the truth in sunny rhetoric is Treasury Secretary Lawrence Summers. Harvard's youngest-ever tenured professor got to show off his skills last fall to an international audience of the finance ministers of the world's seven richest nations.

He gave the global economy a clean bill of health—putting aside the massive Russian corruption that has impoverished millions of its citizens, the ballooning U.S. trade deficit, Japan's deepest recession since World War II, and those nagging little maladies in Mexico, Brazil, and Colombia.

And while testifying before Congress a week earlier on our disastrous financial involvement with Russia, Summers used his prodigious brainpower like a squid uses ink to obfuscate the seriousness of the current crisis in which up to $150 billion was transferred out of Russia while the West was cheerleading the "reformers" and their ongoing "privatization."

"I think it's very difficult," he said, "to know what the counterfactual would be if different policies had been pursued." "Counterfactual" is a favorite Summers squid word. "And I'm not sure," he continued, "we'll ever know the answer to that counterfactual question."

It's not surprising that Summers maintains this agnostic stance. Since 1993, when he was appointed Treasury undersecretary for International Affairs, he has been responsible for U.S. policy with regard to the World Bank, the IMF, and debt negotiations—including, of course, with Russia. Summers turned a blind eye as Russian "corruptionalists" drove the country's GDP down 40 percent in the past decade to a level lower than the Netherlands, and capital investment fell to 10 percent of what it was a decade ago. As late as the spring of 1997, he called the men turning Russia into a corrupt oligarchy "a dream team."

"This is not a matter of hindsight," Rep. Ed Royce (R-Calif.), who questioned Summers at the hearing, told me. "In 1993 the Russian finance minister asked Summers not to approve a loan of $1.5 billion, on the grounds it would undermine his attempts to impose financial discipline. He warned that unconditional lending would end up offshore in Zurich."

But go tell that to Michel Camdessus, former managing director of the International Monetary Fund. Having learned nothing from being caught completely off guard by the Asian economic crisis, he echoed Summers's head-in-the-clouds pronouncements on Russia, where IMF money has been the root of nothing good. "Remember that for us Russia is a program which has worked and on which Russia, for the time being, is overperforming," he said while the IMF was meeting in Washington last year.

This denial makes sense given the revelation that a U.S. diplomat in Moscow "personally saw dozens of draft reports on economic problems that were never transmitted, while the U.S. Treasury representative blocked a negative assessment of Russia's capacity . . . by arguing it would give Larry Summers a heart attack." To this day, the official administration reaction remains, in the words of Deputy Secretary of State Strobe Talbott, "Calm down, world."

So it has become the Washington rule to withhold any news that would give the secretary of the Treasury—or likely voters—a moment's pause, let alone a coronary. And when withholding is no longer possible, start squirting your ink.

It was a long way from Summers's days as chief economist of the World Bank in the early '90s, when he wrote a memo outlining policy options for less-developed countries. "Just between you and me, shouldn't the World Bank be encouraging more migration of the dirty industries to the LDCs?" he wrote. "A given amount of health-impairing pollution should be done in the country with the lowest cost. . . . I think the economic logic behind dumping a load of toxic waste in the lowest-wage country is impeccable." During his confirmation hearings for Treasury secretary last summer, not a single senator mentioned this callous memo. Clearly, Summers has learned to bury his beliefs in more sanitized lingo. But even if he hadn't, would anyone care?

The war in Kosovo proved beyond a shadow of a doubt that spin doesn't stop at the water's edge. Executives of major newspapers and networks wrote to Defense Secretary William Cohen, complaining about "the current restrictions on the flow of information." When the same concern was raised in a question put directly to the president at the American Society of Newspaper Editors luncheon in San

Francisco, Clinton blamed the "weather," the "terrain," and the "NATO command structure," but assured the editors that "the more information we can get out there the more quickly, the better off we are." It was an eerie echo of Clinton's empty promise in 1998 to provide the press with answers to their Lewinsky-scandal questions—"more rather than less, sooner rather than later." For Clinton, apparently, every day is opposite day.

The culture of concealment also dominated Pentagon and NATO news briefings, which seemed designed to engage in what the Chinese government—a champion euphemizer—calls "guiding public opinion." "Whenever any potentially 'newsworthy' incident occurs," Dai Qing, a former reporter in China wrote, "the first decision to be made by the higher-ups is whether to cover it up." Yet another import from China, I guess.

This appeared to be the philosophy informing the Pentagon the week in April when it turned out that our forces had accidentally bombed a refugee convoy in Kosovo.

"We are quite sure that we only hit military vehicles," Pentagon spokesman Ken Bacon said forcefully on Wednesday. But what about those refugees? Bacon did his best to shift the blame: "We are receiving reports that Yugoslav aircraft have been used to attack refugee convoys in Kosovo." Major General Charles Wald played along, doing his best to silence reporters with his military expertise: "I can tell you that it's easy to tell the difference between a tractor and a tank. If there is any doubt, you just don't drop."

By Thursday morning, the Pentagon had switched from cover-up to a modified limited scapegoat hangout. NATO's acceptance of responsibility for the refugee deaths coincided with news that American-made bomb shrapnel was found amid the carnage. But by Saturday morning, with reports indicating that more refugee convoys had been hit by NATO bombs—including, perhaps, U.S.-made antipersonnel cluster bombs that spray bursts of red-hot, fin-shaped metal shrapnel—a new face appeared to take the heat at the next Pentagon briefing. "The only thing worse than making you wait for the facts," said Captain Steve Pietropaoli, "is giving you facts that turn out not to be facts." And with that Zen-like pronouncement, he took back "the fact" that NATO had bombed the convoy, and replaced it with "the fact" of an ongoing investigation, a classic stall tactic.

President Clinton's use of spin and outright lies has so diminished his credibility that he now sparkles only in venues where credibility is not an issue, like the annual White House Correspondents' Dinner—where year after year he wows 'em with his unflappable affability and polished stand-up delivery. The president may have forfeited his place next to Washington and Lincoln on Mount Rushmore, but he has more than earned the right to sub for Jay Leno. The few memorable lines his presidency has produced have been comedic ones. Intentional and otherwise.

For instance, on Chinese spying at Los Alamos, the president contradicted both his National Security adviser and his Energy secretary when he claimed that "the investigation has not yet determined for sure that espionage occurred." "I was a bit troubled," admitted an incredulous Sen. Bob Kerrey (D-Neb.), "that he said that he doesn't remember being informed of potential espionage at Los Alamos."

On Medicare, the president grandly urged Congress "to adopt what would be the most ambitious set of legislative proposals yet in my tenure," including saving "Medicare for the 21st Century." But in fact, he has refused to support the report of the Commission on the Future of Medicare, chaired by his good friend and ally Sen. John Breaux (D-La.), and has yet to offer a proposal of his own. "I'm disappointed that the president did not endorse the product that we produced," said Breaux. "Some people want an issue out of Medicare rather than solving the problem."

After watching Clinton get away with untruth after untruth, many other public figures have also adopted Spin-glish as a second language. "I'm not a politician," said Elizabeth Dole before she put her presidential campaign out of its misery, a boast as phony as Strom Thurmond's orange hair. How can a woman who served under five presidents, including as head of public liaison for the Reagan White House—as political a job as there is—claim with a straight face that she's not a politician? Maybe if politicians actually served the public, the word wouldn't be something to be ashamed of.

The only Republican presidential contender who could have walked from her Watergate apartment to the White House, Dole was allowed to get away with this kind of disingenuous talk only because the public has come to expect it from the political class. If people got this kind of chronic dissembling from family members, they'd have them committed.

And as if it isn't bad enough that politicians feel they can con us into believing anything, they also betray their innate contempt for the legislative process by baldly hijacking it for their own ends, piggybacking selfishly motivated spending allotments onto sure-thing bills—convinced that as part of the mutual protection pact known as bipartisanship, no one will ever call them on it. This auctioning of public policy to the highest bidder is as rampant as it is repulsive. And among the High Priests of Pork, none sits higher or stoops lower than the chairman of the Transportation and Infrastructure Committee, Rep. Bud Shuster (R-Pa.).

Shuster is under investigation by the House Standards of Official Conduct Committee for allegations that he steered federal funds to big campaign contributors, and for his association with his former chief of staff, Ann Eppard. Eppard, who left the Hill in 1994 to become a lobbyist, has profited handsomely from the relationship. Her firm reported more than $2.5 million in lobbying fees in 1998 alone, much of the money coming from companies with transportation interests.

Last November, Eppard pleaded guilty to one charge of corruption for accepting illegal payments from a lobbyist while working for Shuster. "Our trust and respect for Ann remains intact," said Shuster. Sure—what's a little corruption between friends?

And in the culture prevailing on Capitol Hill, Eppard, far from being shunned, was thrown a party. "Everything

she did was aboveboard," said party host Rep. John
Murtha (R-Pa.). "When Joe McDade went through his little thing"—translation: federal indictment—"we had a little reception to say, 'good work,' 'nice going,'" said Rep.
George Gekas (R-Pa.). You may remember Gekas as one
of the House managers, relentless in his prosecution of
President Clinton for not walking the straight and narrow
path.

Being under an ethical cloud hasn't stopped Brazen Bud
from ramming through the 105th Congress a $218 billion
highway bill so clogged with fat that even his fellow
Republican Rep. John Kasich (R-Ohio) was prompted to
say, with unintentionally comic understatement, "I think
the Republican Party lost its way on this bill." Shuster was
at it again in 1999, with an $18 billion set-aside for
increased aviation spending that passed the House last
March.

Wallowing on the other side of the feeding trough is
Sen. Robert Byrd (D-W.V.). Last spring the courtly,
white-haired Democrat engaged in two incidents of
attempted highway robbery—one of justice, the other of
taxpayer money.

The first occurred on a Friday afternoon in May, when
Byrd rear-ended a 1990 Ford Econoline van with his 1999
Cadillac in Fairfax County, Virginia. According to Fairfax
Commonwealth's Attorney Robert F. Horan Jr., when the
senator was charged, he pulled out a copy of the U.S.
Constitution and showed the police officer Article I,
Section 6, which states that while Congress is in session
members "shall in all cases, except treason, felony and

breach of the peace, be privileged from arrest." Duly impressed, the police officer tore up the ticket and sent Byrd on his merry way.

And that would have been the end of it, gentle readers, had the story not gotten full-page treatment in the *Washington Post*. At that point, it dawned on the senator that he "didn't want special treatment"—something that must have escaped his mind when his ticket was being voided and his court date canceled. Inside the Beltway, intelligence is often measured by the ability to change one's mind in the face of media ridicule.

The other incident occurred off-road, inside the halls of Congress. When an emergency spending bill to provide funds for the war in Kosovo, tornado victims in Oklahoma, and hurricane victims in Central America was introduced, Byrd hijacked it in order to piggyback several of his pet projects, including $140 million for the steel industry, $20 million to build three new jails (one in his home state), and $2 million for the National Center for Cool and Cold Water Aquaculture—a line item that received the Cold Shower Award from Citizens Against Government Waste. When criticized for riding shotgun so extravagantly on an emergency bill, Byrd replied, "That great philosopher Mae West once said, 'Too much of anything is simply wonderful.'" What a statesman.

Byrd may have been the most audacious, but he wasn't the only offender. Rep. Fred Upton (R-Mich.) was appalled by the legislative ambulance-chasing: "The word was that at one point 99 senators had projects for their states attached to the emergency bill." So Upton intro-

duced a resolution that called on Senate and House nego-
tiators not to add more projects to the bill before it went
to the floor. It passed 381 to 46. "We did get a lot of the
pork out, including Byrd's steel provision," Upton told
me. "If it had stayed in, a bunch of us in the House would
have been able to take the bill down. But a deal was struck
to let Byrd bring his provision back as a separate emergency measure, not to be counted against the spending
caps." So even when the good old boys lose, somehow
they win.

Then there's arm-twister extraordinaire, Majority Whip
Rep. Tom DeLay (D-Tex.). Even as the House Ethics
Committee was chastising DeLay for threatening a trade
association that had the gall to hire a Democrat as its president, he continued to shake down the Washington lobbyist
establishment. He demanded $20,000 from each of his two
dozen dearest lobbyist friends by June in exchange for an
exclusive party with Speaker Dennis Hastert. Either
Hastert's cocktail chatter skills have skyrocketed lately, or
that $20,000 is about something else. "That's chump
change," one lobbyist said. "If DeLay needs it, we'll get it for
him." "When DeLay asks," said another, "we deliver." After
all, what are a few more pearls before swine? And when a
lobbyist asks, DeLay, Byrd, Shuster, and their Beltway bud-
dies almost always return the favor.

The gap between our leaders and those they govern
yawns wider every day. How else to explain their 1998
decision to give themselves yet another pay raise, claiming
it was no longer "politically risky" to do so? Just in case,
though, some of them decided to plead poverty, appar-

ently unaware of how ludicrous it made them sound. "I pay the same money for soap that a woman out on Pennsylvania Avenue does," said Rep. Carrie Meek (D-Fla.). "I work just as hard as she does." The congresswoman also makes just as much money as the average woman on Pennsylvania Avenue—as long as you only count those local gals making $133,600 a year. Rep. DeLay played the Compassion Card, tugging our heartstrings with tales of House members "living in their offices," adding, "It is difficult to raise a family and serve under those conditions." Which only begs the question of whether someone who can't raise a family on $133,600 a year has the judgment to vote on a budget bill.

Still, secretive habits die hard. Although they no longer try to pass pay raises in the middle of the night, as they did in 1989, members still thought it prudent to smuggle the salary hike through in a huge Trojan horse Treasury appropriations bill. It's too bad we don't have trained dogs to sniff this stuff out—or maybe we should just be asking, "Has this appropriations bill been left unattended since you entered the building?"

Even those who arrive with good intentions aren't immune to becoming infected with the Washington bug (which apparently is contracted through direct contact with money). Consider the case of Rep. George Nethercutt (R-Wash.), whose promise to limit himself to three terms was central to his 1994 underdog win. Now that his run is up, poor ol' George is singing a different tune. Here is Nethercutt in 1994: "No one is indispensable in this district. We don't need a permanent Congress. I think I can have a large impact on the Republican majority in six years." And in 1999: "You have to have time to change the system. Do you give up and give your seat to somebody who wants to go back to the old days, or do you work incrementally?"

Does Nethercutt really expect us to believe that it took six years before it dawned on him that it takes time to change the system? Would he have bought that from the man he defeated, Speaker Tom Foley (D-Wash.), whom Nethercutt charged over and over with becoming "part of the Washington, D.C., establishment instead of the establishment that is represented by us in the 5th Congressional District"? He should at least have the guts to issue a formal apology to Mr. Foley.

Nethercutt is one of ten "self-limiters" whose time runs out at the end of the 106th Congress. Six of them—Reps. Charles Canady (R-Fla.), Matt Salmon (R-Ariz.), Helen Chenoweth (R-Idaho), Tom Coburn (R-Okla.), Mark Sanford (R-S.C.) and Jack Metcalf (R-Wash.)—are honoring their pledge. Three—Nethercutt, Rep. Scott McInnis (R-Colo.), and Rep. Marty Meehan (D-Mass.)—have reneged. Taking a cue from Henry Hyde, Meehan called his decision to voluntarily limit his terms a "youthful indiscretion." His alternative excuse is the standard one for all those unwilling to give up power. He now describes himself as "obviously more effective today than I was when I arrived."

Another member, Tillie Fowler (R-Fla.), remains "officially undecided." As a leader of Florida's 1992 "Eight is Enough" term limits initiative, she had promised during her campaign that "the 1998 election will be my last." But eight years may not be enough for Fowler, who now seems to be searching for the best way to spin her betrayal. She calls it having "a more open mind."

Rep. Tom Coburn (R-Okla.), a doctor-turned-legislator who is keeping his word, identified the problem: "People become addicted to the morphine of power and ego. We've made the rules so you only have careerists, and the careerists are killing us." Or as Paul Jacob, national director of U.S. Term Limits, puts it, "A few who come to Washington to drain the swamp decide it makes a great hot tub."

U.S. Term Limits has turned up the heat in the congressional Jacuzzi. It is spending $20 million during the 2000 election cycle to point out the benefits of term limits and the hazards of not keeping your word. The campaign includes television and radio ads in Nethercutt's 5th Congressional District, comparing his promise to serve only six years to President Nixon's "I am not a crook," President Bush's "Read my lips," and President Clinton's "I did not have sexual relations with that woman."

This latest breach of the public trust was actually supported by Republican Party elders, fearful that the price of keeping one's word will be losing the House in 2000. "We're going to encourage them to back out of the pledge," said one top Republican aide. One self-limited freshman, Rep. Jim DeMint (R-S.C.) was warned that his position on term limits may hurt his ability to raise campaign funds and to get the committee assignments of his choice.

How does this square with the much-touted Contract with America, which promised to limit terms, not punish limiters? It doesn't, but then neither does all the behind-the-scenes maneuvering to find a way around the GOP majority's rule limiting the tenure of House committee chairmen to six years.

Another factor contributing to the degradation of political discourse is the raising of what I call the "Guffaw Threshold"—the point at which you just can't help but burst out laughing at a politician's latest spin. The brazenness of our public figures has grown in direct proportion to the blithe indulgence they receive from a distracted and complacent electorate. It doesn't, of course, help that the media, eager to chase any sex scandal they smell, have all but abdicated their role as the public's B.S. detector.

So one whopper is followed by another—and fewer and fewer make us spit our milk back up through our noses. The public has clearly forgotten one of the vital components of democracy—our right to laugh at the most ludicrous statements of our political leaders. Remember Dan Quayle?

Yet we greet with studied solemnity Donald Trump. Of course, there have always been joke candidates—but the joke used to be the point. Now the joke is on us. Trump's White House fantasy would be pure comic relief if only the media could resist the ratings temptation to treat it seriously, adding gravitas where a laugh track should be. Do we really need Larry King asking Trump if he would reappoint Alan Greenspan? Is Donald Trump's answer any more meaningful than Donald Duck's?

At first Trump couldn't stop talking about how great he was doing in the polls. In fact, it's apparently what first made him think of running. "The polls have been unbelievable," he told King. Pundits scratched their heads trying to figure out what poll he was referring to; it turned out to be from the *National Enquirer*—running alongside a story on a new diet that lets you eat all the fatty foods you want, provided you have your stomach removed.

When he was asked how he could relate to working people, the bumbling billionaire replied without batting an eye, "I employ thousands and thousands of people . . . and the people that like me most are the so-called construction workers, the taxicab drivers." It takes a special kind of self-delusion to confuse the look on an employee's face when he gets his paycheck—or a cabbie's thumbs-up when you overtip him—for affection.

The sole qualification Trump put forward for the highest office in the land is that he once got a skating rink in Central Park refurbished. Which isn't to imply that he doesn't have opinions on the important issues of the day. He believes, for example, that he's the perfect guy to address campaign finance reform because he's already stuffed the coffers of every politician in sight: "You know, I'm a very big contributor. . . . I'm maxed out every year."

There is actually a clinical term for such baffling behavior—and views: "Self-Destructive Intelligence Syndrome." One of its primary symptoms is the "Disconnect Effect." "There is no better place to study the Disconnect Effect than Washington, D.C.," says psychologist Mortimer Feinberg. "Anyone listening to the Watergate tapes might note the impersonality with which Nixon, Haldeman, and Ehrlichman address the Watergate issue. . . . The trio speak in third person to create detachment and insulate the consciousness from reality."

Enter The Donald. "If they think Donald Trump can be walked on," says Trump, "if they think Donald Trump is a rollover, like most people are, then the litigation will increase tenfold."

In fact, detachment from reality and a lack of self-examination appear to be occupational hazards for presidential candidates. "I'm running as a Ronald Reagan Republican," Gary Bauer proclaimed again and again, clearly preferring to adopt another's identity rather than search for his own. Steve Forbes has followed suit. "If it was good enough for Ronald Reagan, it is good enough for Steve Forbes," he answered when asked if he would support a pro-life plank in the GOP platform.

Now, unlike the budding third-party movement, which Arianna—I'm sorry, I mean "I"—see as a sign of political health, the third-person movement is clearly a sign of a troubled system, and maybe a troubled soul. It is an indication that our would-be leaders have surrendered to the notion that they have become political products to be sold on the open market. Thus we have George W. Bush explaining his consumer appeal by declaring, "We've now got nearly 80,000 Americans who have said we want George W. to be the president. It's a huge groundswell." (Less than one-third of one percent of the population is a groundswell?) It's as if even he can't help hopping on the careening bandwagon speeding this "George W." character toward the nomination.

Candidates operating under the double stress of switching to a third party while defending themselves from a barrage of criticism seem especially likely to lapse into a third-person state. Hence Pat Buchanan trying to explain that people were so eager to "bash Pat Buchanan," as he put it, "because they fear that Pat Buchanan may move to the Reform Party and take the conservative movement with him." As for those pesky charges that he was an anti-Semite, he claimed they arose because "Pat Buchanan is probably the only leader in this country that will stand up to the Israeli lobby"—and not because he would have been in favor of appeasing Hitler. As a topper, he added this third-person non sequitur: "They know Pat Buchanan is not a hater or a bigot. He's done 3,000 shows on *Crossfire*.'"

Bob Smith, the Republican-turned-independent-turned-Republican-again-turned-former-candidate, needed all the help he could get with name recognition. Maybe that's why he tried to set himself apart from the pack by informing his audience that "only one—right here, Bob Smith—voted against funding for the UN." Or claimed that one of his adversaries "went on *Crossfire* the other night to debate Bob Smith, but Bob Smith wasn't there to answer for himself. He took the anti-Bob position."

Giving rise to the theory that this annoying malady is actually a sexually transmitted disease was Elizabeth Dole's fondness, when she was running for president, for the third-person way. Her husband was, of course, the king of the "thirders," who spent much of 1996 talking up this fella Bob Dole. Who'll ever forget his doleful attempt to cast the election as a contest to determine who should become Babysitter of the Free World: "If you had to leave your children with Bob Dole or Bill Clinton, I think you'd probably leave them with Bob Dole." When informed this summer that the South Carolina primary had been moved

up a week, the Mrs. didn't miss a beat: "That means victory is just one week closer for Elizabeth Dole."

Then there's the near epidemic use of the "royal we"—a
first cousin of the third person—which allows the user to
foster the impression that he's speaking for many others
besides himself. It's been a favorite of Bill Bradley's. "We
had a plan we laid out in January," he said last fall. "We
met every checkpoint along the road. And I think we're
moving forward." "We" can also be used to deflect blame.
"We're in a new phase of the campaign," Al Gore said in
announcing his decision to move his campaign headquar-
ters from K Street to Tennessee. "We've laid the ground-
work. We've invested in the organization. We've largely
completed the fund-raising."

Anxious to make his mark before the Bush juggernaut flat-
tens him, Orrin Hatch has used both the third person and the
royal we: "We plan on running for president. . . . We're
going to give it everything we have. . . . Reducing taxes is a
very, very important part of Orrin Hatch's agenda."

As a collector of political humbuggery, I have had to
rent a hangar out by the airport for storage. Beyond my
1999 Third Person and Royal We collection, I have some
other all-time favorites. In 1997, it was the White House's
explanation for having kept Janet Reno in the dark about
the discovery of forty-four videotaped fund-raising coffees
until after the Justice Department had issued its final
report exonerating the president. It was Rosh Hashanah,
the White House said. The chutzpah of playing the Jewish
holiday card came on top of the impudence of using the
increasingly common "the computer ate my homework"

excuse. This was the reason the White House put forth for not finding the tapes earlier: that anonymous minions had failed to type the right code word into the computer system. That one wins the Rose Mary Woods Award for convenient technological incompetence.

Or how about the time the president rushed back from Martha's Vineyard to speak to the nation from the Oval Office after dropping bombs on Sudan? "Our target was terror," he said. "The factory was involved in the production of materials for chemical weapons. The United States does not take this action lightly." The president's National Security adviser, Sandy Berger, told the nation that he knew "with great certainty" that the Khartoum factory was producing a nerve gas precursor. Berger's great certainty was based on a handful of dirt from the factory's yard.

The administration was later forced to admit that the factory was actually manufacturing medicine, not terror. In fact, it appears that the United States took this action not just lightly but also recklessly and under extraordinary circumstances—to wit the exclusion from the decision-making process of four of the five members of the Joint Chiefs of Staff as well as FBI director Louis Freeh, who at the time had four hundred men in the field investigating the embassy bombings. The attack on Sudan was supposed to be in retaliation for the very bombings the FBI was investigating.

And as if the deluge of lies isn't bad enough, there are also the seemingly endless betrayals of decency, ethics, and core values. If you're a Republican who joined what you thought was the party of Lincoln, you've been betrayed by

the specter of high-ranking GOP elected officials—such
as Rep. Bob Barr (R-Ga.), Sen. Trent Lott (R-Miss.), Sen.
Jesse Helms (R-N.C.), and Mississippi Governor Kirk
Fordice—getting involved with the racist Council of
Conservative Citizens, including speaking before the
group and meeting with its leaders. Lott, the most powerful man in the U.S. Senate, went so far as to endorse the
group in a 1995 promotional mailer as a needed "national
organization to mobilize conservative, patriotic citizens to
help protect our flag, Constitution and other symbols of
freedom." Lott's uncle, Arnie Watson, reported that the
senator was "an honorary member of the group." "I would
probably go again," Gov. Fordice told me. "They are very
delightful people and just because of a few views they
hold, that wouldn't keep me from attending their events
again."

A visit to the CCC's Web site—revealing articles describ-
ing Martin Luther King as a "depraved miscreant" and
America as turning into a "slimy brown mass of glop"—
should have given Fordice, Lott, and others plenty of reasons to stay away. In fact, a few Republicans—including Rep.
Michael Forbes of New York, who recently switched to the
Democratic Party—stepped up to the plate with a resolution
condemning the CCC. The Republican leadership, however, had other ideas. "When you start naming one group
over another group, or this group or that group, the list is
going to get pretty long, and that would be the wrong
approach," said Lott. Yet Lott has taken just that tack when
it suited his needs, voting for a 1994 resolution condemning
just one individual, Khalid Abdul Muhammad of the Nation

of Islam, for spewing the same kind of hateful rhetoric. The anti-CCC resolution was actually patterned after the Muhammad one, which passed the Senate unanimously and the House 361 to 34.

But Lott's not the only establishment Republican that, to borrow a phrase, just doesn't get it. Fordice, the man who found the CCC such "delightful people," was later named national cochair of the now defunct Dan Quayle for President Committee. But the former vice president seemed to have no trouble with Fordice's racist sympathizing. He asked him to resign only after Fordice was caught committing adultery. Clearly, the Republican Party establishment believes that rolling around in the sheets with a mistress is more damaging politically than traipsing around with people wearing them. Maybe at the next convention, the GOP should start handing out bracelets engraved with WWLD ("What would Lincoln do?").

Now, if you're a Democrat who joined the party because you cared for the neediest among us, the picture isn't much better. How are you supposed to feel when the party's presidential front-runner spearheads what the State Department has called "an assiduous, concerted campaign" to stop South Africa from making low-cost AIDS drugs available to its 3.2 million infected citizens?

Allowing South Africa to license domestic production of the lifesaving drugs, known as "compulsory licensing," is one of those rare issues—such as child abuse and drunk driving—on which there cannot possibly be two sides. After all, although sub-Saharan African nations account for 70 percent of the world's new HIV cases and 90 percent of all

AIDS deaths, less than 1 percent of all AIDS drugs are sold there. Moreover, World Trade Organization (WTO) regulations allow for the compulsory licensing and parallel importing—i.e., shopping for the best price—of AIDS drugs, and are particularly liberal when it comes to national emergencies such as epidemics. But Al Gore, who has helped raise at least $1.4 million in drug-company campaign contributions over the course of his career, aligned himself with pharmaceutical companies that are suing the government of South Africa and invoking WTO rules. I guess in this case, lobbying plus legislation equals death.

It's no wonder that a political system characterized by such greed, graft, duplicity, and out-and-out lying has led millions of citizens to turn away from democracy in disgust and resignation.

But how much longer can we afford to turn away?

3

VOTING FOR DOLLARS

There's an old joke that goes like this: A drunk is on his hands and knees, crawling around under a streetlight. A policeman comes up to him and asks, "What are you doing?" The drunk answers, "Looking for my keys." "Where did you lose them?" asks the policeman. "Back at the bar." "Well, why are you looking for them here?" "Because the lighting's so much better," he replies.

Ever wonder why politicians pass the laws they do? Why certain groups are fawned over while others are ignored? Why certain issues are deemed crises while others aren't even granted the status of issues? The answer is simple. Like the drunk following the light, politicians follow the money and the clamor of noisy special interest groups—leaving the real crises, like so many car keys, forgotten and far behind.

Some people look at laws and ask, Why not? I look at them and ask, Who paid for them?

The growth in the number of registered lobbyists in Washington has produced a succession of designer give-aways, like the one specially crafted (handmade and giftwrapped) by Rep. Jennifer Dunn (R-Wash.) for the Nordstrom retail chain, headquartered in her district, which would provide department stores with tax-exempt subsidies from mall developers.

One hundred thirty-eight of Washington's registered lobbyists are former members of Congress, two-thirds of whom left the Hill after 1990. Democrats? Republicans? It really doesn't matter. As legendary lobbyist J. D. Williams once said, "I'm prepared for anything except a Communist takeover—and I could get ready for that in twenty-four hours."

Exiting politicians are spinning through Capitol Hill's revolving door in record numbers, quickly reappearing as glad-handing, arm-twisting lobbyists. Under current law, former members of Congress cannot directly lobby their colleagues for one year after leaving office, but that doesn't stop them from setting up their lobbying shops and beginning to peddle their influence. Last year alone, former Representatives Gerald Solomon (R-N.Y.), Vic Fazio (D-Calif.), and Bill Paxon (R-N.Y.), as well as former Senators Dan Coats (R-Ind.) and Wendell Ford (D-Ky.), were actively recruiting lobbying clients while chomping at the bit for their year-long moratorium to expire.

Sen. Russ Feingold (D-Wisc.) recently tried to extend the ban to two years, saying, "By putting a lock on this revolving door for some period of time, we can send a message that those entering government should view public service as an honor and a privilege—not as another rung on the ladder to personal gain and profit." But to listen to the reception he got, you'd have thought he was taking on God, country, and Mom's apple pie. "The Speaker is opposed to it," said Denny Hastert's spokesman. "In his view, it is unfair to members and staff." "Our leadership will be against it," echoed Rep. Ed Pastor (D-Ariz.). Finally, some bipartisanship!

The truth is that former members can get plenty done long before their year on the sidelines is up. Look at ex-congressman Bob Livingston, who took that short stroll from Capitol Hill to K Street in March and soon thereafter was using the expertise and power he amassed as chairman of the Appropriations Committee to recruit clients for his Livingston Group—among them defense contractors seeking some of the taxpayer dollars Livingston used to dole out. So Livingston is on the go, building his client list, organizing trade shows to lobby Congress, schmoozing over golf with erstwhile colleagues like Rep. Tom Davis (R-Va.), and generally amassing his forces and awaiting the signal to begin Operation Money Storm. "The pay is a little better," Livingston concedes. "I'm eating in all kinds of restaurants I'd never heard of before."

On the other side of the aisle, former New York Congressman Thomas Downey, who was defeated in 1992, is well into the lucrative game. In 1998, his firm collected $1.8 million in lobbying fees from forty-seven clients. They know they will all be well positioned should his pal Al Gore become president.

Of course, politicians never admit that their votes are on the trading block. "Prove it," Sen. Mitch McConnell challenged Al Hunt on CNN's *The Capital Gang.* "I am involved in so many issues," said Senate Majority Leader Trent Lott (R-Miss.), "I could almost not accept a contribution from anybody." Almost.

Here are just a handful of examples that prove the corruption. If McConnell and Lott cannot see it, it's because they and their colleagues are swimming in it.

Lott scored nearly a million dollars in contributions for his party from casino interests following a trip to Las Vegas with McConnell aboard casino magnate Steve Wynn's corporate jet. Afterward, Lott tucked a ten-year, $316 million tax break for the casino industry into an IRS reform bill. "No other industry benefits from it," says Frank Clemente, director of Congress Watch.

Sen. Bob Smith (R-N.H.), who chairs the Senate Environment and Public Works Subcommittee on Superfund, Waste Control and Risk Assessment, has introduced a number of bills that would weaken Superfund cleanup laws. Over the last five years, according to Public Campaign, he has also collected more than $100,000 in PAC and large contributions from companies named as "potentially responsible parties" at Superfund sites in his home state.

Sen. Ernest "Fritz" Hollings (D-S.C.) received more than $250,000 from the banking, insurance, and securities industries during that same period. He was—coincidentally?—the only Democrat to vote for a bill that would eliminate the firewall between banks, insurance, and securities companies, and would water down laws requiring banks to serve low-income communities, according to Public Campaign.

Nine of this year's top ten Senate recipients of PAC contributions from the Health Benefits Coalition, representing managed-care and business interests, voted against allowing patients to sue their HMOs.

The list goes on and on. And then, of course, there are the hundreds of lobbyists whose lives revolve around influencing members of Congress. And they aren't just anybody. They're players in the same political game, just fielding different positions. And if you keep your eye on the legislative scoreboard, you'll see just what All-Stars they are.

For instance, in 1998 Sen. Tom Daschle (D-S.D.) introduced a one-year pilot program requiring meatpackers to reveal the prices they pay for livestock. But lobbyists hired by the American Meat Institute—including heavyweights like former House Minority Leader Bob Michel, former Agriculture Secretary Clayton Yeutter, and former Republican National Committee Chairman Haley Barbour—sprang into action and persuaded lawmakers to kill the provision.

In fact, since leaving the RNC in 1997, Barbour has emerged as one of the hottest lobbyists in Washington, having corralled a list of blue-chip clients—including Microsoft and the American Financial Services Association—that other lobbying firms might have taken years to attract. Some of his new clients, such as Philip Morris and BellSouth, contributed huge amounts of soft money to the Republican National Committee under Barbour's tenure. According to Barbour's partner, Edmund Rogers, "Haley likes to raise money. He doesn't get mealy-mouthed. He doesn't shuffle his feet, and his eyes don't shift to the ground."

This straightforward—some might call it shameless—approach has helped keep Barbour's friends in high places happy, well funded, and well looked after by the public's legislators. For instance, in early 1998 Barbour was master of ceremonies and a top fund-raiser at a special tribute to his fellow Mississippian Trent Lott. The gala raked in more than $1 million. And Barbour was a key organizer of a May 1999 fund-raiser thrown for Lott in Austin that featured a special appearance by Barbour confidante George W. Bush. The event, which was attended by plenty of D.C. lobbyists, raised close to $300,000 for the Senate Majority leader.

Now, lobbyists—even those as well connected as Barbour—don't always get their way. But even in their failures we get a picture of the magnitude of the abuse. In 1997, Barbour was hired by Big Tobacco to help shepherd through Congress its $368 billion settlement with state attorneys general. The deal fell through, but in the process of working out restitution by the tobacco industry to the public, Barbour managed to convince his GOP cronies—including Lott—to give the industry a $50 billion tax break. This Beltway bounty was slipped into the final conference report, away from prying eyes. And it would have become law if Sen. Dick Durbin (D-Ill.) hadn't blown the whistle. Once the tax ploy was exposed in broad daylight, no one was willing to defend it publicly, and it died a quick death.

Few such giveaways ever see daylight, but sleazy episodes like these make Big Tobacco's efforts to keep its product on the lips and in the lungs of Americans a primer on the corrupting influence of money in our political process.

As the proposed anti-tobacco bill made its way toward a Senate vote, the tobacco industry was under siege on many fronts—agreeing to record financial settlements with state attorneys general across the nation, and watching as one of its favorite sons, Joe Camel, was sent out to pasture by the Federal Trade Commission for intentionally targeting teenage smokers. It looked like Big Tobacco was finally going to be stubbed out.

But then the bill hit the Senate floor—a smoker's sanctuary where lawmakers still celebrate the economic glories of the weed and the quiet nobility of those who puff it. Jesse Helms, normally not one to anguish over the plight of the working classes, grew so impassioned during the cigarette-tax debate that he began to sound like Cesar Chavez. "Any increase in the cigarette excise tax," he bellowed, "will fall disproportionately on low and middle-income consumers—the citizens least able to pay." Of course, he was strangely silent on the fact that it would also fall on the tobacco companies—those *most* able to pay.

Helms, who has received over $175,000 in tobacco contributions over the past decade, went on to quote a statistic from a 1994 study—funded by the tobacco industry—about the effect of a cigarette-tax increase on the job market: "The anti-smoking zealots do not care about the 18,000 people in North Carolina alone who stand to lose their jobs." What the good senator neglected to point out was that just last year 400,000 Americans lost their jobs by dying of tobacco-related illnesses.

After Helms gave the tobacco companies their money's worth, punched his time card, and yielded the floor, the level of debate dropped even further. It did, however, remain bipartisan. Sen. Wendell Ford, the Kentucky Democrat, wrung his hands over the possibility that increasing the cigarette tax would lead to reduced smoking. That's clearly an undesirable outcome, especially when you've received—as Ford has—$94,773 from the tobacco industry.

But it fell to a Republican again to underscore the dreaded class repercussions of the proposed tax. North Carolina's Lauch Faircloth ($162,050 in tobacco contributions) sounded downright apocalyptic as he described the plight of the smoking poor, wheezing under the burden of a cigarette tax. Faircloth called the tax "the most regressive tax there is," nothing less than "an opportunity to further gouge the working people of this country." What a great day for the poor of this country. Suddenly they'd been discovered by both parties. But they've barely been mentioned on the Senate floor since.

Barbour buddy Trent Lott ($88,000 in tobacco contributions to his campaign and PACs) even went so far as to call the president twice and warn that raising taxes on cigarettes was "a deal-breaker." In the budget agreement that was eventually produced, the GOP swallowed new entitlements and the removal of the discretionary spending cap—but balked at raising cigarette taxes. Poor people all over the country leapt for joy.

Republican leaders may think symbols are for sissies, but how tone deaf could they have been to draw a line in the sand to protect the tobacco industry? Frankly, millions of Americans would be in favor of raising taxes on cigarettes even if the money were given to kindergartners to shred into confetti. After all, studies show that for every 10 percent increase in the price of a pack, cigarette consumption by youths drops by 10 to 12 percent.

No wonder the tobacco people worked so hard to kill the amendment. "It was a close call," a tobacco lobbyist told me. "We worked the phones all day. Even we could hardly believe we won." Yeah, what a shocker.

There is hardly anything a few million dollars slipped into the right palms will not buy these days. Another addictive substance—easy credit—has found its own enablers on Capitol Hill. In fact, last November fifty-nine senators voted down common sense by defeating Sen. Chris Dodd's (D-Conn.) amendment to the bankruptcy reform bill. It would have required credit card companies to ensure that new customers under the age of twenty-one either have a qualified cosigner such as a parent or show independent means of paying off their debts.

I asked Sen. Dodd if he was surprised that his amendment lost. "Frankly, I was," he said, "because so many of my colleagues had told me privately that I was absolutely right."

But clearly, massive spending from finance and credit companies—nearly $3 million in PAC and soft money contributions and $30 million on lobbying in the last election cycle—has made it much easier for our political leaders to ignore the devastating effects of the credit pushers on our youth.

Following the philosophy that it's never too early to turn our nation's young people into irresponsible consumers, credit card companies have been wallpapering the halls of academia with plastic—enticing college students with free gifts, low "teaser" introductory rates, and huge credit lines approved on nothing more than a signature and a student ID. "It was walking into the University of Connecticut Student Union and seeing tables set up by every credit card company that made me decide that something had to be done," Dodd told me. "The heavy marketing that is going on is staggering to me. An intern in my office had received fifty applications from credit card companies offering her all sorts of enticements, including a 'spring break sweepstakes,' if she signed up." Hardly the "extra credit" most parents hope their kids will earn.

One study found that one in four college students carries credit card debt in excess of $3,000. And this debt is a gift that keeps on giving long after graduation. How far credit card companies have gone was illustrated recently when a mother in Rochester, N.Y., filled out an unsolicited application her three-year-old daughter had received. She listed the child's occupation as "preschooler." Under "income," she wrote nothing. The toddler was promptly sent a Platinum Visa card with a $5,000 limit (which she, no doubt, quickly maxed out on Barbies and Pokémon toys).

The rising tide of youthful indebtedness hasn't deterred the credit companies, especially since they've discovered that, on average, people hold on to their first card for up to fifteen years. "We are in the relationship business," says one major card issuer, "and we want to build relationships early on." Indeed, at one card marketing conference, one of the key sessions was titled: "Targeting Teens: You Never Forget Your First Card!" What's next? Perhaps a MasterCard commercial extolling the virtues of on-campus credit: "Cost of this year's textbooks: $500. Dorm-room decorations: $750. Back-to-school wardrobe: $1,500. A lifetime of crushing credit card debt: Priceless."

The correlation between special interest payoffs and public policy takes many forms. Sometimes it kills good ideas, and at other times it paves the way for indefensible decisions. The tax bill the House passed last summer is a perfect case study of the latter. It doled out almost $100 billion in tax breaks to big contributors—including an $8.4 billion tax break for the restaurant and hotel industries. Does anyone seriously believe that the restoration of the food lobby's beloved 80 percent write-off for business meals has nothing to do with the $9.9 million the industry has forked over in campaign contributions?

"Republicans promised to change this kind of behavior," said Sen. John McCain (R-Ariz.). "Now we're going to see this big thick tax code on our desks, and the fine print will reveal another cornucopia for the special interests and a chamber of horrors for the taxpayers." Included in the cornucopia were $30 billion in tax breaks for banks and securities firms in exchange for $34.6 million in contributions, and a $5 billion windfall for the oil and gas companies in exchange for $14.3 million. "If you're a business lobbyist and couldn't get into this legislation," said one lobbyist of the House bill, "you better turn in your six-shooter. There was that much money around." And if you're a congressman, you'd best turn in your integrity.

Just ask Mr. Special Interest himself, Dwayne Andreas, the chairman of Archer Daniels Midland. Over the last four election cycles, Andreas and ADM have heaped over $3 million in soft money on both parties—$2.1 million to the GOP and $1.1 million to the Democrats—in an effort to protect federal subsidies for ethanol.

Well, guess what—this generous spreading of financial manure has proven to be the best investment in town. Of the $600 million taxpayers will be forking over to ethanol-producing companies every year until 2007, half will go to ADM—which no doubt will turn around and reinvest a portion of it in enormous campaign contributions.

Not a bad deal. Drop half-a-million annually into the political wishing well and get $300 million back—that's a rate of return that would make Warren Buffett drool. Buying a few senators and congressmen—or, what the heck, an even dozen—is clearly the most prudent investment a company can make. How this differs from Al Capone buying off judges in Chicago is a topic worthy of debate in civics classes.

Given all this, it's no wonder that, with the exception of John McCain, the 2000 presidential candidates all support continued ethanol subsidies—even Bill Bradley, who shamelessly changed his stance on the issue midstream yet still claims to be taking the high road. As did Andreas's pal Elizabeth Dole, who stands as living proof that you don't have to be a man to be a good ol' boy.

As Secretary of Transportation, Dole testified before a Senate committee in 1986 that the ethanol subsidy "loophole," as she called it, should be ended immediately. But something made her change her mind between then and now. Could it be the millions of dollars that Andreas has contributed to the Doles' PACs, think tanks, foundations, and campaigns over the years? And the loopholes will continue to get wider, reinforced with concrete, steel, and greenbacks, so long as campaign cash remains the drug of choice in Washington.

It doesn't take long for politicians to develop a big-time habit, especially during election years. According to the Center for Responsive Politics, George W. Bush raked in $10.3 million from the finance, insurance, and real estate industries, $2.3 million from the health industry, and over $1 million from the oil and gas crowd in the first nine months of 1999. Lobbyists and lawyers ponied up $4 million. Will Bush now show that, in the words of former California Assembly Speaker Jesse Unruh, he can "eat their food, drink their booze, screw their women, take their money and then vote against them?"

He's off to a rocky start. Despite his widely reported admonition to House Republicans not to "balance the budget on the backs of the poor," when Bush had a chance to demonstrate true independence from the Capitol Hill system, he blew it. Without expressing any reservations about the government giveaways the 1999 House tax bill was loaded with, Bush said if he was president he would sign the bill into law. How can voters believe that, if elected, he will respond to their needs, even if they never turn up on his contributor list or attend his fund-raising parties? Maybe he'll try to fit them in on the last day of his administration, after he's taken care of all those "participating in the political process."

Perhaps the public isn't buying it. An NBC News/*Wall Street Journal* Poll found that 56 percent considered Bush's fund-raising total "excessive and a sign of what's wrong with politics today," compared to 29 percent who saw it as "impressive and a sign of broad-based support." It's not hard to understand why, when one looks at the connection between money and power. House incumbents took in nearly ten times as much from political action committees as their challengers in 1998, and they waltzed to victory in all but a few races.

For an example of what happens to a politician who tries to go cold turkey from special interest money, one need look no further than the short-lived presidential run of reform-minded Rep. Kasich. While chairman of the House Budget Committee, Kasich teamed up with Ralph Nader to target twelve of the most galling government giveaways. Though he could find few allies among House members, Kasich pressed on, scaling back the list to ten, then to five, and finally in the summer of 1999 to three. The Three Kings of excess were the Market Access Program, the Advanced Technology Program, and the Partnership for a New Generation of Vehicles.

Over the past ten years, MAP has frittered away $1.5 billion of taxpayer money promoting the products of such hard-luck cases as Dole, Sunkist, and Ocean Spray. Not to be outdone, the ATP has spent over a billion dollars in taxes on research and development handouts to struggling underdogs like General Electric, Xerox, DuPont, Caterpillar, and United Airlines. Then there's the Partnership for a New Generation of Vehicles, launched in 1993 by the president, the vice president, and a few needy domestic automakers to develop a "Supercar." Would it have gone from zero to sixty mph faster than a speeding bullet? Leapt potholes in a single bound? We may never know, for after subsidizing Ford, Chrysler, and General Motors to the tune of a billion dollars, taxpayers have nothing to show for it.

"If you can reform welfare for the poor," Kasich said, "you clearly ought to reform it for the rich." A good message, but the price of the public's attention has been bid up by those who stand to lose if this message gets out. Given such a dispiriting reality, it was ironic but not surprising that on the same day the corporate welfare reformers were meeting on the Hill to announce their list, it was reported that Kasich was pulling out of the presidential race before it had even really started—overwhelmed by the Bush fund-raising juggernaut.

It's becoming harder and harder to attract the attention of our political leaders, mesmerized as they are by the crinkling of campaign cash and distracted by the clamoring of special interest groups.

This legislative pandering could be seen rearing its ugly head in the Maternity Stay Amendment, a congressional initiative that mandated a forty-eight-hour hospital stay for new moms and that Bill Bradley spotlighted in his first presidential ad. It garnered a lot of media attention, but did little to address the real problems plaguing our health care system. It was yet another example of an apparently benign bill that was actually grossly misconceived—a microscopic legislative initiative that made everyone feel warm and fuzzy while ignoring both the real needs of women and the appropriate role for government. It was another example of political malpractice.

As Dr. Roy Pitkin, editor of *Obstetrics and Gynecology* and until recently chairman of ob-gyn at UCLA, told me: "Medically, there is no reason for a woman who has given birth vaginally to be in the hospital beyond the first three to four hours, during which any danger—mostly of hemorrhaging—will have manifested itself. As for the baby, a problem like jaundice is often not evident until after the forty-eight-hour period. When government demands that women stay in the hospital for forty-eight hours, it's a very expensive way of providing a service that is not medical but more about patient education and psychological support."

In other words, this bill only gave new moms a very costly way to postpone being at home without help. But it offered politicians a great opportunity for gas-bagging. "Too many new mothers," Hillary Rodham Clinton said, jumping on the bandwagon, "are asked to get up and get out after twenty-four hours, and that is just not enough time." But forty-eight hours *is*, Mrs. Clinton?

With both my children, I left the hospital in less than twenty-four hours. What I needed is what every new mother needs: help *at home* so I could devote myself to my babies during this critical bonding period.

To quote Mrs. Clinton, new mothers do need a village—not a village of doctors and nurses, but an extended family. It's a sad commentary on our families and our neighborhoods that so few women have these networks of support, and sadder still that we're trying to paper over the gap with half-baked legislation.

Meanwhile, services are springing up around the country to provide the kind of help mothers can actually use.

One in Santa Barbara sums up the need in its brochure: "Dishes are stacked up in the sink . . . laundry is piling up in the bedroom—and you want nothing more than to curl up with your baby and hide away from the world." Their daily fee is $45.

If the Senate really wanted to do some good, it could have urged insurance companies to pay for this kind of practical postpartum support. The average cost of one day's stay in the hospital ($800 to $1,000) could buy new moms three weeks of at-home care.

Meanwhile, the Congressional Budget Office estimated that the forty-eight-hour maternity stay will cost the federal government $223 million over four years, and the private sector $790 million over the same period. And since there's no such thing as a free lunch, inevitably some other benefits will be cut, some other premiums will be raised, and some other people will be left uninsured to absorb the new costs. And they'll be the ones without powerful groups speaking up for them.

In the end, pandering to single-issue constituencies improves little—except the length of the politicians' stay in their comfy offices.

Nowhere is this mindset more evident than in our misplaced priorities on education. Speaking at the National Urban League convention in Houston last August, Vice President Gore tried to needle Governor Bush by asking his audience: "Here in Texas, can we be satisfied when African-Americans are twice as likely to drop out of school when on a national basis the black and white high school graduation rates are just about equal?"

In point of fact, according to the National Center for Education Statistics, African Americans are just about twice as likely to drop out as whites at the national level, too. Our public education system is fast moving toward racial resegregation. And Gore's selective number-crunching ignores the fact that half as many blacks (17.9 percent) as whites (34.5 percent) graduate from college—underlining the education crisis that is now at the heart of the nation's racial divide.

Black children are "decaying academically," Hugh Price, president of the Urban League, has said. "To illustrate how scandalous the situation is, do you realize that the average A student in an inner-city school knows about as much and tests about as well as the typical C student in the suburbs?"

There are few areas in which radical reform is more urgently needed than K-through-12 education, yet we're more obsessed with polishing our ivory towers than with repairing our bullet-ridden schoolhouses. We've spent billions to make it easier for middle class parents to send their kids to college, while completely ignoring the millions of children trapped in a system that denies them even the hope of higher education. How can we in good conscience justify allocating $40 billion for higher education over five years and only $100 million more—to be spent on new charter schools—for K-12? This is social Darwinism at its worst.

What a bizarre sense of priorities. The president keeps repeating that K-12 are the most important years, and then completely belies this by the way he allocates resources. But in our poll-crazy political life, any proposal that commands two-thirds of popular support joins the untouchables—the latest addition to the list being college loans. As a result, other dire needs—like those of students not bound for college and whose needs will be accordingly greater in the future—are ignored.

What accounts for the startling disconnect between the president's good intentions and his practical failure to attend to the plight of those most in need? Once again, the road to this hell is paved by special interests. For all his lofty rhetoric, Clinton knows better than to cross the powerful teachers' unions—which stubbornly and consistently resist educational reform even as voter confidence in public schools continues to tumble.

In a tragic twist, over forty years after the *Brown v. Board of Education* decision, public schools have never been less equal or more segregated. Albert Shanker, the late president of the American Federation of Teachers, pointed to the "devastating" fact that 57 percent of parents surveyed would choose a private school for their children if they could afford it. The parents who can, like the president and vice president, have already voted on the sorry state of public education by taking their children out of it.

A Gallup poll released last August showed that 48 percent of white Americans—and 71 percent of African Americans—support school choice. Black parents are motivated by growing anxiety about their own children's welfare, while Al Gore and Bill Bradley, their own children safely in private schools, seem more concerned with the welfare of the system—and their college-educated donors—than the welfare of the children who cannot escape the system.

It's a simple, dark truth: baby boomer politicians are standing in the doors of crumbling schools telling poor children they can't get out, just as George Wallace once stood in the schoolhouse door telling black children they couldn't get in.

While our public schools are crumbling, prison building is booming, with more of our citizens—two million—living behind bars than in any other country. Over $35 billion in public funds are being spent to house them, in conditions that are often barbaric.

Last October in a California courtroom, Eddie Dillard, a first-time offender at Corcoran State Prison, told a chilling story of being placed by guards in a cell with Wayne Robertson, a convicted murderer with a long history of prison rapes. In sickening detail, Robertson, known as the "Booty Bandit," testified that despite Dillard's pleas that his life was in danger, the guards just laughed and walked away. Asked what happened after that, Robertson responded that he proceeded to beat and sodomize his cellmate for the next two days.

This is not an isolated incident. In 1998, a Corrections Department panel found that nearly 80 percent of shootings by Corcoran guards were not justified. Despite this, no district attorney in California has ever prosecuted a prison guard for one of the thirty-nine shooting deaths of inmates statewide in the last decade.

How could this be? As is so often the case these days, the answer can be found by following the money. "Whenever a local D.A. would go after guards aggressively," says *Los Angeles Times* reporter Mark Arax, who first uncovered these crimes and their cover-ups, "the guards' union would try to run the D.A. out of town with record amounts of campaign contributions to his opponent. After our stories, the union came after me and my colleague Mark Gladstone with personal attacks and investigations."

Here we have a particularly noxious example of the nexus between campaign contributions and policy. The California Correctional Peace Officers Association, the powerful prison guards' union, gave nearly a million dollars to former Governor Pete Wilson and former Attorney General Dan Lungren, and $2.3 million to help Governor Gray Davis win the 1998 election. Predictably, Davis did nothing to intervene as a bill that would have made it easier to investigate and prosecute corrupt prison guards was quietly given a death sentence in the state Assembly. According to Attorney General Bill Lockyer, "The CCPOA torpedoed this thing." One of the assemblymen who led the fight against it had received more than $100,000 in campaign contributions from the union.

So contributions from the prison guards' union—ranking right up there with the massive sums doled out by Big Tobacco and Archer Daniels Midland—are directly linked to miscarriages of justice that, in less self-involved times, would have led to a collective uproar. It's yet another glaring example of how our campaign financing system directly influences public policy.

Not even foreign policy is free from the old quid pro dough. Last spring, politicians raced each other to the cameras to show their concern for the nuclear espionage at Los Alamos National Laboratories. Trent Lott called the Cox report on U.S. National Security "scary. . . . The hair on the back of my neck stood up." But the most hair-raising aspect of the report had nothing to do with Chinese spies sneaking around in our labs. It's the damage American businessmen were doing to our foreign policy in broad daylight, in their frantic pursuit of new markets and bigger profits.

The sections in the Cox report involving the Hughes Electronics Corporation and Loral Space and Communications garnered very little publicity compared to the sections detailing Chinese espionage. Yet, according to the Cox Committee, a classified report by the Pentagon in 1997 concluded that Hughes and Loral gave the Chinese expertise that significantly increased "the overall reliability of their launch vehicles and ballistic missiles and in particular their guidance systems."

Isn't this what we're accusing the Chinese spies of doing? Energy Secretary Bill Richardson assured us that the strong counterintelligence measures he instituted will make it impossible for spies to transfer nuclear secrets in the future. But who will assure the nation that American corporations will be stopped from selling off our national security—while both political parties obligingly clear the way?

In the waning days of Ronald Reagan's presidency, his administration approved the launch of three Hughes satellites on board Chinese rockets. It was a reversal of long-standing U.S. policy, but when congressional Democrats complained about the expedited timetable, the State

Department responded that any delay would put $300 million in U.S. contracts at risk.

And when concerns on Capitol Hill focused on China's trustworthiness after its sale of Silkworm missiles to Iran, then–Defense Secretary Frank Carlucci called the technology transfers "a trade issue," not "a national security issue." He added, in the now familiar language of Clinton administration apologists, that China has "given us all the assurances that we need on safeguarding this technology." Less than a year later, the same government that Carlucci was "fully satisfied" would behave in a "thoroughly responsible way" rolled its tanks through Tiananmen Square.

In 1993, Hughes CEO C. Michael Armstrong complained to President Clinton that the sanctions imposed on dual-use technology were hurting his company. In a memorandum marked "for discussion with David Wilhelm," then-chairman of the Democratic National Committee, a lobbyist for Hughes flagrantly tied a request to the president "to release these satellites from the sanctions" to the fact that "Hughes has stood publicly by the president on the budget, NAFTA and health care, and C. Michael Armstrong was a supporter during the campaign." Instead of saying "too bad," two months later the president did as he was told. Extortion accomplished!

But it gets even cozier. After contributing $116,000 to Democratic congressional candidates in the 1993–94 election cycle, Hughes was rewarded with the appointment of its CEO as head of the president's Export Council. Not satisfied with the return on its investment, Hughes proceeded to

lobby the Clinton administration to "transfer the responsibility for commercial satellite export licensing from the
State Department to the Commerce Department," where
trade always trumps national security. Over objections from
the State Department, in March 1996 Clinton authorized
the unprecedented transfer.

Vindicating the State Department's stand, Hughes and
Loral, following the failure of Chinese launches of their
satellites in 1995 and 1996, forwarded to China sensitive
analyses of the crashes with no clearance from the State
Department. This led to the Justice Department's criminal investigation of both companies. Yet in 1998, over the
fierce opposition of Justice, the president authorized a
waiver to Loral for another launch.

Chastened by the Cox report, and by the Pentagon's
conclusion that national security had been compromised,
the House and Senate last year passed a law to solve the
problem. But lawmakers still haven't yanked out the root
cause of the controversy: the voracious appetite for dollars
that has put our foreign policy on the trading block just as
it has our domestic policy. And so Hughes continues to
lobby with a vengeance ($2.3 million in the last election
cycle, according to the Center for Responsive Politics).
And Armstrong, who has left Hughes for AT&T, is a life
member of the Council on Foreign Relations and on the
board of the president's National Security Telecommuni-
cations Advisory Committee.

Three years ago, China assisted Pakistan in building a
factory for medium-range nuclear missiles. And now the
Pakistani army has overthrown a democratically elected

government—seizing complete control of the country's nuclear arsenal. A useful lesson for anyone who believes that the exchange of money for policy is just the harmless price we pay for democracy, and according to Senator McConnell, free speech.

4

THE PUBLIC OPINION RACKET

Vaclav Havel, in his book *The Art of the Impossible*, has called for a generation of "post-modern politicians" who will have the courage to speak the truth and put principle above party loyalty. "First-hand personal insight into things" and "the courage to go the way one's conscience points" are two of the qualities he identifies as essential for the politician of the future.

No two qualities could be less characteristic of American politicians' secondhand, expedient, and above all poll-driven style of leadership. Today's political landscape is littered with ersatz leaders who can't even get dressed in the morning without consulting the latest numbers. God forbid they should put on boxers if 65 percent of the public "strongly agrees" they should wear briefs.

Our political system is being brought to its knees by this obsession with polls. Far from being out of touch, our leaders are way too aware of the public's every passing whim. But what people want, or think they want, from moment to moment and what they need long term aren't always the same thing—and the way they answer questions often says more about the way they were asked than about what the people believe. Politicians have become pathological people pleasers, addicted to the short-term buzz of a bump in the polls and indifferent to the long-term effect. And pollsters are their dealers, providing the rush of an instant—but ephemeral and highly manufactured—consensus.

Today's new poll-happy pol has replaced the old-fashioned leader—one unafraid to make difficult, unpopular decisions. If Lincoln had surrounded himself with modern-day pollsters, he would more likely be known for something uncontroversial—creating Secretaries' Day, say—than for freeing the slaves.

The industry's notoriety dates back to 1936, when George Gallup proudly claimed that a random sampling of a few hundred people could predict elections. His claim was borne out when the Gallup Poll predicted Franklin Roosevelt's reelection, while the *Literary Digest* survey of two million readers picked Alf Landon.

Even so, our politicians' addiction to polls began slowly, as most addictions do. John F. Kennedy's administration was the first to be infected with the polling disease. "We were not unlike the people who checked their horoscope each day before venturing out," wrote Evelyn Lincoln, Kennedy's longtime secretary.

The 1976 election was the first time a presidential campaign was dominated by one pollster: Pat Caddell. "Jimmy

Carter is going to be president because of Pat Caddell," said Hamilton Jordan, Carter's chief of staff.

In 1992, Bob Teeter was the first pollster to be named manager of a presidential campaign. And the vacuity of the Bush campaign owed much to Teeter's determination to poll every question and issue before coming up with a stand to match the results.

Four years later, the Dole campaign had no overarching vision, choosing instead to run on "three top priorities" created and fine-tuned by extensive polling and focus group testing: pushing for tax cuts, blaming Clinton for teen drug use, and attacking Clinton as a tax-and-spend liberal. They read like those tests your guidance counselor gave you in high school to tell you what career you should have—and were about as successful.

It's a scourge with tragic political consequences—turning our leaders into slavish followers of the most shallow reading of the electorate's whims and wishes.

The election results should have taught Dole and his staff a thing or two about the perils of leading by polling— but it seems they derived the wrong lessons from the experience. When it was all over, Tony Fabrizio, Bob Dole's chief pollster (it's now customary to have a small army of them) and a key strategist for the strategy-less '96 campaign, held a post-defeat press conference at the National Press Club to tell the world what—according to his post-mortem numbers—the Dole campaign should have said and didn't.

The pollster proclaimed that the 15 percent tax cut Dole ran on "was ill-timed and ill-conceived." But wasn't

Fabrizio present at its conception? Or was he ill that day, stricken with a specialized laryngitis that rendered him unable to speak up at any of the several thousand strategy sessions where the tax cut was crafted as the centerpiece of the campaign? Has he ever done a poll on the fave/unfave opinions people have of scapegoaters?

Fabrizio then announced that his polling indicated that there are, in fact, five Republican parties—not one, as we'd all naively assumed. Fabrizio's GOP Quintet was made up of the Deficit Hawks, the Supply-Siders, the Cultural Populists, the Moralists, and the Progressives.

This earth-shattering news was delivered, along with two dozen pages of backup polling data, to all Republican members of the House and Senate, all Republican Party state chairmen and executive directors, GOP governors, and the Republican National Committee leadership.

One hopes they didn't waste their time reading it, but they probably did. The words "supplemental polling data" make politicos, unlike other mortals, jump for their letter openers.

What Republican leaders need is to give their heads a good spring cleaning, not hang old cobwebs in their cranial corners. Fabrizio's Eureka Moment is nothing more than Politics 101 wrapped in charts, graphs, and gimmicky conceptualizing—a multimedia term paper. *Every* major party is a coalition. And what keeps a coalition from splintering is a solid core more powerful than the individual parts.

After submitting his banal revelation to rigorous numbers-crunching, Fabrizio came up with an eye-opening prescription that is classic GOP boilerplate: Balancing the budget, reducing government spending, and promoting a strong moral climate.

And for this he had to disturb thousands of Americans during dinner? What the Republican Party needs, Fabrizio went on to say, is "a wedge issue that polarizes our way." Wouldn't that make Lincoln proud—a party in search of a "wedge issue"? I think what the Republican Party really needs is fewer pollsters hawking disembodied lingo and pushing pseudoscientific analyses. Fabrizio and pollsters like him are a major part of the problem, for their livelihood depends on pretending to possess some secret alchemical wisdom that will conjure up gold on voting day. They don't. And the sooner elected officials making policy and candidates running for office realize this, the more likely they are to find the issues, the vision, and the voice that will move the electorate. The day politicians need pollsters to help them find a "wedge issue" is the day they should turn in their office keys, disconnect the phones, and close up shop.

Fabrizio bemoaned the scarcity of urgent issues Republicans could rally around. This is rich. If suburban Republican pollsters bothered to get off the interstate on their way to the next focus group, they'd find plenty of urgent issues in our collapsing cities to stir all but the most torpid. But when you talk about poverty or crumbling schools, there's no one to demonize.

"Their symbols were far more powerful than our symbols," Fabrizio whined at his press conference. Apparently, it never occurred to him that the Democrats' cosmetic approaches and empty symbolism—the *V-chip?* school *uni-forms?*—worked at the polls because the empty-headed opposition couldn't muster the merest alternative, and forfeited the match.

As we march into the next century, the motto of every politician seems to be: "I am their leader; I shall follow them."

Both parties, with their scores of poll-tested plans, are unable to beat their addiction. Yet this is a moment when the nation needs leaders with the wisdom to see what does not show up in the polling data, and the passion to build a consensus for reform. In the 1950s, Jacques Soustelle, a close aide to French President Charles de Gaulle, returned from Algiers, where he had taken an informal poll. He told the president that all his friends were bitterly opposed to de Gaulle's policies. "*Changez vos amis,*" de Gaulle responded. Change your friends.

De Gaulle's attitude echoed the sentiments of American political leaders going back to the founding fathers. Representative democracy was intended, in James Madison's words, to "refine and enlarge the public's views." If we wanted politicians to enslave themselves to opinion polls, we could have followed Ross Perot's suggestion and converted to a referendum state, with the electorate voting on every issue with little electronic boxes, like the audience polls on *America's Funniest Home Videos.* As it is, we're not much better off. Our modern variation—government by focus groups—exaggerates both the significance of an often blurry snapshot of public opinion and its predictive value.

Poll-quoting has actually become a substitute not only for leadership but for debating and for thinking. We have accustomed ourselves to politicians who, when asked to render the most cursory opinion, reach for the only lifeboat in sight—the latest polling data. I remember Nancy Pelosi (D-Calif.) being asked by George Will on *This Week* why Bill Clinton was fit to lead and Bob Packwood wasn't. "I continue to be impressed by the wisdom of the American people," she shot back, substituting the latest polling data for any kind of intellectual argument.

It is interesting how selective our politicians' admiration for the wisdom of the American people can be. I don't remember, for example, Pelosi being overly impressed with the public's wisdom when the majority of Californians approved of Proposition 187 against illegal immigration or of Proposition 209 against affirmative action. Nor did the fact that the majority of the public approved of the president's trip to China prevent her from exercising leadership in opposing it.

Not only do we depend on polls as an alternative to reasoning, we ascribe an almost magical authority to them, though everyone who has ever participated in a poll understands how easily results can vary depending on the wording of the questions, or even the order in which they are asked. In an ABC News/*Washington Post* poll taken during the Clinton impeachment crisis, the president's favorability was 39 percent when the question followed one about the First Lady's favorability. It jumped to 56 percent when no question about the current scandal was asked before it, then dropped to 45 percent when a question about the scandal preceded it. Such results *are* significant, but more for psychology than politics.

And of course there is the well-established tendency of poll respondents to give the socially acceptable answer. In 1980, for example, a significant number of Jews in New York could not bring themselves to admit to pollsters that they were for Ronald Reagan, so they said they planned to vote for Carter; yet Carter, in the end, failed to win a majority of Jewish votes.

Supporters of extreme candidates also lie. Not too many people are eager to admit in public that they'll vote for David Duke, but he always draws more votes than his polling indicates. And blacks are often loath to admit that they would vote against a black candidate. When Doug Wilder was running for governor in Virginia in 1989, polls showed him with much higher support in the black community than his razor-thin victory revealed.

Of course, the industry argues that polls are not supposed to "predict" elections. They are "snapshots" of a given point in time, we are told. If so, the pollsters' 1998 electoral photo album must be filled with images of blurry thumbs.

In a leading Minnesota poll conducted three days before the election, Hubert Humphrey III was beating Jesse Ventura 35 percent to 27 percent. But Ventura put the polling industry in a chokehold. When asked during the National Governors Association meeting what message he had for his fellow governors, Ventura replied: "They can learn from me that the American dream is still alive. They can learn from me: Don't ever believe the polls."

But the pollsters need you to believe in them. "With all due respect," said an unabashed Del Ali of the Mason-Dixon poll, "I think we were right on the money. One thing a poll is not going to predict is Hillary Clinton coming into California and the voters being as energized as they were." Mason-Dixon's final poll had showed the Boxer/Fong senate race to be a virtual dead heat; Boxer won by a 10-point margin. In polling circles, this is called "right on the money."

Writing for his peers in the "Polling Report," Humphrey Taylor, chairman of Louis Harris & Associates, confessed that, contrary to polling spin, "the possible margin for error is infinite. . . . All surveys, all opinion polls . . . are estimates, which may be wrong." In the 1998 race in New York for U.S. Senate, John Zogby, acknowledged as one of the more accurate pollsters, showed Al D'Amato up by 3/10ths of a point on election eve. "I, personally, was kind of mesmerized by history," he said. "I saw him do it in '92 and I probably spun it more D'Amato's way than I should have."

"Spun?" But isn't "spinning" the realm of partisans and pundits, not scientists? Not exactly. As we've seen, polls can be spun in myriad ways—by changing the phrasing or order of the questions, by monkeying with the sample design, by inappropriately weighing the data.

Zogby and Taylor notwithstanding, most pollsters in 1998 blamed not themselves but the voters for not complying with their conclusions: the turnout was too low; the turnout was too high; the unions got their voters to the polls; the Christian Coalition stayed home.

There is also the little matter of the undecided voter, who was rarely mentioned by the media but who, in many instances, became the decisive factor on Election Day. Take the poll that 10 days before the election had Wisconsin Sen. Russ Feingold losing to Rep. Mark Neumann 43 percent to 46 percent, with 10 percent undecided. The undecided voters broke Feingold's way and turned an incumbent upset into a two-point victory.

Despite these pitfalls, the media remain in thrall to polls' powers of prediction. Lengthy articles are written about such horse-race polls, which are then circulated by handlers and fund-raisers to convince donors and PACs that the other candidates are already out of it. This leads to more money and more endorsements, fewer resources left over for rival candidates, more positive snapshots by the pollsters, and so on, and so on.

Unfortunately, this emphasis on the horse race—often months or years before Election Day—changes the landscape itself. Polls showing George W. Bush beating Al Gore by 20 points or more were used to build a huge edge in money and endorsements over his nearest Republican rival long before the year 2000 dawned. Polling thus becomes another tool in the hands of the establishment front-runners. Snapshots harden into portraits; predictions become coronations. And reform is put off for another time.

But the best reason polls should be relegated to the back of the newspaper, alongside the daily horoscope, is the pollsters' dirty little secret: plummeting response rates ("trending downward," they would say). In what is undoubtedly a response to the mushrooming number of opinion polls and irritating telemarketing calls, an ever-increasing number of Americans are expressing their disgust by refusing to participate in telephone polls. Response rates are down to 20 percent in some recent cases, compared to 50 percent or more a decade ago, according to a recent *New York Times* story.

This is not good news for pollsters. The key to accurate polling is the principle of "equal probability of selection"; that is, if the selection of respondents is large enough, it's likely that a random sampling of opinion will reflect that of the entire population. But if more and more of the randomly selected voters refuse to participate, the principle eventually breaks down. Dubious results begin "trending upward."

It turns out that polling companies are glad to talk about anything except the response and refusal rates on their latest polls. Here's a sampling from a little poll of the pollsters we conducted in my office, which should help demonstrate the unscientific nature of polling.

Ours was a one-question inquiry: "Can you please give us the response and refusal rates for your most recent national poll?" ABC News pollster Jeff Alderman's first response was to say he didn't understand the question. When it was repeated to him, with minor refinements, he growled: "That's proprietary information. . . . I've got another call. Good-bye." In pollster lingo, that was a refusal—but a very revealing one. After all, we weren't asking ABC's pollster if he wanted to change telephone services or presidents. We weren't even calling him at home during dinnertime.

Tom Riehle of Peter Hart Associates also played the "proprietary information" card. He called their methods "our secret recipe," and explained usefully, "that's not your business." Our little poll was batting 0 for 2—a 100 percent refusal rate (in the spirit of openness, I'm not being proprietary about my refusal rates). CBS's Kathy Frankovic was reluctant to release response and refusal data without knowing the information her competitors were giving out. She added helpfully that it was a complicated issue. But then, hiding behind complexity and jargon is second nature to most pollsters.

At Gallup, senior methodologist Rajesh Srinivasan promised to fax us response rate data right away. And indeed, we did receive reams of data right away—on everything except response rates. A representative for Roper-Starch-Worldwide, who did not want his name used, explained that "that information is not available."

Only Mike Kagay of the *New York Times* released an actual response rate—43 percent—but it wasn't, as we had asked, of their most recent poll.

Pat Caddell is now appalled by the monster he played a part in unleashing. "The dodging of such basic questions is alarming," he says. "When pollsters are talking to themselves, they express their worries about the progressive decline in response rates. But when they talk to the public, they clam up. It's ludicrous to suggest that response and refusal rates are any more proprietary than the size of the sample or the date of the interviews."

It's the polling industry's paradox: This most public-centered of the political arts is also one of the most secretive. Pollsters will throw out truckloads of irrelevant and often misleading information—but they will withhold one of the most significant numbers of the poll. And the pollsters have become masters at playing the inside game and getting themselves exempted from some of the laws that apply to mere mortals.

Here's one example. Consumers whose dinners have been interrupted for years by unsolicited sales calls may not know it, but they have a powerful tool at their disposal—the Telephone Consumer Protection Act, a law that allows us to request that our name be placed on a "do-not-call" list.

Yet the law conspicuously, maddeningly, excludes pollsters. Polling surveys, you see, are said to have a "higher social purpose" than commercial speech. A higher impact, maybe—but a higher purpose? Not only are they as much of a nuisance as unsolicited commercial calls but they enable a habit that is hazardous to our political health. Switching long-distance carriers isn't going to shape the politics of the new millennium, after all.

But hey, no sweat, say the pollsters. "If being called at home is annoying," John Zogby told me, "there is a simple solution: Don't have a telephone. Just have a beeper. Or a telephone just for outgoing calls." I'm sure even the shoddiest poll would show that 99 percent of people aren't all that eager to rip out their phones.

Here's a better idea: Let's fight back against the pollsters. Contact your congressman and demand that he or she work to get telephone polling added to the Telephone Consumer Protection Act. This would not only offer consumers one more tool to protect their privacy, it would also give citizens a valuable weapon to protect democracy from its ongoing hostile takeover by pollsters. Given the collective nature of politics, people always ask, What can one person do? Well, you can start by removing yourself from the polling pool.

Even without an expansion of the Telephone Consumer Protection Act, several state legislatures—among them Texas, Idaho, Nebraska, and Louisiana—have introduced statewide "do-not-call" list bills. The only problem is, most such bills, which start their legislative life containing no exemptions, eventually fall prey to the lobbyists who manage to get them defanged and declawed by demanding the same old exemptions for pollsters and political campaigns. That's what happens when you have the dealers and the users running the courthouse. ("We've decided to let ourselves off with a warning this time.")

But there's more than one way to skin a poll-cat. What's stopping us from demanding that polling companies reveal the response rates of every poll they publish? If we can force food processors to tell us how much riboflavin is in a hot dog, why can't we know how many people didn't approve of being asked questions about approval ratings?

And what's stopping the media from investigating the polling industry instead of just quoting it—from trying to get to the truth behind all the smoke it's been blowing? Any industry that has proven so instrumental in shaping national policy is *long* overdue for investigation. Of course, part of the problem is that quoting polling data is now synonymous with reporting at many news organizations. It's so much easier to reprint a fax than to go out and talk to real people.

One of the inherent difficulties with polling is a problem described by G. K. Chesterton with regard to voting, but infinitely more true when it comes to polling: "The question is not so much whether a minority of the electorate votes. The point is that only a minority of the voter votes . . . the average man votes below himself; he votes with half a mind or with a hundredth part of one." In other words, even among the dwindling numbers who consent to participate in polls, how many are willing to ponder them deeply, and how many are just trying to plow through the exercise as quickly as possible and get back to *Ally McBeal*?

Personally, when I read poll results, I feel more uninformed with every number. If "disenlightenment" were a word, it would describe my poll-induced state. Maybe a warning label should accompany polling results: "Contemplating this data for too long may actually kill brain cells and impair your ability to think critically. Read at your own risk."

So much of what we supposedly learn from polls is really just a convoluted mix of uninformed speculation and hypothetical supposition, all carefully designed and packaged to generate a camera-ready result for the nightly newscast. "We don't have all the facts yet," we're told again and again. Yet what make the headlines—and what we remember—are the bogus poll results, treated as if they were hard facts, announced with all the respect ancient Romans reserved for the reading of chicken entrails. A year away from an election, is any purpose actually served by a question that begins, "If the election were held tomorrow . . ."?

Remember the ten minutes, right after the Gulf War, when George Bush was anointed with a 91 percent approval rating? And remember when he was soundly defeated by the "Comeback Kid" governor of Arkansas less than two years later? What about the amazing story of Dick Thornburgh, who ran for the Senate in Pennsylvania in 1991? According to the pollsters he was 40 points ahead of his opponent Harris Wofford when the race began—but he finished 10 points behind Wofford after all the votes had been counted: a 50-point swing.

Where's the accountability? Nobody asks pollsters to explain these swings—least of all the politicians who rely on these phony numbers year after year. For instance, how was it possible for Bob Dole to go from trailing Clinton by 17 points late in the '96 campaign to just 2 points behind a week later, only to end up losing by a whopping 22 points less than a month after that? Are we really supposed to believe that 20 to 30 million voters changed their minds, then changed them back again, in a few weeks' time?

And it isn't just elections that get thrown off by misleading polling data. The real reason that polls have become so hazardous to our political health is that today almost all policy decisions—even life-and-death ones—are made with one eye on the latest polling data. At the beginning of the Kosovo war, for example, a much-publicized consensus emerged in favor of deploying ground troops. Less than two months later, a Zogby poll found that only 15 percent of likely voters favored using ground troops. Zogby called it "a dramatic reversal of public sentiment." And in this most poll-driven of administrations, it quickly led to a dramatic reversal of military objectives.

While the poll numbers were in their favor, administration officials cited popular support to deflect criticism of their policy. But when the support diminished and the poll numbers plummeted, a sudden drop of NATO demands—previously considered essential at Rambouillet—immediately followed. It was a retreat that should have come as no surprise to students of contemporary political decision-making.

The latest twist on the theme of political leaders as slaves to public opinion is the hot political trend of lending an ear—"listening" not in order to lead, but in order to avoid leading.

So as soon as Hillary Rodham Clinton set up her Senate exploratory committee, she embarked on a "listening tour" of New York State. She began by, as she put it, "listening to probably the wisest New Yorker," Sen. Daniel Patrick Moynihan—the same wise man who had helped torpedo her cherished health care plan, and who endorsed Bill Bradley on the grounds that, according to the polls, Al Gore "can't be elected."

Then the tympanic tour rolled on. What wasn't immediately clear was how the "ordinary people" she listened to were plucked out of their ordinariness and brought into her zealously protected earshot so she could hear them. Perhaps a "listening lottery"?

And Hillary wasn't alone. Elizabeth Dole was all ears as well, steadfastly refusing to voice any opinions because, as she said, "I want to hear from people. Then we're going to be laying out positions on all of these issues."

Refusing to be outlistened, the vice president also got in touch with his inner ear—amplified, at the time, by his inner circle's four pollsters. "I'll be offering my vision when my campaign begins," Al Gore said, "and it will be comprehensive and sweeping, and I hope that it'll be compelling enough to draw people toward it. I feel that it will be. But it will emerge from my dialogue with the American people."

Here's a hint: You don't develop a comprehensive, sweeping, and compelling vision by listening alone. Sure, you can sharpen or fine-tune a vision or learn how best to put your vision across, but *overhearing* a vision? Just imagine Abraham Lincoln going on a listening tour of the Union states to determine whether slavery was, on the whole, a bad thing—"I want to hear what the people have to say." Or Thomas Jefferson hitting the Colonial hustings to see if folks preferred "all men are created equal" over "some men are more equal than others." The presidency might just as well be replaced by an Internet chat room.

Listening without having a point of view to filter what you're hearing can be a very confusing experience— instead of going with your heart, you end up following whoever is blowing in your ear. And we all know that the clearest voices are the closest ones. You only need to whisper if you've paid enough to get up really close.

If you think about it, there's something very passive-aggressive about just listening. It is engagement without commitment, like going on a date determined not to reveal anything about yourself ("before I tell you if I liked the movie, I want to hear what *you* have to say"). It is also extremely expedient. If your primary function is to listen, then you can't be blamed for what you've said. So if you're Hillary Clinton and you flip-flop on the Middle East—saying Jerusalem is "the eternal and indivisible capital of Israel" just a year after declaring that the "territory that the Palestinians currently inhabit . . . should evolve into a functioning modern state"—you can simply respond that, well, you listened, and you're accountable not for what you say but for what you hear.

"He who molds public sentiment," Lincoln said, "goes deeper than he who enacts statutes or pronounces decisions." But our vision-impaired and hearing-endeared leaders are working on the opposite principle. Nowadays it's only the most obvious of public sentiments that our politicians have the confidence to embrace. We've hit upon a new kind of politician—the leader as world-class flirt, locking onto the public's eyes and becoming, as *Cosmopolitan* once called Pamela Harriman, the "consummate listener."

Cosmo described Harriman's infallible rule of seduction: "Her legendary ability to convince the man she is with at the moment that he is the most fascinating in the room has led to a series of spectacular liaisons." Taking a page from Harriman's little black book, Hillary Clinton worked on her own spectacular liaison with New York, trying to convince the state she was with at the moment that it was the most fascinating in the Union, even subscribing to the local papers in the Hudson Valley to bone up on those always stimulating dairy prices. Isn't that proof that she really wants a long-lasting relationship?

During one listening session in Oneonta, Mrs. Clinton nodded, made notes, and like a seasoned courtesan, kept her tongue in check even when a remedial-education teacher blasted politicians for making it harder for her students to get into college.

Our modern politicians have forsworn leading in favor of seducing—batting their eyelashes for money, giggling for our votes, flattering us by lending an ear, and endlessly soliciting our opinions as if asking for our hands. Our founding fathers would not, to use a polling term, approve.

The irony is that this craven, ham-handed attempt to pander to the public has resulted in a nation whose people feel condescended to rather than heard—and in a set of leaders who have proven themselves utterly unable to lead.

5

DEMOLITION DERBY 2000

The president calls it "the politics of personal destruction." To win-at-all-cost campaign consultants it's known as "going negative." And to a scandal-driven media, it's that sure-fire ratings grabber known as the "Gotcha!"

American politics is becoming a sewer, the stench of which is driving countless voters away from the political process. Every campaign season, we worry that the negative ads will start earlier and get uglier. And every campaign season these fears are confirmed.

Even when they're not negative, campaign ads are still just a well-dressed version of the degraded, vapid display modern campaigns have become. When Al Gore and Bill Bradley rolled out their "positive" ads last November, both camps immediately cried foul over their contents. If this is the high road, what's it going to look like when desperation sets in and someone decides to go negative?

Bradley's sixty-second commercial, put together by his team of Madison Avenue All-Stars, started off with the traditional biographical puffery, then took a quick turn for the bizarre—and the deceptive. In a sound bite worthy of a tabloid headline, Maureen Drumm, a mother of three, made an extraordinary claim: "Thanks to Senator Bradley, my daughter is alive today. That's the type of man I want in the White House."

And just what heroic, lifesaving act did Super Bill perform? Pull her baby from a burning building? Dive into an icy river? Perform the Heimlich maneuver to dislodge an errant jujube? No, his derring-do consisted of sponsoring legislation mandating forty-eight-hour hospital stays for mothers and their newborns.

But it turns out that the child who developed complications after delivery was born two years before the bill was a gleam in Bradley's eye. When confronted about the veracity of the claim, the Bradley campaign responded, "That's how Maureen feels."

By the logic of Madison Avenue, feelings trump facts every time. ("What's your opinion of Bill Bradley as a brand?" Bradley asked the group of admeisters that he put together to sell him to the American public. The Crystal Group, as it was dubbed, answered by giving him a tagline: "It can happen.")

While the Gore Brand was quick to pounce on the inaccuracies of Bradley's commercial, it served up a Whopper of its own with extra chutzpah on the side. "I think it's just unconscionable," says a shirt-sleeved Gore in the ad, "at a time when we have the strongest economy in history, we're the wealthiest nation on earth, to have millions and millions of children who have no health care coverage at all. We ought to change that."

Yes, Mr. Vice President, we certainly ought to. But when, precisely, during the seven years of the Clinton-Gore administration did the thought first occur to you? It's tough to be both an accomplice and an outraged bystander.

Now it was the Bradley camp's turn to be upset, accusing the vice president of political plagiarism, charging that the ad was too close for comfort to a Bradley speech in which he had called it "not acceptable" to have "14 million of our children" living in poverty "at a time of unparalleled prosperity." As if Bradley holds the copyright on caring for the poor. What, did he call dibs on them just before the campaign started? I wonder how many candidates will be fighting over the poor once campaign season ends.

This petty back-and-forth sniping had all the intellectual depth of a schoolyard squabble: "You stole my idea! Did not! Did too!" Team Gore responded by trying to smear Bradley with the fact that one of his media advisors, Alex Kroll, headed the Young & Rubicam ad agency when it had the Joe Camel account. It was an attack of almost indescribable stupidity, since it allowed Bradley's staff to remind the world that top Gore consultant Carter Eskew had been instrumental in creating the ads that helped Big Tobacco defeat anti-smoking legislation that had long been one of the veep's legislative priorities.

What's most troubling about this petty bickering is that it came so early in the campaign, when both candidates were still stressing their commitment to staying positive. You can almost hear the opposition research teams in the background revving to life: "Gentlemen, start your search engines!"

What is certain is that long before Election Day, political ads will have morphed from the shameless positive to the poisonous negative. Once an intellectual battlefield of opposing beliefs and agendas, the modern political campaign has come to resemble a demolition derby. After rounds and rounds of innuendo-fueled background bashing and slanderous reputation ramming, the last candidate left standing is given the checkered flag of high office. Only at this spectacle, there aren't many cheers.

Sadly, politics is no longer about stepping forward with a will to lead—it's about managing not to step on the land mines laid out by your opponents' campaign team. It's no wonder that today's candidates all sport the wide-eyed look of a five-year-old caught up in a game of "Simon Says," a terrified expression that says, "I'll do whatever you want, but please God, whatever you do . . . let me make it out of this alive!" With every new election season we face a lineup of candidates who are a little more wrinkle-free, a little more foible-free, a good bit less interesting—and considerably more idea-free.

Who's responsible for this sorry state of affairs? It's an unholy trinity: cynical campaign consultants only too happy to lie, distort, and destroy lives for a quick victory; tabloid media that don't even aspire to anything more than sex, scandal, and ratings; and the political elites of both parties, who seem perfectly content to cook up ever more cartoonishly fiendish depictions of their opponents, even as they watch the size of their audience shrink and shrink.

Election '98 was a dispiriting example of how the game is now played: low on substance—and voter turnout—and high on sleaze.

In California, Barbara Boxer did her darndest to paint her pro-choice, pro–gun control opponent Matt Fong as an extremist by dramatizing the fact that he wasn't quite as pro-choice or as pro–gun control as she is.

Fong was a bland candidate through and through—even he joked about his blandness—but Boxer's $9 million of negative campaign ads transformed bland into beastly. One left-wing wag joked that Fong would probably wet his pants if left alone in the same room with an AK-47. But if the postelection polls were to be believed, the public bought Boxer's bull, helping her win reelection. This kind of campaigning is a little like a lawsuit—you ask for ten million and hope to get two. Here, you call your opponent the Antichrist, and hope to get his negatives up three points.

In New York, Republican Al D'Amato took a nugget (more of a pebble, actually) from Chuck Schumer's past and turned it into a scary commercial that tried to make Schumer seem like an enemy of the people. The ad centered on a federal investigation into allegations that Schumer's Assembly staffers had illegally worked on his congressional campaign in 1980. What the ad didn't mention was that the investigation took place almost twenty years ago, and that no charges against Schumer were ever brought. After this failed, the sum total of D'Amato's Plan B was to call Schumer a "putzhead." If this was the best D'Amato could do (it was), he didn't deserve to be reelected (he wasn't).

Meanwhile, in Maryland, free speech became hate speech when an ad by Democratic Gov. Parris Glendening claimed to reveal "the real Ellen Sauerbrey"—the one who's supposedly opposed to civil rights, and "freedom and tolerance." They might as well have thrown in "puppies" and "all things good and true." This ad was too much even for Baltimore's black mayor, Kurt Schmoke, who observed that he could tell the "difference between a political conservative and a racist."

It may be easy for Mr. Schmoke to make these distinctions, but the media can't. Nor could the Missouri Democratic Party, which must have thought black voters in the Show Me State needed some help; hence the language of one ad it ran: "If you don't vote, you let another church explode . . . you allow another cross to burn." So the two choices open to Missouri voters were simple: pro-Democrat or pro–cross-burning.

Negative campaigning has even begun to edge into the criminal. Last August an Alabama grand jury indicted Garve Ivey Jr. and his private investigator, Wes Chappell, on counts of bribery, witness tampering, and criminal defamation for allegedly orchestrating rape and assault charges against Lieutenant Governor Steve Windom. Seven weeks before the 1998 election Melissa Myers Bush, a former prostitute, filed a lawsuit alleging that Windom, running for lieutenant governor at the time, had five years earlier beat, raped, and sodomized her. But apparently, at least according to the grand jury (a phrase we're likely to hear more of in the new politics), Melissa's prostitute days weren't quite over—it was just a matter of what she was selling.

The phony rape charges were blast-faxed to the media two days after the release of the Starr report and one week before a critical fund-raising reporting deadline. By the following Monday, Windom's campaign was in a tailspin. The immediate objective of the charges was clearly not to put Windom in legal jeopardy but to cut off his air supply— that is, his money. And it worked: fund-raising dried up while the candidate found himself engaged in full-time damage control.

The man who stood indicted as the mastermind of this latest political campaign technique is—was—a respected Alabama citizen and former vice president of the Alabama Trial Lawyers Association. So what could have been the motive? As it turns out, Windom was a major proponent of tort reform legislation that could have slashed trial lawyers' incomes by putting a cap on punitive damages. So the trial lawyers, who had already funneled more than $300,000 to Windom's opponent in the Republican primary, proceeded to contribute more than $1 million to the state Democratic Party, which, being a good Southern host, laundered it and turned it right over to Windom's opponent in the general election.

But not satisfied with exercising their Supreme Court–protected "free speech" rights to contribute millions to defeat Windom, his opponents then allegedly orchestrated a smear campaign to destroy him. Perhaps this, too, will be found a constitutionally protected form of free speech, and we can look forward to bribe-induced character assassination—funded by soft money, of course—becoming just another tool to be used by the professional political class.

Now that private behavior has become public currency, candidates are shifting their attention from their opponents' voting records to the more fertile field of their private lives. And what's to stop unscrupulous political opponents or special interests from crossing the line between revealing past indiscretions and manufacturing them? If you can buy a candidate, how hard can it be to buy a "witness" to the other guy's low character and general perfidy?

With so many billions of dollars hinging on whose cronies are in or out, few things seem easier than trampling on the truth on the way to defeating any man or woman who stands in your way. As the *Birmingham News* put it, even if Ivey isn't convicted, he "was definitely instrumental in a sleazy, trashy effort to ruin Steve Windom's run for lieutenant governor." Despite the lucky appearance of a whistle-blower, the effort still nearly succeeded: Windom won by a mere 7,000 votes out of 1.2 million cast. What if there's no whistle-blower next time?

Tactics like these make the idea of entering the political fray less appealing than visiting a proctologist with a hangnail. As do those hatchet men—a.k.a. campaign consultants—who whisper in their employer's/candidate's ears like some crazed political version of the Sean Connery character in *The Untouchables*: "The other guy pulls a knife, you pull a gun . . . he sends one of yours to the hospital, you send two of his to the morgue. That's how you win an election! That's the American Way!"

Our political selection process is fast becoming a hideously efficient Darwinian showdown, with normal flesh-and-blood human beings selecting themselves out of the process. How long will it be before the field is filled with only psychopaths—candidates immune to the cost, to their families and themselves, of round-the-clock sleaze and slander? It's the survival of the unfittest.

The new campaign hit men view politics as a blood sport. And the odd thing is, season after season, most of them manage to get paid a lot of money to win elections, no matter how many times they actually lose them. They can be found in both parties, and unlike personal injury lawyers—who work on contingency—political pros win whether their candidate does or not. In fact, like Hollywood studio bosses, the more spectacular the failure, the more likely they are to get promoted to the next level.

In the race for the Republican presidential nomination, Steve Forbes's three armored divisions of consultants will no doubt set new spending records trying to prove that George W. Bush was no Boy Scout. Then they'll stroll away from the inevitable Forbes conflagration with millions in fees and media-buy commissions, ready for the next dramatic failure. So far, the correlation between the spending on Forbes's early ads and his poll ratings is a negative one, but no matter—political consulting is a risk-free profession.

Campaign professionals have become our political rain dancers: No matter how many times the dance fails to produce rain, villagers keep believing in its mystical power. And no matter how many elections pollsters and consultants lose, empty, insecure candidates, fearful of defeat and willing to try on any "vision" or personality they're told to, will keep hiring them.

Take Al Checchi's woefully mishandled 1998 run for governor of California. Armed with the most expensive consultants money could buy, Checchi proceeded to spend $40 million of his own money on a losing effort—thankfully, for those of us named Huffington, replacing Michael Huffington as the poster child of campaign profligacy.

Checchi's free-fall began when his dream team of Mark Penn, President Clinton's pollster, and Bob Shrum, Clinton's friend and the darling of Washington consultants, started producing godawful ads aimed at destroying Checchi's opponent, Jane Harman. Leaving aside for the moment that Bob Shrum had previously run Harman's campaign (Clinton's never been a role model for loyalty), the style of the ads was Early Sledgehammer, complete with hokey music and B-movie announcers.

Then came the spectacular defeat, with Checchi mustering a pitiful 13 percent of the vote. Ironically, his concession speech was unquestionably the best, most emotional, most authoritative, most heartfelt speech Checchi had made. He looked liberated—perhaps from having to follow the dictates of all those pros.

As for Shrum? What else—he got promoted, and can now be found writing expensive, inscrutable speeches for Al Gore ("Gandhi once said you must become the change you wish to see in the world. I want this campaign to become the change that we're fighting for in the country"). Ca-ching, ca-ching. But then Gore has even overlooked major ethical flaws in bringing on board such usual suspects as Tony Coelho. He wants the rain so badly, he doesn't care what the rainmakers have been up to.

One specialty of pollsters like Penn is slicing the electorate's concerns into transparently fine baloney through the use of so-called wedge issues. Team Checchi came up with a real heartwarming zinger for his rotten run: death to serial rapists and child molesters. The electorate was meant to believe, I suppose, that his opponents wanted molesters fed caviar in four-star hotels with free Spectravision. It is the kind of panderfest fabricated in sterilized political labs, completely disconnected from the brain, let alone the soul (sent to a safe house for the duration of the campaign), of the candidate—and even further from the hearts of real voters.

But there are growing signs that the public has finally begun to tire of mud-slinging TV ads. So a lot of the negative energy is now being channeled into direct mail, used to disseminate—under the radar screen—ghoulish caricatures of one's opponents and their dark motives. These black-hearted missives represent the last sub-basement on the ever-descending escalator of Dirty Politics.

Today, candidates intent on winning are all competing for the middle of the road—until it's time to pad the coffers. Campaign consultants know that the easiest way to raise money is to raise donors' blood pressure. Sex sells, but fear funds—and this is where direct mail slithers into the picture.

Thanks to the latest demographic research techniques, campaigns are finding ever more sophisticated ways to target those voters most likely to agree with them on hot-button issues, zeroing in on would-be donors by sending out fund-raising smart bombs through the mails.

Hillary Clinton's campaign is a high-profile example. At Sen. Pat Moynihan's farm last summer, she preached the need for common ground, claiming she was "very much concerned that we work together to try to find answers to the challenges." The very same day, she sent out a fund-raising letter in which she wrote, "The Republican Party and its powerful right-wing allies . . . are now going all out to strengthen their grip on the U.S. Senate. If they succeed, America will be virtually defenseless against their extremist agenda." And you thought they were just out to fluoridate the water.

In the same packet was a letter from Sen. Bob Torricelli (D-N.J.), listing the enemies lined up against Hillary: "The gun lobby, the tobacco lobby, Pat Robertson and the Christian Coalition, the right-to-lifers, the corporate polluters, the allies of Ken Starr. . . . We cannot let them win."

Equally overheated was a letter I received from the National Republican Congressional Committee apprising me of "an emergency situation" (read: the GOP needs money). The letter used the word "liberal"—that bugaboo that worked so well against Michael Dukakis a decade ago—four times in the space of three sentences: railing against the "ultra-liberal establishment," "liberal spin-doctors," "media liberals," and "no-holds-barred liberal news commentators."

Meanwhile, Al Gore's direct mail makes it sound as though he's running against George Wallace, not George W. Bush. "Will our nation succumb to the forces of divisiveness, extremism and personal destruction that threaten to engulf Washington as I write this?" he asks ominously. Faced with this onslaught, he pleads, "I need you by my side. I need your moral support. I need your advice. And most important, I need your prayers." P.S. And your money.

To its credit, when I asked, the Gore campaign provided me with its direct-mail pieces. Gary Bauer's campaign, on the other hand, informed me that it is "campaign policy not to give out copies of the letters." "I'm not sure of the reason," said his spokesman. The Democratic Senatorial Campaign Committee also failed to come through, even refusing to give me the phone number of its direct-mail consultant.

Fortunately (for these purposes), I seem to have made it onto plenty of other mailing lists, including that of Rep. Dick Gephardt (D-Mo.). The minority leader wrote to me lambasting "the Newt Gingrich–led 105th Congress." Fine, but there's one problem: We're well into the 106th Congress, and Newt is but a painful memory. Why not include the dastardly Herbert Hoover—or, what the hell, George III?

Even as the millennium approaches and candidates pay lip service to new Big Ideas, their fund-raising machines flash back to the moldy oldies of campaigns past, pandering to voters' basest instincts in the privacy and comfort of their living rooms. From the Right, it's warnings about "radical homosexual activists," "Big Labor," and "Hollywood liberals." From the Left, it's dire predictions about a "return to the time" of "segregation . . . loyalty oaths . . . and dying at the hands of a back-alley abortionist." It's like a middle-aged guy at a singles bar trotting out his tired old pickup line: "If I said you have a beautiful body, would you hold it against me?"

This year's hottest direct-mail come-on is expressing interest in my opinion. Letters come dressed up as important-sounding policy surveys. The Republican National Committee needs me for an "Official RNC 2000 Presidential Pre-Primary Ballot." Gore needs me to become "one of the first members" of his "National Steering Committee, a nationwide alliance of my closest and most loyal friends." Pat Buchanan sends along a "Referendum on Immigration," Gary Bauer a "Moral State of the Nation Survey," John McCain a "National Defense Readiness Survey," and Steve Forbes a "Specially Commissioned Presidential Agenda Survey Registered in Your Name Only."

Of course, the most important question these "surveys" ask is, How much will you donate? In other words, they don't just want my money, they really care what I think—as long as I'm thinking of sending them some money.

So how do we take back our mailboxes? By asking that campaigns send nothing to one group they would be uncomfortable letting another group read. And by demanding that copies of all direct mail be posted on the Internet for everyone to see. That way, candidates won't get to make like political versions of peanut M&Ms—sweet and centrist on the outside, crazed and crunchy on the inside.

Another direct-mail ruse that's on the rise is the use of phony intimacy—apparently to eliminate the anonymous, money-grubbing feeling of most political begging letters. Last year a friend of mine received a beautiful card with two adorable little twin girls smiling from it, beneath the inscription, "Happy Birthday Dad!" Enclosed was a letter from Congressman Jim Rogan's (R-Calif.) wife.

"Dear Carole," it began, "can I ask you a big favor? I need you to keep it secret. You see, my husband Jim's birthday is coming up, and I wanted to do something special for him this year. *And I need your help.* I have enclosed a birthday card for you to sign and send back to me so I can give it to Jim at the family birthday party Dana, Claire and I are having for him on September 5th."

The true purpose of this warm family letter is exposed in the fifth paragraph: "I hope that when you send back your signed birthday card, you will include a special birthday contribution to Jim's re-election campaign. Perhaps you could send $100, $75 or even $42—as a special gift on Jim's 42nd birthday."

Despite the massive fund-raising edge this gives Strom Thurmond, the birthday mailer is catching on. Around the same time as Rogan's, a letter went out from Sen. John McCain's wife. "I'm excited about my plans to surprise him with a special birthday gift," Cindy McCain wrote. "I've arranged with the Senate staff and the campaign staff to give John a gift he can desperately use—a solid three days off from worrying about politics to spend some quiet time with me and our children, Megan, Jack, Jimmy and Bridget." Of course, it's hard to throw a surprise party when the invitation is posted on the Internet.

This time, the real purpose of the letter appears in the eleventh paragraph: "I'm also hoping you can contribute at least $63, along with your birthday greetings. Your contribution of $63 —just $1 for each year—will be a special way to thank John for all he's done for our state and nation. . . . Thanks again for being such an important part of our extended family." At last, we know what politicians mean when they refer to strong family values.

Christine Rogan gets even more intimate. "Carole," she wrote my friend, "you have been such a good friend to Jim." In fact, Carole barely knows Jim. But that didn't prevent Mrs. Rogan from underlining the following sentence: "*I know how much your friendship means to Jim. . . .*"

The Rogan birthday mailer was sent to twenty thousand special friends on his donor list, the McCain one to forty thousand. "We have already exceeded our goal of raising $63,000," Rick Davis, John McCain's campaign manager told me. "Because it's signed by Cindy, it reminds people that John McCain is a human being who has a birthday and a family."

But what to make of a mailer signed by someone barely old enough to write? "Hi. My name is Julia and I am eight years old," begins another five-page missive, produced in 1998 by The Lukens Cook Company, the direct-mail consultants behind the Rogan piece. It was written in a child's scrawl with, yes, a teddy bear at the bottom of the page. "I know that you don't know me, but you do know my Grandpa. His name is Jim Bunning, and he's running for the U.S. Senate, and October 23rd is his birthday. . . . We usually get him a sweater for his birthday. But after talking to my cousins, we decided to write this letter to you and some of Grandpa's other friends."

It's good to see such a practical-minded third-grader. No wonder she was a trusted member of the campaign's inner circle: "I talked with Miss Debbie (Grandpa's campaign manager) and Mr. David (his finance director) and they told me we must raise $50,000 to get Grandpa on TV more.... We can't wait to see Grandpa's face when we give him your cards at his surprise birthday party and then call the people at the TV stations and tell them we have the money to get Grandpa's commercials on TV for the last week of the campaign."

If you can accept this with a shrug, as just more politics-as-usual, it simply means that you have completely given up on any expectation of authenticity in politics, that you're content to let politicians farm out their families' faces and lives to win your votes—or just your money. This shameless exploitation is so insidiously effective that it's lured in even so righteous a reformer as John McCain. The political world has finally been taken over by a cadre of sophisticated carnival hucksters: the consultants, pollsters, ad men, media buyers, direct-mail men, private eyes, and astrologers to whom even good men find themselves helplessly turning for advice.

The shenanigans won't stop until the targets of these hollow pitches decide they must be stopped. I don't mean you have to go to your window and yell, "I'm mad as hell and I'm not going to take it anymore" (though who could blame you?). But at least you can mark these letters "Return to sender."

When confronted about their noxious behavior, politicos are all too quick to point the finger of blame at the other guy—some opponent or predecessor who opened the door to new strategies of fraud and filth. Well, the "everybody's doing it" defense is getting lamer by the minute; it has all the intellectual depth of a schoolyard squabble: "He did it first!" After all, if everybody does something nobody should be doing—polluting the political environment with negative ads and direct mail—that just means that everybody should be *on* the hook, not that everyone should be let off it.

What we need is a good revenge-crazed fisherman to clean up these sleazy practices with a zero-tolerance message: "I Know What You Did Last Campaign." And an especially sharp scythe should be reserved for politicians who practice that time-honored campaign con game, "You scratch my backside and I'll blow smoke up yours"—also known as the political endorsement.

You know the drill: Two bitter rivals pummel each other mercilessly for their party's nomination until one is finally knocked out. Beaten, bloodied, and usually in need of a loan to repay campaign debts, the vanquished candidate suddenly sees the light and anoints his erstwhile opponent—whom he has spent much time and money painting as evil incarnate—"The Best Man For The Job."

So the next time you hear Gary Bauer accusing George W. Bush of "running as a wobbly moderate," or see Al Gore sending his surrogates out to call Bill Bradley a "quitter," make a mental note. Because those are the very words they'll be dining on when it comes time to trade the slugs for hugs, playing kiss-and-make-up in the name of party unity.

We saw one of the more egregious examples of this practice in the last presidential race, when Pete Wilson's opinion of Bob Dole went from "loathsome" to "laudable" in less time than it takes to cook a Thanksgiving turkey.

Before his own hopes of becoming president bit the dust, Wilson sent his opponent Dole a letter—which he also happened to release to the press. In the pointed missive, Wilson wrote, "I find it troubling that you would compromise on so many things, but stand firm in defense of the squandering of taxpayers' dollars on individuals whose only disability is self-inflicted drug addiction and alcoholism." At the same time he said of Dole's senatorial achievements, "If your child brought that kind of report card home from school, even in today's schools, he wouldn't be getting a promotion. And a legislator with a record like that doesn't deserve a promotion either."

Turn the clocks ahead two months, and what happens? Out of the race and sniffing around for a vice presidential nod, Wilson declared that "Dole is clearly the best general to lead Republicans into battle against Bill Clinton." He also claimed that Dole stood "head and shoulders above the rest of the Republican field."

Wilson's opportunistic endorsement was not only meaningless but comic—almost as funny as the eagerness Dole displayed in celebrating the endorsement of the same man who had been hammered by Dole's press secretary only weeks before as a "back-in-the-pack liberal" spouting "politically motivated rhetoric." Wilson had "precious little credibility to attack Bob Dole," his campaign maintained—at the time.

A little over a month later, Dole called Wilson's endorsement "a tremendous asset." How did Wilson suddenly overcome his credibility gap? It might have been nice if Dole or Wilson had filled us in on the details of such a miraculous transformation.

Adding to the general sense of surrealism in this sorry spectacle was the media's coverage of Wilson's newfound admiration for his former nemesis: completely straight and at face value—as though journalists' memories had been extinguished, and Lexis-Nexis had never been invented. The *New York Times* even concluded that "the Wilson endorsement gives Mr. Dole's campaign . . . an aura of inevitability."

Rounding up political endorsements produces an aura of inevitability only among those who've been in the political game for so long they've stopped asking the simple questions—such as, Why couldn't Wilson see these great qualities in Dole before? Or perhaps, Wait—was he lying then, or is he lying now? For the rest of us, it only adds to our sense that politics in America has degenerated into a world where there's no integrity, no principles, and no truth. A world where endorsements are traded for post-campaign financial help and paraded as a substitute for vision and enthusiasm.

Of course, you may say, this is just how the game is played. But the contempt it shows for the public can only deepen our cynicism with politicians. Candidates and their consultants aren't the only ones leading us down the slippery slope of political degradation. They are getting plenty of help from the media. What passes for objectivity today is the relentless pursuit of bursting bubbles and raining on parades.

When unfounded rumors of George W. Bush's cocaine use cropped up last summer, the media, instead of waiting until they had done some actual reporting and found, say, a shred of proof, pounced. "We need to ask the cocaine question," a *Washington Post* reporter said to Bush in a classic show of convoluted reasoning. "We think you believe that a politician should not let stories fester. So why won't you just deny that you've used cocaine?"

Then came the brow-furrowing pundits discussing whether we should be discussing the cocaine question—and, in the process, keeping the guilty-of-cocaine-use implication alive.

After failing to find any hard evidence of drug use by George W., some in the media decided they didn't really need any. Enter James Howard Hatfield, author of *Fortunate Son*. Over the course of just ninety-six hours, St. Martin's Press, the respectable mainstream publisher of Hatfield's book, went from hailing its flagship title of the season as "a balanced, engrossing portrait" to suddenly withdrawing it. And good riddance to it. But the far-reaching implications of how this book came to be debated all over the media are chilling for our politics.

In *Fortunate Son*, Hatfield—heretofore best known as the author of an undistinguished biography of *Star Trek*'s Patrick Stewart—alleged that Bush was arrested for cocaine possession in 1972, was taken to Harris County jail, and then used his father's political pull to have the record expunged. "Within hours, dad was there," Hatfield flatly stated.

And what hard evidence did the author offer as proof of his combustible claims?

None. Zero. Zilch.

Not the time, date, or location of the arrest. Not the name of the cop who made the bust, or the judge who supposedly let young Bush off. Not a single verifiable fact. Instead, Hatfield relied on three anonymous sources—a "Yale classmate," a "longtime Bush friend," and a "high-ranking advisor to Bush"—who, he professed, had contemporaneous, independent knowledge of the purported arrest.

Hatfield asserted that the judge who helped clear Bush's record was "a fellow Republican." When this claim was challenged on the grounds that there were no Republican district judges handling criminal cases in Bush's home county at the time, Hatfield replied, "Maybe it was a Democratic judge. Maybe he switched parties later." And maybe he never existed—until Hatfield created him.

He also conceded to fictionalizing details about one of his three sources to protect his identity and "help him out a bit." Even his own editor admitted that the allegation was based entirely on hearsay. "I know [Hatfield's key source] hasn't given Jim anything in a formal document or physical piece of proof or evidence," said St. Martin's Press's Barry Neville at the time.

But none of these red flags stopped newspapers from reporting the story, pundits from analyzing the political fallout, or the White House press secretary from keeping the arrest rumor in play by saying that if it was true, "it is for the American public" to decide if Bush is fit for office. As it would be, I suppose, if a rumor had been floated that

Gore had been killing babies and burning them in the Rose Garden.

No doubt this slow-drip character assassination would have dragged on for days had the *Dallas Morning News* not broken the story that Hatfield was actually the one with the criminal past—a felon on parole, convicted of hiring a hit man to kill his employer with a car bomb in 1987. He served five years of a fifteen-year prison sentence and was released in 1993. Quite a few public documents on that paper trail—but I guess the media felt it could better serve the public with rumor mongering instead of doing some actual reporting.

At first, Hatfield brazenly denied the story: "It's not me, and we're supposed to be pursuing the governor of Texas." Really? I thought we were supposed to be producing "a balanced, engrossing portrait" of the governor.

By the next afternoon, after a frantic morning of lawyer-filled meetings, St. Martin's Press issued a press release: "At 9:00 A.M. this morning, we suspended publication of Mr. Hatfield's book. We have stopped all sales, promotion, and other publishing activities, and are not filling orders we have already received."

The message this sends is outrageous: Political reporters no longer feel compelled to follow the classic "who, what, when, where, why and how" as long as they can offer up a scintillating "wow!" "This kind of nasty, groundless attack is the reason that many good people are unwilling to enter politics," said former President Bush. Indeed it is, and it's got to stop.

For the moment we're left with a sordid synergy:

Campaign opposition researchers spend bags of money digging up dirt on their opponents, then promptly feed it to story-hungry reporters. And for headline-seeking journalists, dirt is good, sex is better, and dirty sex is best of all—it trumps every other hand.

"In an effort to compete with TV and supermarket tabloids, we've adopted their methods and print anything," said one journalist at the 1997 American Society of Newspaper Editors convention. "Nothing's too sleazy to omit." The following dishonor roll confirms his assessment: Anita Hill, Gennifer Flowers, Paula Jones, Monica Lewinsky, Juanita Broaddrick—all names that in another time would have been lost to history, but that now fill our history books.

The prevailing attitude was best expressed by Fox News Channel news director John Moody at an editorial meeting last February. According to the *Los Angeles Times*, despite a plethora of news stories to choose from—including the Salt Lake City Olympic bribery scandal—there was no question what Fox's priorities were that day. "Remember, let's stay on the impeachment trial," Moody told his staffers. "That's the story which got us this far."

It's the classic defense: Well, the public likes it, so we cover it. The implication is that ratings are the ultimate news ethic. If that's the case, then why don't we just fill the evening news with hard-core pornography and live executions?

Media critics and pollsters smugly believe they've caught the public in some sort of lie when they juxtapose negative poll numbers about scandal coverage with higher ratings. But is it that hard to understand that a lot of peo-

ple watch scandal coverage exactly because the media
make such an event out of it?

Clearly, our media feel about sex and scandal the way
Vince Lombardi felt about winning—it isn't everything,
it's the only thing. So even though the Clinton years
should have taught us that the public overwhelmingly
rejects "bimbo eruptions" and long-gone bong hits as the
means tests for selecting our leaders, Campaign 2000 is
already offering up more of the same prurient pandering.

"Is the personal side of someone's life our business?"
Larry King asked Bob Woodward last summer. "Well,
obviously, some of it is," he replied. But is it really? Is the
desire to know the same thing as a *right* to know? The idea
of reporters and/or political opponents having the right to
rummage through candidates' sexual closets and drug histories before every election is truly depressing. Isn't it
clear by now that the big questions for the body politic
have nothing to do with politicians' private lives?

Apparently not. "Everyone is going to get the question.
The press is going to ask that question," erstwhile candidate Dan Quayle said on *Meet the Press*. No, the question
isn't, How many fingers am I holding up? It's, Have you
ever committed adultery? Or, for more euphemistic aspi-
rants, Have you ever caused pain in your marriage?

In case you're interested, Quayle's readily volunteered
answer was no. But I'm not interested. Dan Quayle's marital fidelity did not in the slightest increase my desire that
he lead the country. "Does not stray" might be a wonder-
ful attribute in a husband—or a dog—but history has
clearly shown that it says nothing about what kind of

leader a person will be. Quayle's words remind me of the feeling I get when real estate agents try to increase my interest in a lousy house by insisting that I look in the master bedroom's fabulous closet. If I don't care about the house, why should I care about the closet?

"If you've committed adultery," cultural watchdog Bill Bennett has pronounced, "I don't think you're going to get the nomination." Which might have meant, if we wanted to be absolutely sure, that in 2000 we would have been left with the choice of a sexually pure Mr. Quayle or the sexually pure Mr. Gore. Both of these men give sexual purity a bad name. Personally, I'm willing to countenance a little infidelity in order to expand the field.

Just as we were getting used to the media's fixation on whether our politicians are adulterers—as if marital fidelity is the sine qua non of leadership—it's gotten even worse. It now appears they're out to uncover whether a candidate is the kind of guy you'd want to go on a date with. Wondering who to vote for? Ask Miss Manners.

In their never-ending search for Issues That Don't Matter, last fall the media created a firestorm over the weighty question of whether Sen. John McCain has "the temperament" to be president, given his "fiery temper" and propensity to call people he disagrees with "liars" and "idiots." (Shocking. I'm gonna tell Mom!)

It takes an assiduously cultivated lack of knowledge of history to claim that a temper is a disqualifier for high office. Even the revered George Washington was known to blow a gasket now and then. One Washington biography describes a time during the battle of Monmouth when he lashed out at Gen. Charles Lee so furiously that "the leaves shook on the trees."

I mean, is this the worst they could dig up on McCain—that he gets hot under the collar now and then? The press coverage sounded less like political analysis and more like a nursery school report card: "Johnny is smart, honest and is good with scissors, but lacks self-control and doesn't play well with others. Not sure he has the temperament to be bathroom monitor."

So now that the Temper Question has been raised, how far will it go? Is Jim Lehrer going to ask him, "When was the last time you got really miffed?" or "Are the rumors true that you turn beet red every time the Arizona Cardinals lose?"

"Do I insult anybody or fly off the handle or anything like that?" said McCain. "No, I don't." Now, I have too much respect for the senator as a man of deeply and passionately held convictions to believe that. Personally, I could never trust a man who does not occasionally see red.

Also, by at first denying the charges instead of laughing at them, McCain legitimized this line of questioning. Haven't we had enough of politicians falling into the trap of answering questions about their private lives by issuing fake denials or splitting hairs? Are we now going to have to endure finger-wagging declarations—"Sure, I got my nose out of joint, maybe even bent out of shape, but I don't consider that flying off the handle"? Fortunately it did not take McCain long to start making fun of the charges: "I'm having trouble hearing you, Maureen," he kidded *New York Times* columnist Maureen Dowd. "Those voices in my head. Stop those voices!"

This media fixation on personal peccadilloes is a perfect example of what G. K. Chesterton warned us about: "If there is one thing worse than the modern weakening of major morals, it is the modern strengthening of minor morals." But now that we've started down this road, in the same way that we had former lovers crawling out of the woodwork to tell tales on our philandering politicians, we'll have complete strangers spilling the beans about the ill-mannered behavior they've observed. How long before we get an eyewitness account ("Customer Jane Doe") of McCain chewing out his dry cleaner because he wasn't able to get a coffee stain off the senator's favorite shirt? ("He really blew his stack," said an unnamed but highly placed source familiar with the stain. "He bent a wire hanger and stormed out.")

Had we used these new, refined criteria for selecting our leaders we would have been spared the unpleasantness of, say, Winston Churchill (drank too much and smoked foul-smelling cigars indoors) or Andrew Jackson (prone to putting his muddy boots on White House furniture).

According to *Campaigns and Elections* magazine, 81 percent of candidates surveyed say that press scrutiny keeps qualified people from running for office. By spotlighting our political leaders' private weaknesses, we're in danger of limiting our pool of potential leaders to a group of men and women with no private weaknesses—or, indeed, private thoughts or ideas. We'll eliminate any number of potential Jeffersons or Lincolns and what we'll get instead will be a parade of smiling, handshaking automatons, programmed with the requisite poll-tested policies and focus group–approved sound bites.

And by allocating so many of their resources to covering the scandal du jour, the press is in danger of asphyxiating any story that didn't have its start in an after-hours office hallway or cheap motel room. For instance, while obsessively covering every lurid detail of the Lewinsky affair, reporters all but overlooked the 1998 conviction of three executives of Archer Daniels Midland—including Michael Andreas, the son of ADM chairman and political kingmaker Dwayne Andreas. The verdict marked the end of a three-year FBI government investigation into ADM's global price-fixing schemes.

What made this story particularly important is the fact that Dwayne Andreas is a master manipulator of our political system. When he's not busy feeding the world, Andreas keeps the campaign finance trough brimming for any peckish politician who cares to stop by.

Archer Daniels Midland had "no comment" on the verdict, but that was hardly surprising. What *was* surprising, and dispiriting, was that the media had almost no comment either. An analysis of media coverage since the end of the trial reveals only brief mentions of the case by Tom Brokaw and Jim Lehrer—whose show has received more than $30 million from ADM—and colorless reportage on cable business shows.

National Public Radio's *All Things Considered*—which owes its extension from ninety minutes to two hours to a generous grant from ADM—did do a report on the story, but failed to draw any connection between ADM's criminal activity and its octopus-like political and media influence, which extends to the Sunday political shows.

So a big story involving a company at the center of our political-media-industrial complex died a quick death in the mediasphere, while all the oxygen was diverted to Monica and that spunky blue dress. If only, after a long day of price-fixing, one of those ADM execs had had sex with a politician.

And remember the cruise missile attack Bill Clinton launched against the al-Shifa factory in August 1998? The one where we obliterated a supposed chemical weapons plant that, in fact, turned out to be manufacturing medicine?

Well, last May, the administration reluctantly unfroze the assets of the Saudi businessman who owned the plant. It declined, however, to apologize to the Sudanese people, whom it deprived of life-saving medicines, and to the American people, whom it deceived.

But despite such behavior—far more scandalous than anything involving Monica Lewinsky—the media largely ignored the story. "This story had all the wrong odors from the beginning," Bill Moyers told me. "It reminded me of decisions to retaliate in the Johnson White House during Vietnam on slim evidence of uncorroborated personal reports."

So our commander-in-chief, operating on evidence so flimsy even James Bond would have thought twice, launched a massive—and massively expensive—attack against an innocent target . . . and reporters were too busy to look up from their dog-eared copies of the Starr report to take notice.

Or were they too lazy? As the Washington bureau chief of a great metropolitan newspaper confided, "Frankly, it's easier to plow through thousands of pages delivered at their door than to make a hundred calls to get a tough story."

Whether it's due to lethargy or lechery, reporters are more and more frequently choosing the salacious over the significant, the expedient over the essential. And as if to justify their choices, they've also begun exaggerating the importance of even the most inconsequential stories they choose to tell. It's as if they're saying to the public, "Hey, we're serious people . . . and if we take something seriously, so should you."

Last summer's Iowa straw poll was a perfect example. It was sound, fury, and a whole mess of free barbecue signifying nothing. Six hundred credentialed journalists breathlessly reported a contest whose winner was never in doubt, and whose results are nonbinding and famously meaningless: No outright winner of the poll has gone on to win the Republican nomination, let alone become president.

Yet there were the media, devoting days of air time, thousands of column inches, and hundreds of thousands of dollars to an exercise that has nothing to do with democracy. "There was one thing we couldn't control: how many votes Mr. Forbes could buy," said one Bush advisor. Who needs "one man, one vote," when you can have "Here's twenty-five bucks and a Sloppy Joe—now go vote and cheer for me"? Richard "Boss" Daley must have been smiling down from that great overstuffed ballot box in the sky.

Steve Forbes spent $2 million and received 4,921 votes, which means each vote cost him a little over $406. His voters got gold and silver lapel pins, reserved seats on an air-conditioned bus—"nice, thick seats," his aide stressed—free barbecue, carnival rides, and face-painting for their kids.

For his part, Bush shelled out more than $800,000. He served his voters lunch and dinner; featured a world champion bass fisherman at his party; recruited fifty Washington lobbyists to get Iowans to the poll; and erected a 60,000-square-foot tent on a plot of ground his campaign rented for $43,500—approximately $10 per grass root. And Bush's victory speech contained the preposterous claim that he "won the straw poll the Iowa way—neighbor to neighbor." In point of fact, he won it the Washington way—donor to donor.

But the lowest point was watching the media become such an unwitting accomplice in legitimizing the takeover of our political process by big money.

With no one stepping up to question whether this was any way to pick the leader of the free world, we were left with the "breaking news" that Iowans preferred Bush's barbecue to Forbes's, that Liddy Dole's buses were plusher than Pat Buchanan's, that Dan Quayle really wasn't electable after all, and that Hawkeyes reacted to Lamar Alexander the same way most everyone does—with a shrug and a yawn.

And when, during the same week as the straw poll, Quayle, Forbes, and Gary Bauer endorsed the Kansas school board's decision to eliminate evolution from the curriculum, there were no hoots of derision; not a soul ventured a follow-up on, say, whether the earth was flat. Where was Bill Nye the Science Guy when we really needed him?

Another disturbing journalistic trend is what I call the "Marmaduke Syndrome"—reporters rolling over and playing dead simply because a public official scratches them behind the ears and tosses them a bone of carefully chosen information to chew in time for their deadline.

Marmaduke was in full effect during the war in Kosovo, when the media showed a frightening tendency to accept uncritically the cover stories of the administration's spin doctors, no matter how they defied belief. Many of the standard rules of journalism, including allowing for sources' biases, were suspended for the duration of the conflict by the journalists themselves.

The Sunday after the Pentagon denied responsibility for the destruction of the refugee convoy, no one on the political shows took the opportunity to pose a single question about this stunning display of news manipulation to Secretary of State Madeleine Albright, her deputy Strobe Talbott, British Prime Minister Tony Blair, German Chancellor Gerhard Schroeder, or NATO spokesman Jamie Shea.

It all hearkened back to the summer of 1964, when reporters politely refrained from asking government officials the hard questions about our policy in Vietnam. "Acquiescent journalists," wrote James Aronson in *The Press and the Cold War,* "were in effect acting as propaganda agents for the State and Defense Departments in distorting and confusing the facts. They kept from the American public information it needed to weigh and form opinions on the war in Vietnam." The chokehold on the flow of information and the media's complicity paved the way for near-unanimous editorial support for the Gulf of Tonkin resolution—one of our most disastrous foreign policy deceits.

It's a bitter and tragic irony that the same ruling elite that covers up negative information to protect its own power has no compunction about going negative to achieve that power in the first place. This may be a great way for individual members of the political elite to rise to the top, but it's dragging democracy downhill fast.

We need to break the iron grip negative campaigners—and manipulative spinmeisters—have on the political process. Until that battle is won, the true contest of ideas cannot even begin.

6

Two Parties as One

As the skies over Washington grow crowded with the trial balloons of third-party candidates, those familiar with the current political scene can be forgiven for scratching their heads and wondering, How about launching a second party first?

Today's Democrats and Republicans have become like Beltway versions of the identical cousins on the old *Patty Duke Show:* they walk alike, they talk alike, sometimes they even think alike. In fact, the differences between the two parties have become so narrow that they should consider changing their names—as Marc Cooper of *The Nation* has suggested, how about the Pro-Life Corporate Party and the Pro-Choice Corporate Party?

Better yet, they could just follow in the footsteps of their Big Business corporate masters and make the merger official. One gentle nod from the FTC and they could become the Time Warner or Sprint/World Com of politics. Take your pick: Republicrats? Demopublicans? The Fund-Raising Party? Elites Incorporated? Now, that would be a merger Wall Street would love.

As Bob Dole so passionately defined the debate during the last presidential campaign: "The Republicans want government to grow by 14 percent while the Democrats want it to grow by 20 percent." Wow, I guess we're lucky we avoided civil war. No wonder so many Americans are sick of the political process—how can you get excited when all you're offered is a choice between two versions of the same outdated agenda? It's like going to a car dealer and finding that all they have on the lot is one battered Studebaker and another, even more battered Studebaker.

One prominent businessman summed it up for me: "It's like the Mafia. You've got to be protected. So we have people in our company giving to anyone in both parties who has any chance of winning."

The leaders of both parties, who are convinced that any reform would undermine their current hegemony, should stop playing games and start listening to Granny D. "No political party," she wrote in a letter hand-delivered to Sen. Mitch McConnell last year during the debate over campaign finance reform, "has an advantage in the present campaign financing system, because no party can prosper if it cannot engage the hearts of the people. Right now, the people are saying a pox on both your parties. How can that be an advantage worth preserving?"

Even party leaders themselves are having a hard time remembering what they're supposed to stand for. It was fascinating last summer to hear the head of the Democratic

National Committee, Joe Andrew, on CNN criticizing George W. Bush's call for legislative action to help those left behind. "Where is he going to find the money?" Andrew sputtered, sounding like an old-time GOPer. "This is fiscally irresponsible." Given their reluctance to actually stand for anything, and their overwhelming desire to beat the other side, it's a wonder the two parties haven't done what sports teams do to win: deal and trade for each other's stars. We'll give you John McCain for Bill Bradley and three mayors to be named later. Then we'll just throw all state legislatures into a pot and have a draft each spring.

This bipartisan identity crisis has already begun to shred the fraying coalitions that have defined the two parties for years. Traditionally loyal factions on both sides of the political spectrum seem readier than ever to pick up their marbles and play the third-party game.

"I have not gone to a meeting where someone has not gotten up and asked me to leave the Republican Party and go third party," said Pat Buchanan before he finally heeded the call and left last October. Buchanan's defection is good news for the GOP, which should be all too happy to rid itself of this divisive demagogue. And it's good news for the Democrats, too, who believe Buchanan will siphon off conservative support from George W. Bush. But it's simply awful news for everyone who believes that our present political system needs to be shaken up.

Just as our two-party system is showing unmistakable signs of exhaustion, and the public's suppressed discontent is ready to be tapped, a disaster in reform's clothing stands poised to take advantage. Like the townsfolk in an old

Western, the millions who feel shut out of our "unprecedented prosperity" may thrill at the sight of a masked man
riding to their rescue—until it turns out he isn't the Lone
Ranger, but a racist punslinger bent on turning them
against one another.

There's something uniquely depressing about hearing a
message you approve of delivered by someone you abhor.
There was Buchanan on *Meet the Press*, telling America that
"what we have is a one-party system . . . masquerading as a
two-party system. And I think what we need is a real opposition party, a party that can become a second party and
maybe a first party." Well . . . yes, we desperately need something other than two corporate parties—but hearing it from
Buchanan makes the status quo stolidity of Bush and Gore
seem downright reassuring. A classic twist on that
Washington specialty—the lesser of three evils.

The two-party system, incidentally, seemed fine with Pat
as long as he thought he might get to lead one of them. Now
he has reinvented himself as a reformer—giving reform a
bad name. "He would bring an organization to bear on what
is fundamentally a disorganized political party," Bill
Hillsman, Jesse Ventura's media man, told me. "Right now
the Reform party is ripe for a hostile takeover, and Buchanan
is certainly a hostile enough guy to pull it off."

So why does Buchanan appeal to so many average
Americans? Indeed, how can they stand Pat? Thanks to his
gift of gab (and his gift of a contract on a twenty-four-hour
news network) Buchanan seems domesticated—more like
an exotic pet than a viper. It's been called the "Green-Room
Effect"—with many of Buchanan's friends in the media still

beguiled by his impish charm. From the *Wall Street Journal* to the *Village Voice,* he's been described as "marvelous and witty," "very engaging," "warm and self-deprecating," "a bon vivant," and "very likable." You wonder if Pat's pundit pals would give his fellow anti-Semite Louis Farrakhan such sweet write-ups if only he had a better way with chat-show repartee.

Buchanan's way of slithering out of trouble is to claim that his ravings were made "tongue-in-cheek," as he did when he was confronted with a column he had written in November 1998: "Non-Jewish whites—75 percent of the U.S. population—get just 25 percent of the slots. . . . Now we know who really gets the shaft at Harvard—white Christians." That's tongue-in-cheek? Another Buchanan ploy to slough off his racist statements is to call them, with a chuckle, his "golden oldies"—as if racist views can be dismissed as youthful indiscretions: "Cut me some slack, I haven't disputed the Holocaust since I was twenty-eight!"

It's been harder to cut him some slack since the publication of his latest book, *A Republic, Not an Empire.* "Had Britain and France not given the war guarantees to Poland," Buchanan argues, "there might have been no Dunkirk, no blitz, no Vichy, no destruction of the Jewish populations of Norway, Denmark, Holland, Belgium, Luxembourg, France or even Italy."

On what did he base this view that Hitler was appeasable? Well, on the writings of Hitler. On *Face the Nation,* Buchanan's defense of the indefensible began with, "If you read a lot of Hitler. . . ." *Read a lot of Hitler?* Like we're supposed to explain the deeds of a madman by the writings of the madman? If they ever decide to remake Mel Brooks's *The Producers*, Buchanan would be perfect casting for the role of the Führer-loving playwright: "Hitler was better looking than Churchill . . . a better dresser than Churchill, he had more hair, he told funnier jokes, and he could dance the pants off Churchill!"

Buchanan is a viable candidate only because both established parties have ignored voter frustration and discontent. They have made it possible for such a demagogue to arise, using passionate language like a sword, cutting right to voters' unspoken fears and dark emotions.

In the long season of bloodless, focus group–tested sound bites, he will no doubt lead many a news cycle. "Mount up and ride to the sound of the guns," he said in his announcement speech in New Hampshire last year. "It is our calling to recapture the independence and lost sovereignty of our republic, to clean up all that pollutes our culture and to heal the soul of America."

Read between the lines of this florid language, though, and you'll find a troubling call for "a national campaign of assimilation." "America," he said, "is not some polyglot boarding house for the world; this land is our land, this home is our home."

Buchanan's rhetoric is not only reckless and divisive, it is all too frequently disconnected from facts and history. "Free trade is the philosophy of nations on the way down," he roared to the adoring crowd in New Hampshire. This, as America's postwar prosperity proves, is completely false— but demagogues don't need truth to whip their audiences into a frenzy.

"Free traders are traitors," proclaimed one of the hand-made signs at the announcement rally. So there you have it: three easy steps from inflammatory false diagnosis to pithy placards to the treatment of scapegoats as the traitors inside the gate. And, as we all know, there is no limit to what you can do to traitors.

Like Father Charles Coughlin, the 1930s radio commentator who started his own political movement on the principles of economic nationalism, Buchanan finds his strength in the existence of a legitimate issue that mainstream politicians have left unaddressed. Father Coughlin preached about the collapsing economy, and blamed it on Old World bankers and Jews. Buchanan is addressing the problems of economic dislocation and the plight of the American worker, and blames them on the New World Order and immigrants.

"He's the one well-known person," said a fifty-five-year-old bookkeeper for a steelworker's union in New Hampshire, "who is taking an interest in what is happening to us." And that was a Democrat speaking.

It may be hard to discern economic anxiety amidst the running of the bulls, what with record low unemployment and record high prosperity grabbing the headlines. But Buchanan is tapping the fears of those left out of the good times and those worried that when the downturn comes, they will be its first victims. "Americans believe," he wrote, "that they are richer than they have ever been, that they are getting richer by the minute, and that the good times are here to stay. Let me concede it: mine is a sense of deep foreboding."

And there is no shortage of Americans who feel alienated and apprehensive. Unless mainstream candidates or legitimate third-party candidates address their concerns, based on a shared sense of national purpose rather than on mass finger-pointing at imagined enemies, demagogues like Pat will fill the vacuum.

New Hampshire Senator Bob Smith also bolted the Republican Party (only to return weeks later). Will Gary Bauer be next? Calling George W. Bush "indistinguishable from Gore," Bauer is effectively saying that only a pro-life position that involves an all-out assault on *Roe* v. *Wade*—including a right-to-life constitutional amendment and a pro-life litmus test for all federal and Supreme Court judges—counts as Republican. Bauer is extremely unlikely to follow Paul Weyrich and abandon politics altogether. But these right-wing defections are leaving a void. And Bush and the GOP will have to decide how to fill it.

The waters are no less choppy at the other end of the political pool. For most of this century the Democratic Party has been the home of social progressives—even when they were only casting a lesser of two evils vote. Now, however, even longtime loyalists are beginning to have serious doubts as they watch the Democratic National Committee launch an unprecedented drive to raise $200 million in soft money. What is now the price tag on public policy? *Everything must go—even our most sacred priorities!* Candidates start losing their reform impulse pretty fast after they've raised $200 million from wealthy contributors.

But the major parties' problems hardly end there. In fact, if younger voters' opinions are any indication, their troubles are just beginning. Recent surveys suggest that no more than a third of young adults identify with either Democrats or Republicans, and only a quarter vote a straight-party ticket. They see the differences between the two parties as far less significant than the similarities. "The old left-right paradigm is not working anymore," writes novelist Douglas Coupland, who coined the term "Generation X." Young people understand that the two-party system is rigged against their interests, and want to replace it with a more responsive democracy.

Even African Americans, once the most loyal partners on the Democrats' dance card, are reevaluating their relationship. Nearly one-fourth of all blacks now identify themselves as Independents, including 30 percent of those aged eighteen to twenty-five, according to the Joint Center for Political and Economic Studies. In the 1998 election, turnout among eligible black voters fell to 29 percent.

"After Lincoln's election," NAACP president Kweisi Mfume told me, "black people were Republican nine to one. In the 1920s some thought the Republican Party was taking the black vote for granted. Now the Democratic Party takes the black vote for granted, and the Republican Party doesn't do enough to cultivate it. It's the flip side of what King used to say: 'The problem is the Negro in Alabama doesn't have the right to vote, [and] the Negro in New York doesn't have anything to vote for.'"

With a broader selection of parties competing for office, politics might become reinvigorated enough to interest the disenchanted younger generation of would-be

voters who now believe—quite rightly—that in most elections their votes just don't count. It's not that they don't
have enough votes to determine who wins, it's that it no
longer matters who wins. Because even when they bother
to vote, their voices are nullified by the special interests
that dictate policy after the election.

A 1999 report by the National Association of Secretaries
of State confirms that in the eyes of young people, the system isn't working at all. "America is in danger of becoming a
divided nation of voters and non-voters," the survey con-
cludes. "Young people have the distinct sense that politics is
not about them." Indeed, the report found that two-thirds of
the young people surveyed believe that their generation has
an important voice, "but no one seems to hear it."

Sixty-four percent believe that "government is run by a
few big interests looking out for themselves, not for the
benefit of all." And fifty-eight percent believe that "you
can't trust politicians because most are dishonest."

The report is filled with troubling statements from
members of Generation X and the millennial generation—
otherwise known as Generation Y, comprising those born
between 1984 and 2000. Here's one I found particularly
disheartening: "All I know is that when I went to get my
driver's license, the DMV asked me if I wanted to register
to vote and I said, 'no.'"

Yet as a group they are far from selfish. In fact, they are
more concerned about the steady decline of American social
conditions—rising rates of child poverty, infant mortality,
teen suicide, homelessness, and functional illiteracy—than
other generations. They volunteer in higher numbers and

their political agenda is a mixed bag—fiscally conservative, but socially progressive.

But we're not going to reconnect young people to the political system through old-fashioned local outreach programs. It will take fundamental campaign finance reform and a major overhaul of the way we run campaigns before we can get politicians to turn their sold-out attention to the millions left behind by the much touted good times. This is our best chance to reenergize young people, 94 percent of whom, according to the survey, believe that "the most important thing I can do as a citizen is to help others." With fewer than one in three eligible Xers presently engaged in the political process, they're clearly a sleeping giant—an electoral leviathan just waiting for a candidate, or a party, or anything, to speak to their idealism and their pent-up political frustrations.

In the meantime, the powers that be seem content to offer up stale solutions, like the Republicans' umpteenth bid to abolish the estate tax—this time in the populist name of saving the family farm. In point of fact, the first $650,000 of any inheritance is automatically exempt from estate taxes, so less than 2 percent of all estates are hit with any tax at all. And of those, only one-half of one percent are farm property of any size. This "populist" proposal would actually save the wealthiest Americans $330 billion over the next ten years. Shilling for the Gateses while hiding behind the Waltons.

Just in case you possess some sort of super election microscope that allows you to still tell the two parties apart, consider for a moment the issue of crime. Once the sharpest of wedge issues, crime is now an afterthought that doesn't even merit a demagogic mention in the "issues" sections of the presidential candidates' Web sites. Both parties seem intent on ignoring the two biggest—and interrelated—crime problems America faces: the exploding prison population and the failure of the war on drugs.

Despite being funded to the tune of $18 billion annually—with another $15 billion spent by state and local governments, the war on drugs has been a disaster.

The proof? Among other things, a 72 percent increase in drug use among children ages twelve to seventeen since 1992. "Drug use is soaring among our 12th graders," reports Rep. John Mica (R-Fl.), Chairman of the House Criminal Justice Subcommittee. "More than 50 percent of them have tried an illicit drug and more than one in four is today a current user." The administration, for its part, claims a "leveling off" in teen drug use "after years of dramatic increases." What both parties refuse to address are their misplaced priorities in the drug war.

Only one-third of the Clinton administration's anti-drug budget is earmarked for education, prevention, and treatment programs; the remaining two-thirds go to the higher-profile trio of interdiction, supply reduction, and law enforcement. Rep. Rob Portman (R-Ohio), an author of anti-drug laws in Congress, believes the Clinton administration has reneged on its pledge to emphasize education and treatment: "My concern is that the president's budget priorities don't match the rhetoric from the White House."

David Rosenbloom, program director of the Boston community advocacy group Join Together, told *Alcoholism and Drug Abuse Weekly* that "the federal government's continuing emphasis on supply reduction is ineffective and contrary to what most 'in-the-trenches' substance abuse advocates want." It also is the only market in which the government thinks it can suspend the laws of supply and demand.

These misplaced priorities are coupled with the inhumane policy of mandatory—and arbitrary—minimum sentencing. In the name of drug war toughness, mandatory federal sentences of five years without parole are meted out to anyone caught with more than five grams of crack cocaine. To merit the same sentence, you'd need to be caught with five *hundred* grams of the more upscale powder form of the drug. According to federal sentencing guidelines, first-time cocaine possession is a misdemeanor, punishable by probation (or six months' jail time at the most); first-time crack possession is a felony. And crack is the only drug under the guidelines subject to mandatory sentences for possession.

This has disproportionately affected the "other nation." The percentage of African-American men who have been arrested for drug crimes has tripled over the last twenty years. Black men are arrested for drugs five times as often as white men, even though only 13 percent of all monthly drug users are African American, according to federal statistics. And according to the Justice Department, almost 60 percent of the people serving time in state prisons for drug offenses are black. The result is appalling: One out of fourteen black men in America is in prison or jail, sure to face economic and social disenfranchisement when he does return to society.

Thanks in part to mandatory minimum sentencing, our drug war's casualties have also been predominantly nonviolent users. Nearly eight out of ten recently sentenced inmates have been sentenced for nonviolent offenses, according to the Justice Policy Institute. And in 1997, 80 percent of drug arrests were for possessing drugs, not selling them.

A look at individual states is equally depressing. According to the Massachusetts Department of Corrections, over eight out of ten inmates serving mandatory sentences on drug charges are first-time offenders. The inmates, overwhelmingly black or Hispanic, are serving an average of five years—about one year longer than the average violent criminal. In New York, 95 percent of inmates incarcerated for drug offenses were black or Hispanic.

Over the last two decades, the number of incarcerated drug offenders has skyrocketed from one out of every sixteen inmates in state prisons to nearly one out of four, according to the Sentencing Project. In federal prisons, the percentage of drug offender inmates has climbed to 60 percent.

Overall, our state and federal jails are currently holding nearly two million inmates, despite a violent crime rate that has fallen to a thirty-year low. By the end of 1998, our federal prisons were filled to 27 percent overcapacity; in terms of incarceration rates, the U.S. is now second only to Russia. Given how expensive it is to build enough prisons, this has become our new space race.

An American Bar Association report last February found that despite increased arrests for drug possession—up 73 percent from 1992 to 1997—and higher incarceration rates—the number of users has risen to 14 million people.

"Of all the things I was involved in during my nine years on the House Judiciary Committee, my role in the creation of mandatory minimums was absolutely the worst, the most counterproductive, the most unjust," says Eric Sterling, a former congressional lawyer who wrote the federal mandatory minimum sentencing laws in 1986. "Thousands of men and women are serving many years in prisons unjustly as a consequence of these laws." Even law-and-order conservatives—including Supreme Court Chief Justice William Rehnquist and Associate Justice Anthony Kennedy, former Reagan Attorney General Ed Meese, and criminologist John DiIulio—are reconsidering. "There is a conservative crime-control case to be made for repealing all mandatory-minimum laws now," DiIulio wrote in *National Review.* "With mandatory minimums, there is no real suppression of the drug trade, only episodic substance-abuse treatment of incarcerated drug-only offenders, and hence only the most tenuous crime-control rationale."

"It seemed like a good idea twenty-five years ago, but the sad fact is they haven't worked," says former Bush Assistant Attorney General and New York State Senator John Dunne, a Republican who coauthored one of the nation's first mandatory minimum drug sentencing laws in 1973. "They're ineffective, unfair and extremely costly to taxpayers." Nevertheless, only a handful of members of Congress have had the guts to cosponsor Rep. Maxine Waters's (D-Calif.) bill to abolish federal mandatory minimum sentences for drug offenses.

Millions of underprivileged minors are crowding our prisons, all the result of crowd-pleasing but cowardly sentencing laws. This is modern politics at its worst. Such bad policy, defended on fraudulent grounds by *both* parties, can only serve to erode the public's already shaky trust in democracy.

Even the most entrenched Washington insiders are now trying to distance themselves from the stench of our current politics. Enter, stage center (the entrance of choice these days), Vice President Al Gore, who proudly announced last fall that he would be relocating his sputtering campaign "lock, stock and barrel" from the Beltway to Nashville, Tennessee—or, as he put it, "from K Street to the aisles of Kmart." Well, you can take the campaign out of K Street, but you can't take the K Street out of the campaign. Especially when it's run by Washington lobbyists, five pollsters, and Tony Coelho. Gore's pledge to "show that a campaign can be an ennobling experience and not one that drives people away from politics" was immediately undercut when two days later Coelho, his campaign chairman, was accused in a State Department inspector general's report of misusing government funds while he was commissioner general for the U.S. pavilion at the 1998 World's Fair.

A decade ago, Coelho, then House Majority Whip, resigned from Congress under an ethical cloud when the U.S. Justice Department began an investigation to determine whether he had traded legislative favors to a Beverly Hills savings and loan executive for an unorthodox $100,000 "junk-bond" investment. Not only did Gore hire him for the top campaign job despite this history, but the vice president dismissed the new allegations as just "inside baseball." Ennobling indeed!

Also let us not forget Carter Eskew, now in the Gore campaign's top echelon, but as recently as last spring, testing new television ads for Big Tobacco. Just the thing, as Gore promised, to "breathe new life into our democracy."

"Since 1960," the vice president has said, "Americans have been voting in fewer numbers and turning their backs on the process. Let's shake this thing up." The problem is Gore embodies the very system he wants to shake up. It's hard to think of a more absurd and less convincing spectacle (unless you count Dukakis riding around in that tank) than Al Gore positioning himself as the alternative to politics-as-usual.

No other campaign can boast as many pork-fed Washington insiders. But apparently, after seven years of assuring us that we never had it so good, Gore suddenly wants to stop "doing things the same old way."

Wake up, Al: Cosmetic changes—moving your offices to another state, replacing one of your four pollsters, trading pinstripes for earth tones—aren't going to convince anyone you're just a good ol' Tennessee newsboy. It's only going to make us feel played. And badly at that. America has had enough of self-proclaimed "true believers" and ersatz "outsiders." It's time for politicians to stop playing dress-up and start taking our problems seriously.

But that would take political courage. And unfortunately, that's a scarce commodity these days, when both parties are afraid of offending their shrinking slice of the electorate. Days after Pat Buchanan began sending his loony theories about appeasing Hitler coursing through our TV cables, Republican National Committee Chairman Jim Nicholson went to Buchanan's home to ask him to stay in the party. George W. Bush's spine also turned to mush as he tried to placate Pat: "I don't want Pat Buchanan to leave the party. . . . I'm going to need every vote I can get among Republicans to win the election." True Profiles in Courage. I guess in a close race you cannot afford to lose the crackpot vote.

One politician who isn't afraid of upsetting people is Jesse Ventura. His eye-opening victory in Minnesota rode a wave of disenchantment with the two major parties that threatens to wash away their long-standing dominance. The Ventura factor has Democratic and Republican leaders alike running scared. What if other candidates, inspired by "The Body," started seeking political office without submitting to the strictures of the two parties? What if, instead of weighing whether to please the unions or the New Democrats, James Dobson, or the Christian Coalition, they just decided to play outside the parties' sandbox and please the disaffected majority?

As establishment candidates continue to fight over the dwindling numbers of the public who are still listening, they're ceding the largest slice of the electoral pie—the more than 60 percent of eligible voters who skipped the last midterm election—to insurgent candidates who might be able to reignite them.

Take the not-so-dear, but definitely departed, Newt Gingrich. It wasn't so long ago that he promised in his first speech as Speaker "that there will come a Monday morning when for the entire weekend not a single child was killed in America. That there will be a Monday morning when every child in the country went to a school that they and their parents thought prepared them as citizens. . . . That there will be a Monday morning when it was easy to find a job or create a job and your own government didn't punish you if you tried."

So what happened to that Monday morning? Newt turned it into—honest to God, he did—the Monday Morning PAC, one more tool for raising money and staying in power. It's the kind of cynical move that can suck the air right out of a room, or a nation's capital.

Then there was the letter I received, personally signed by Sen. Mitch McConnell, chairman of the National Republican Senatorial Committee: "Dear Mrs. Huffington: On behalf of my 54 Republican Senate colleagues, I would like to invite you to join the most prestigious private association in the Republican Party committed to expanding our control of the United States Senate—the Senatorial Trust. Membership in the trust is limited to 200 individuals. . . ."

The letter was embossed with a shiny, cobalt-blue coat of arms. The word "Trust" was emblazoned in gold surrounded by stars. Trust—the glue that once held together the democratic social contract—has become just another fund-raising come-on.

Of course, the folks at the other end of Pennsylvania Avenue also put tremendous emphasis on the word "trust"—and on granting important-sounding fake titles. But let's give them some credit. The Clinton administration really tries to offer you some bang for your campaign buck.

In an infamous fund-raising package put together by the Democratic National Committee, you could plunk down $100,000 and become a "Management Trustee." For their contributions, Management Trustees got at least two meals with the president, another two with the vice president, two annual retreats with top administration officials, participation in foreign trade missions, and many other thoughtful little perks.

Johnny Chung compared donating to the Democratic Party to buying a token to get into the subway. And where is this particular gravy train intended to lead? To a position of "trust" inside the power structure, from which you get to rummage around in all the goodies at Uncle Sam's disposal—government subsidies, tax write-offs, regulatory loopholes, government contracts, ambassadorships, and more. And the ever smaller circles of exclusivity and influence come with higher and higher price tags. After all, the haves may not be able to vote more often than the have-nots, but voting's for chumps. Giving is where it's at, and Washington just keeps coming up with ways for the same people to give, give, and give again.

"I repeat," Benjamin Disraeli wrote, "that all power is a trust; that we are accountable for its exercise; that, from the people, and for the people, all springs, and all must exist."

To one accustomed to the fetid air of today's political climate, Disraeli's sentiment sounds refreshingly quaint—a century ago and a world away, before the Lincoln bedroom was farmed out like a Motel 6.

Today, the word "trust" in Washington is worth about as much as a Confederate banknote. The Medicare trust fund is going bankrupt despite the bipartisan budget tinkering, and the Social Security trust fund will hit the wall by 2032. As for the federal workers' pension trust fund and the Native American trust fund—they're in trouble too. At this point, whenever you hear someone from Washington use the word, just assume they need money.

Shakespeare had it right: "Trust none. For oaths are straws, men's faiths are wafer-cakes." And strewn among the wafer-cakes are our fading memories of long-forgotten promises and the instantly contradicted fresh ones.

When the lies become bipartisan, the people look for alternatives. Unfortunately for us all, the most plainspoken politician of the last few years was fictional—Warren Beatty's Senator Jay Bulworth. If you haven't seen *Bulworth*—and a look at its box office gross tells me you probably haven't—run, don't walk, to your local video store and rent it. When I saw it in a movie house, people were clapping and shouting out with revival-meeting fervor. The film struck a nerve because Bulworth is crazy enough to speak the truth—not the truth about what it's going to take to solve the problems, but a more fundamental step before that: admitting that the problems exist. "The real obscenity black folks live with every day/Is tryin' to believe a f***in' word Democrats and Republicans say," raps the senator. Or, as Beatty put it: "The parties have melded; they both represent the top 20 percent who have all the money."

We live in a multichannel, multiplex, multitask universe. We no longer live in a two-anything world—except in our politics, with its two-party system. The greatest weakness of this ossified way of governing is its exclusion of millions of Americans from the democratic process. But as the disenfranchised—or the merely disgusted—showed when they took to the streets of Seattle last November, they may finally be tired of waving the white flag. So unless the two parties expand to include them, with new ideas, fresh thinking, and reordered priorities, they may decide to get on with remaking the government on their own. And to the two parties, they'll just say: "Trust us."

A Case Study in Corruption

The War on Drugs and
the Drug Industry's War on Us

For an object lesson in how money has corrupted the political process—changing and even endangering our lives—just look in your medicine cabinet.

The tentacles of the pharmaceutical industry have nearly every aspect of our public policy in their vice grip: from the health care choices we are offered to the way we treat the troubled souls among us; from the government's much publicized war on illegal drugs to the shadowy battle the legal drug giants are waging to make their mood-altering products an integral part of American life; from the public leaders they pay for endorsements to the public policy they pay to influence.

MONEY → PUBLIC POLICY

Let's start with the money that drug companies are pouring into both political parties. In the last election cycle, according to the Center for Responsive Politics, pharmaceutical manufacturers and wholesalers ponied up to candidates, PACs, and party committees over $9.5 million (that includes soft and hard money—it doesn't matter to the drug makers, just as long as it's absorbed into the system). On top of this, the entire pharmaceutical and health products industry spent nearly $150 million on lobbying in 1997 and 1998, the highest total of any interest group and more than was spent on lobbying by the defense industry and labor unions combined. They know that contributing to politicians is simply a good business investment. Which is why they are investing so much more. Prozac's manufacturer, Eli Lilly, went from zero dollars in 1992 to over $787,000 in the last election cycle. "We do it because we think we have to participate in the political process," says Lilly spokesman Jeff Newton. "They are important institutions, basically, and that's why we do it."

ANTIDEPRESSANTS → CHILDREN

What kind of return are the drug companies getting on their investment? Let's just say they're beating the Dow. First of all, they've bought the benign neglect of our political leaders over the legal drugging of America, starting with our children, who were prescribed antidepressants 1,664,000 times in 1998.

This is despite the fact that no antidepressant—Prozac, Zoloft, Paxil, or Luvox—has been approved by the Food and Drug Administration for pediatric use. Luvox was approved by the FDA in 1997 for the treatment of obsessive-compulsive disorders (OCD) in children, but not for the treatment of depression.

So the question is, why are we trusting the drugmakers? The manufacturer of Luvox, Solvay, declares it "safe and effective." Yet the Physicians' Desk Reference reports that during controlled clinical trials 4 percent of children on the drug developed manic reactions. Another clinical trial found that Prozac, America's most popular antidepressant, caused mania in 6 percent of the children studied. "I have no doubt that Prozac can cause or contribute to violence and suicide," Dr. Peter Breggin, the author of *Reclaiming Our Children* and *Talking Back to Prozac*, told me. "And manic psychosis can lead to violence."

Another example: Even though the National Institutes of Health reported that "there is no current, validated diagnostic test" for Attention Deficit Hyperactivity Disorder, that has not stopped the makers of Ritalin from pushing the drug to three-quarters of the children diagnosed with ADHD in 1996, up 20 percent since 1989. At the same time, the percentage of those receiving psychotherapy dropped from 40 percent to 25 percent.

"The age range for being treated for ADHD has gone down as people think these medications are relatively safe and effective," says Richard Todd, psychiatrist at Washington University in St. Louis. "This is a very important developmental period. The effects of medications on these processes are not well understood."

Such is the crass, bottom-line approach of most health care providers, who prefer relatively cheap drugs to costly therapy. But they also speak to our lazy culture's inclination to medicate problems rather than confront them. "Settling for Ritalin says we prefer to locate our children's problems in their brains rather than in their lives," says Dr. Lawrence Diller, author of *Running on Ritalin*.

Dr. Leon Eisenberg of the Harvard Medical School described the Prozac/Luvox family of antidepressants as "potent medications that change nerve transmission." "What happens," he asks, "after two to three years of that?" No one knows. But even mildly skeptical voices from within the medical community are routinely ignored as if they were attacks on scientific progress itself.

Diller described three candidates for ADHD diagnosis: four-year-old Stevie and his two younger sisters, all of whom get dropped off for preschool at 7 A.M. by their dad and are picked up at 5:30 P.M. by their mom "if she isn't running late." Stevie is overly aggressive, and his parents, whose own marriage is troubled, are desperate, demanding a fix: prescription drugs. Is there really a consensus that this is a *medical* problem?

DRUGS → SHOOTINGS

On April 20, 1999, Dylan Klebold and his friend Eric Harris walked into their high school in Littleton, Colorado, and opened fire on their classmates, killing twelve students and a teacher before turning their guns on themselves. Buried in the saturation coverage of the Littleton massacre was the finding that traces of Luvox were found in Harris's bloodstream. The presence of Luvox, the coroner said, "does not change the cause and manner of death." Well, of course not—he died of a self-inflicted gunshot wound. But did the presence of Luvox change the cause and manner of Eric's life?

Mania is defined as "a form of psychosis characterized by exalted feelings, delusions of grandeur . . . and overproduction of ideas." That pretty much describes Harris's Web site. "My belief," he wrote, "is that if I say something, it goes. I am the law. If you don't like it, you die." This should have troubled any doctor who was following Harris after he was put on Luvox. Or was Harris one of the tens of thousands of children cavalierly put on antidepressants without either a proper psychiatric evaluation or any ongoing monitoring of side effects?

The news that Harris had been on Luvox came on the heels of the revelation the previous summer that Kip Kinkel, the Oregon school shooter, had been on Prozac. Later, Anthony "T. J." Solomon, the Conyers, Georgia, school shooter, took Ritalin the morning of the shooting. Solomon is facing trial for wounding six students just weeks after the Columbine killings; Kinkel was sentenced to 111 years in prison after killing his parents and two schoolchildren and wounding twenty-two others. Kinkel and Solomon were only fifteen at the time. The antidepressants clearly did not exorcise these teenagers' demons. The question is, did they embolden them?

"I have testified as a medical expert," Dr. Breggin says, "in three teenage cases of murder and attempted murder in which antidepressants were implicated in playing a role.

In one case a sixteen-year-old committed murder and tried to set off multiple bombs at the same time. The comparisons with Littleton are obvious and ominous."

At a congressional hearing on media violence last spring, we were reminded that 95 percent of children are never involved in a violent crime. Most children whose parents own guns do not steal them; most children who watch *Natural Born Killers* do not go on shooting rampages; and most children on antidepressants do not kill their schoolmates. But while there is constant coverage about the dangers of guns and media violence, there is no debate about the dangers of antidepressants to the brains of our most vulnerable children, no campaign to examine kids for mood-altering legal drugs in their bloodstream the same way as they are examined for illegal drugs and alcohol.

In the aftermath of the Littleton massacre, President Clinton proposed new laws to restrict the marketing of guns to children, and hosted a conference to examine the entertainment industry's marketing of violence to children. But no one planned a conference or introduced laws to deal with the third problem—the marketing of mood-altering prescription drugs for children.

DRUG MONEY → PRESIDENTIAL SEAL OF APPROVAL

Quite the opposite. Weeks after Littleton, a high-profile White House conference on mental health was held, presided over by the vice president and Mrs. Gore. The conference was hyped as "historic" but turned out to be mostly a cheerleading session for drug manufacturers, with Tipper pumping her fists and giving the thumbs-up from the stage.

It was striking that at a time when, following the rash of school shooting tragedies, parents and communities were being called upon to get more involved in the lives of their children, the conference managed to trace all behavioral and emotional problems to the biochemistry of the brain. Dr. Harold Koplewicz, director of New York University's Child Studies Center, went so far as to say that it was an "antiquated way of thinking" to blame "inadequate parenting and bad childhood traumas" for depression. And the First Lady, who not long ago told the world that it takes a village to properly raise children, backed him up, as if a well-stocked drugstore in the village center was good enough.

Even after Koplewicz blamed the wave of school violence on "depression or other mental health problems" that had been left untreated, no one at the conference challenged the good doctor by reminding him of Harris, Kinkel, or Solomon, who had all been treated. "Both plenary sessions," said Sally Zinman, director of the California Network of Mental Health Clients, "were an infomercial for drugs. There was absolutely no mention of the potential risks."

One place you will find them is in the complaint filed in the Superior Court of California by the estate of Brynn Hartman, wife of comedian Phil Hartman, who killed her husband and herself while on Zoloft. "Although none of the drug manufacturers will admit it," read the complaint, "these drugs pose an unreasonable risk of violent and suicidal behavior for a small percentage of patients. They can also cause a condition known as 'emotional blunting,' or disinhibition." Hartman's estate sued Zoloft's manufacturer, Pfizer, as well as the doctor who allegedly gave her a sample package of the drug without a proper diagnosis. To settle the case, Pfizer agreed to provide a $100,000 college fund for the Hartmans' children, Sean and Birgen. "Our principal goal in pursuing the case," said plaintiffs' attorney Andy Vickery, "was to let them know this wasn't really their mom that did this." Pfizer is also being sued in Kansas by the family of a thirteen-year-old boy who hanged himself while on Zoloft. The trial is set to start in July.

But the White House conference organizers seemed intent on avoiding all the tough questions while engaging in insidious hyperbole. The promotional literature stated that "13.7 million of the nation's children have a diagnosable mental illness." When I asked Mrs. Gore's press secretary how the conference came up with this number, she referred me to the White House press office, which in turn referred me to the Health and Human Services Department, which sent me to the American Psychiatric Association and its director of research, Dr. Harold Pincus. The problem is that Dr. Pincus had never heard of this number. It turns out that it is based on a Florida Mental Health Institute study that states that the upper limit of an estimate of "youth with any diagnosable disorder" is 20 percent. Yet despite repeated warnings in the study that we don't have the ability to project national rates, this number was quickly and conveniently treated as gospel by conference organizers and by members of Congress, who set national health policy and readily cash drug industry checks.

If one in five children in this country is mentally ill, it is time to declare a national emergency. But this is true only in the addled brains of those who lump serious mental illnesses like schizophrenia with the garden-variety depression that comes with being awkward and fourteen.

It is particularly disturbing when drugs are used to keep so-called mentally ill children docile, as occurred in California's foster care and group home system, where children were given antidepressants in dosages that psychiatric experts said could cause irreversible harm. Or in Michigan's Medicaid system, where 57 percent of children aged three or younger diagnosed with attention deficit disorder were taking drugs for it, while only 27 percent were being treated with therapy.

How come no one at the conference mentioned that these little panaceas might actually cause harm? Because, as Dr. Breggin put it, "The drug companies call the tune. The problem with this biochemical model is that by blaming the brain of the child, even for commonplace sadness and anxiety, we take parents, teachers, politicians, and all of society off the hook for the widespread suffering of our children."

Some politicians, including Rep. Sheila Jackson Lee (D-Tex.), who led the Children's Mental Health breakout session at the conference, did not let themselves off the hook. "My focus," she told me, "has been not on drug therapy but on how children can be made whole. I've seen the changes that happen when you put your hands around a troubled child by providing a nurturing environment. In our session we talked about mentoring, and about not coming in and telling parents what to do, but engaging them in a plan for their child."

But the overwhelming impression the White House conference left was that of the Clintons and the Gores endorsing a purely pharmacological view of humanity. The conference was supposed to "burst myths" about mental illness, but it never got to the truth behind the myths: that human beings consist of a soul as well as a brain. And there will never be a drug to cure a troubled soul.

DRUG COMPANIES → DAMAGE CONTROL

Buying politicians' silence and seal of approval is one thing. But sometimes it's not enough—not with a world of potential new customers out there.

So when President Clinton called on pharmaceutical companies in 1997 to test all drugs likely to be prescribed for children, Lilly signed up Leo Burnett of Chicago, the ad agency handling Reebok and McDonald's, to target consumers directly. The company sent its spokespeople out to radio shows to debate its critics (myself included) with measured talk of Lilly's "partnership with the academic community," "peer review medical journals," and the need to establish "whether the benefits outweigh the risks." Guess which side they came down on.

The pharmaceutical giant also sent misleading letters to every newspaper in America that ran my column critical of its practice of pushing Prozac on kids. Lilly executive Christina Hendricks was upfront at a drug industry conference in May 1997 about company policy toward anyone who dares be disrespectful of almighty Prozac: "We go after these people with a very serious intent to get them to cease and desist from their activities." Any attack on Prozac is countered as "belittling those suffering from depression."

Lilly's damage-control strategies include settlements that require plaintiff confidentiality, preventing any adverse Prozac side effects from being aired in public. One of the largest occurred in Louisville, Kentucky, where Lilly quietly reached agreement with the families of the victims of a Prozac user who killed eight and wounded twelve in a printing-plant shooting spree. In the trial, the plaintiffs claimed that Lilly had failed to report to the FDA adverse clinical reactions to Prozac. Judge John Potter allowed evidence of a similar case from Lilly's past, when it pleaded guilty in 1985 to criminal charges and paid hundreds of thousands of dollars in fines for concealing from the FDA the fact that patients in Britain had died after taking Oraflex, another Lilly drug.

Eli Lilly did whatever it could to keep the Louisville jury from hearing those details—including misleading the judge. On May 23, 1996, the Kentucky Supreme Court found evidence of bad faith, abuse of process, and possible fraud on the part of Lilly during the trial. A separate investigation by the Kentucky attorney general's office uncovered a secret deal wherein Lilly assured the plaintiffs' silence in exchange for promising to pay them regardless of the verdict. The plaintiffs' lawyer also agreed to settle a number of other cases he had pending against Lilly.

FDA → OVERSIGHT?

In 1997, Lilly ran a three-page Prozac ad in major magazines around the country, from *Time* to *Cosmopolitan*. Under a storm cloud that on the second page is magically transformed into a bright sun, the ad informed us, "When you're clinically depressed . . . you may have trouble sleeping. Feel unusually sad or irritable. Find it hard to concentrate. Lose your appetite. Lack energy. Or have trouble feeling pleasure. These are some of the symptoms that can point to depression. . . ."

These are also some of the symptoms that can point to life. Is there anybody on this planet who has never lacked energy, felt sad or irritable, found it hard to concentrate, or had trouble sleeping? Because if there is, I would sure like to meet that perfect specimen.

However, the small print of the ad made for much more interesting reading. The adverse side effects listed under "precautions" range from anxiety (I thought Prozac *cured* anxiety) to suicide (a fail-safe cure for depression, though probably not the one Lilly likes to brag about).

Despite a page chock-a-block with small-print warnings and small-print advice to consult a doctor, the ad is part of Lilly's multimillion-dollar campaign specifically designed to bypass doctors and target consumers directly. Treating life as an illness is bad enough. But treating childhood as a disease is tragic. And what made the timing of the ad campaign so disturbing is that it coincided with the publication of the only large-scale study on the effects of antidepressants on kids, which was then used by Lilly to try and get FDA approval for pediatric use of Prozac. The University of Texas study found that about half of the eight- to eighteen-year-olds improved. But then, so did one third of those on a placebo.

We are in desperate need of more information—not just more clinical studies but more data released to the public about the medical histories of children charged with acts of violence. Following the news about Eric Harris being on Luvox, Rep. Dennis Kucinich (D-Ohio) called for "comprehensive clinical trials by the pharmaceutical companies" to establish "the behavioral effects of antidepressants on our youth." Kucinich has been waging a lonely battle to get the FDA and the Drug Enforcement Administration to conduct "deliberate and thorough" research on Prozac's effects on children before it is approved for their use. Isn't this, after all, why these agencies exist?

This is especially important given Eli Lilly's dissembling on the issue. "Prozac is being studied by Eli Lilly and Co.," *F-D-C Reports*, which covers the drug industry, disclosed in 1997, "as an antidepressant for use in patients under 18 years of age. . . . A pre-N.D.A. [New Drug Application] filing was made." This directly contradicted the stance Lilly has assumed for public consumption, denying that it planned an expansion into the children's market.

"Lilly's proactive approach to media management may be smoothing the way for antidepressants in children," *F-D-C Reports* concluded. Indeed. Lilly representative Dr. Gary Tollefson appeared on National Public Radio earlier that year to tell listeners that adult depression "often begins in children and adolescents."

According to the FDA's Melinda Plaisier, the "FDA's decision to market a new drug is based on the answers to two questions: one, do the results of well-controlled studies provide substantial evidence of effectiveness? and two, do the results show the product is safe under the conditions of use in the proposed labeling? Safe, in this context, means that the benefits of the drug appear to outweigh the risks." If this is the case, shouldn't we demand a much fuller accounting and understanding?

Shockingly, many drugs regularly prescribed to children have been tested only on adults. The Pediatric Pharmacy Advocacy Group reports that approximately 70 percent of the drugs used by children have not been tested on them. Even their labels admit as much: "Safety and effectiveness in pediatric patients have not been established." Nonetheless, these drugs continue to be given to children, while unwitting parents and heedless politicians ignore the unknown and potentially disastrous long-term effects.

The FDA's lax oversight of drug companies has triggered terrible symptoms. Every year, two million Americans are hospitalized for drug side effects. David Lawrence, head of Kaiser Permanente, says that approximately 180,000 patients in hospitals die annually due to errors and complications from using prescription drugs.

"Most errors are not caused by stupidity, incompetence or neglect, but by system failures that allow them to occur," Lawrence said, suggesting that the safety tests done by drug companies are not enough, and that the companies fail to educate physicians and hospital workers on the proper administration of the drugs.

Currently, doctors and hospitals are not even legally required to report patients' drug side effects to the FDA. And even if they were, the agency has approximately eighty employees to monitor more than three thousand prescription drugs. In the past two years, the FDA has banned five drugs that it had previously approved but that it now deems dangerous. Why do we tolerate such lax oversight of a powerful industry that affects life and death?

DRUG COMPANIES → COLLUSION

Politicians aren't the only recipients of the drug companies' largesse—or its coercive clout. Doctors, pharmacists, researchers, and consumers are all targeted for persuasion, both subtle and aggressive. For instance, medical journals are funded predominantly by ads they carry from pharmaceutical companies, while much of the research on drugs is paid for by the drug companies themselves.

And what the pharmaceutical companies can't buy, they manipulate. Amazingly, present laws allow them to pick and choose among drug studies. "The public might be shocked to learn," Dr. Breggin told me, "that the vast majority of studies done for the FDA approval of psychiatric drugs such as Prozac show them to be of no value whatsoever. But the companies are allowed to pick out two often marginally or questionably successful studies as 'proof' that the drugs work." On top of this, there is growing evidence that the drug companies, by sponsoring their own research—as well as offering grants, trips, and other perks—are contaminating the conclusions of these vital studies. Examples abound, such as the three doctors who editorialized in the *British Medical Journal* that Prozac is not addictive, after participating in an all-expenses-paid symposium in Phoenix sponsored by Eli Lilly. So Prozac is nonaddictive, but desert golf may be.

Some of the legal drug pushers in the employ of Eli Lilly recently found their way to a suburban Washington high school. "They gave out pens and pads and little brochures pushing Prozac to these high school kids," Sidney Wolfe, director of the Public Citizens Health Research Group, said in a groundbreaking but hardly noticed 1997 *Nightline* show. Everything from fancy dinners to first-class vacations to a lifetime supply of ballpoint pens are doled out by "detail" men and women, as drug sales reps are called, who constitute a formidable grassroots army traveling around the country, leaving a trail of judgment-clouding goodies behind. In the other drug industry, such people are called runners.

Another drug company tactic puts free pens to shame. It's called "drug switching"—doctors and pharmacists induced into substituting one brand of drugs for another. Here's how the scheme works: The major pharmaceutical companies buy up the giant drug management and rating companies, which create preferred drug lists (formularies) for use by insurers and HMOs. If doctors or pharmacists don't choose the "preferred" drugs on the ratings list, the HMO often refuses to reimburse the patient. Moreover, for his refusal to switch to the drugs on the list, the prescriber risks being ejected from the HMO and losing a major source of his income. On the other hand, pharmacists are often given a few dollars as a "bonus"—cynics have another word for it—for choosing the preferred drug. Is your doctor giving you a drug because that's the best one for you? You may never know.

This pharmaceutical arm-twisting was evident in the case of Prescription Card Services, the largest and most influential drug rater in the nation, covering 50 million Americans. In its 1993–94 guidelines, PCS informed doctors and pharmacists that Prozac "is no more effective than other antidepressants and is much more expensive." But in its 1995–96 guidelines, the company claimed that Prozac had fewer side effects than the cheaper antidepressants, which were "more toxic."

Was PCS merely suffering from one of those manic mood swings that Prozac is supposed to alleviate? Or did the fact that Lilly acquired PCS in 1994 have something to do with its "objective" medical conclusions? A PCS spokesperson predictably denied a connection. Still, Prozac sales rose 40 percent—from $1.7 billion in 1994 to $2.4 billion in 1996.

"The takeover of PCS by Lilly converted a powerful opponent of Prozac into an ally," charged New York City public advocate Mark Green. And after evidently ingesting some "nonpreferred" FDA truth serum, a former senior official at Lilly who was reluctant to let me use his name (our own version of *The Insider*) said, "The whole point of buying PCS was to influence the formulary lists and protect Prozac. You make sure your drugs are on the formularies and your competitors' drugs are not. If Lilly bought PCS, there was no way they were going to let Zoloft get ahead of Prozac."

Reports that Lilly was using PCS to promote Prozac were made available to the Federal Trade Commission—which had consent agreements signed by Lilly and PCS that this would not occur. Last year, Lilly got rid of PCS, selling it to Rite Aid, a drugstore chain.

A number of states including California, New York, and Virginia are trying to address the bad medicine of drug switching. But our well-compensated Congress, once again, has been virtually silent on the issue. Recent attempts to reform managed care and health insurance, such as the Patient Access to Responsible Care Act, the Fair Care for the Uninsured Act, and the Health Care Access and Equity Act, among others, completely ignored the issue of pill-ola. When it comes to legal drugs, our representatives in Washington—pacified by dangerous doses of pharmaceutical cash—would rather switch than fight.

POLITICAL ENDORSEMENTS → PROFITS

One tried-and-true way to influence public officials is to buy the services of one. After nearly becoming president of the United States, Bob Dole became a paid spokesman for Pfizer, the maker of Viagra. Pfizer was trying to pump up sales in the wake of flaccid demand (prescriptions falling from one mil-

lion in May 1998 to 346,000 in October 1998) and bad publicity (130 men dying from Viagra-induced side effects).

But such risks can be smoothed over when you have an
underemployed former presidential candidate up your
sleeve. To further imply an official endorsement from the
corridors of power, Dole's television ad was filmed in a plush
office before imposing white columns. He positioned the ad
as a public service announcement, dismissing concerns over
Pfizer's logo appearing on the screen with the improbable
excuse that not "many men know that Pfizer makes Viagra."

He even compared his campaign to Betty Ford's fight
for breast cancer awareness. As far as I know, no drug
company ever paid Betty Ford. Pfizer's chairman, by contrast, not only paid Dole but pompously praised him for
making "men's health issues a priority for 1999" and
"advocating for Americans with disabilities." (So *that's*
why all those handicapped spots are always taken.)

"It may take a little courage," said Dole in his commercial
for Pfizer. But the courage that's needed by our public officials is the courage to turn down lucrative offers from drug
companies with self-serving agendas. Dole's protestations
have a familiar ring in this era of politicians who feel compelled to comically deny any link between the massive donations they take and the public decisions they make.

LEGAL DRUGS → ILLEGAL DRUGS

Which brings us to the government's war on illegal drugs.
You might be surprised to learn that the major pharmaceuti-

cal companies are big backers of the Drug War, helping fund both the Partnership for a Drug-Free America and the National Center on Addiction and Substance Abuse, while 17,000 of their sales reps distribute information to health care professionals to help them identify drug abuse. Isn't it ironic that the same people who are pushing mood-altering legal drugs should be taking up the challenge of alerting doctors to the dangers of the illegal competition? It's not that they don't want us on drugs—they just want us on theirs.

"Why do we have such intense punishment for people who take drugs illegally," Dr. Dean Ornish, clinical professor of medicine at the University of California at San Francisco asks, "while drug companies make billions of dollars in profits every year by selling mood-altering drugs to millions of Americans, including children?"

Dr. Ornish is not the only member of the medical community to note the continuum. Dr. Nadine Lambert, a developmental psychologist at U.C. Berkeley, published a paper in October 1998 concluding that children on Ritalin are three times more likely to develop a taste for cocaine. And a 1995 study in the *Archives of General Psychiatry* by Nora Volkow found numerous troubling similarities between methylphenidate, the key ingredient of Ritalin, and cocaine. The distribution of Ritalin in the human brain was "almost identical," the peak effects of the drugs occurred at nearly the same time, and the drugs' highs were "almost indistinguishable." "We're dealing with a drug that does have properties very similar to cocaine," she concluded.

In fact, the Drug Enforcement Administration reports increased Ritalin abuse among adolescents, who sometimes crush it into a powder and snort it—which can lead to heart failure. And it isn't just Ritalin that's abused. The DEA has collected information indicating illicit use of drugs like Prozac by cocaine and heroin users. As Rep. Kucinich, who sits on the Government Oversight Committee, wrote in a letter to the DEA, "The potential for diversion of Prozac to illegal drug users is real and the DEA's role in this decision should not be swept under the rug."

In 1998 our airwaves were filled with anti-drug commercials—paid for in part by the taxpayer. The Office of National Drug Control Policy in cooperation with the Partnership for a Drug-Free America and the Ad Council launched a billion-dollar, five-year ad campaign against drugs.

According to drug czar Barry McCaffrey, the project includes a "scientific" component that has as its goal to "try to talk" to "90 percent of the American people four times a week with a scientifically credible anti-drug message." "I think that this phase will be even more effective than the last phase of the campaign," said President Clinton last August in announcing the second year of the ads. "And I think you will see real impacts on the behavior of our young people, and that teen drug use will continue to decline."

"We're enormously proud of it," boasted McCaffrey. "I think we know what we're doing. We've got a real professional group running it for us now. They do this for a living." So at the same time that we are bombarded with hamfisted public service commercials trying to convince the young that it's "uncool" to do drugs, we're being seduced with ads making it very cool to respond to every emotional pain, stress, and discomfort by taking an exotically named pill. As heroin user Heather said on *Nightline*, "What's the difference between heroin and Prozac? . . . If you live in a neighborhood where you can't afford a therapist who costs $150-an-hour, and you've got brown tar heroin down the street, and you know that's going to make you feel better and get you through another day without killing yourself, that's what you're going to use."

We will never win the war against drugs unless we stop wilfully ignoring the connection between a culture that offers a pill for every ill and a culture that cannot wean itself from illegal drugs. But that will never happen until our political culture weans itself cold turkey from special interest money. In the end, after all, it's all about supply and demand.

DRUG COMPANIES → GOVERNMENT POLICY

Our unwillingness to look at the continuum between illegal drug abuse and legal drug abuse can be traced back to the power of the prescription drug industry, always cloaking its self-interest in language about pharmaceutical research and the public good.

One of the most chilling illustrations of the drug companies' misplaced priorities was the collective silence from the leaders of both parties over the efforts of the drug industry to stop production of inexpensive AIDS drugs in

South Africa. The story—involving powerful drug companies, powerless victims of disease, cash-hungry politicians,
a hidden army of revolving-door lobbyists, and policies
dictated more by profit than public interest—presents an
anti-civics lesson on America's broken political system.

Vice President Gore is the cochair of the U.S.–South
African Binational Commission, coordinating trade policy
between the two countries since 1994. South Africa, suffering an AIDS epidemic that our own surgeon general
has compared "to the plague that decimated the population of Europe in the 14th century," passed the Medicines
Act in November 1997. The act was intended to make it
possible for its infected citizens, many of whom live in
extreme poverty, to obtain inexpensive AIDS drugs.
"American drug companies want some of the poorest people in the world to pay U.S. market prices for drugs," Rep.
Jesse Jackson Jr. (D-Ill.) says. "But AIDS drugs can cost
$500 per week—which happens to be the annual per
capita income of sub-Saharan Africa."

Three months later, the big international pharmaceutical
companies sued South Africa, preventing the law from taking effect, and lobbied for severe trade sanctions to be placed
on the country. Among them were the three major AIDS-
drug manufacturers, Glaxo Wellcome, Bristol-Myers
Squibb, and Pfizer—companies that in 1998 alone made
$4.43 billion, $3.64 billion, and $3.35 billion, respectively.

That the drug companies are acting out of pure self-
interest is not surprising. After all, these are the same
companies that, despite making the largest profits of any
industry, are eschewing spending research money on the

lethal diseases of the poor in favor of antidepressant drugs and designer cures for "lifestyle" maladies such as baldness and toenail fungus. Malaria, which the World Health Organization describes as "closely linked to poverty," has made a fierce comeback in Africa, Latin America, Southwest Asia, and several former Soviet provinces, after nearly being eradicated decades ago. But a survey of the twenty-four largest drug companies found that none of them has an in-house research program on malaria. Meanwhile, U.S. sales of pharmaceutical drugs for pets are approaching $1 billion annually. The Pharmaceutical Research and Manufacturers of America's boast that they aim to "set every last disease on the path to extinction" may ring hollow, but at least Fluffy will never shed again!

The drug industry's unadulterated self-interest is also governing public policy. Despite two years of complaints from public health groups, Gore remained steadfast on the industry's side until embarrassing public protests at campaign stops forced him to issue anemic defenses of his position.

Who would defend leaving hundreds of thousands to die because lifesaving medicines are priced out of reach? Certainly not the same administration that spared no expense in waging a "humanitarian" war over Kosovo. Or so one would think. But Gore, wedded to a trade policy that is anything but humanitarian, aligned himself with his pharmaceutical donors.

In explanation, the vice president's office served up a bureaucratic cocktail of words—to be taken only with an empty head—claiming that it was trying "to help AIDS patients by making sure drug companies maintain profit levels to develop new AIDS medications." But what good are AIDS medications if they can't get to the people with AIDS? It looks as though Gore's vaunted "livability agenda" stops at the suburbs' edge.

Why did Al Gore go to bat for the drug companies and against AIDS patients? One answer lies in the web of Gore aides, friends, advisors, and lobbyists moving seamlessly between his inner circle and the pharmaceutical industry. Among them are Anthony Podesta, a top advisor and close friend of Gore and one of the Pharmaceutical Research and Manufacturers of America's chief lobbyists; Gore's chief domestic policy advisor David Beier, previously the top in-house lobbyist for Genentech; and Peter Knight, Gore's main fund-raiser, who made $120,000 lobbying for Schering-Plough.

Congress was equally paralyzed. In July, the House of Representatives approved the African Growth and Opportunity Act, a bill that liberalizes trade between the U.S. and Africa but contains no protections for AIDS victims— and, in fact, does not even mention the AIDS epidemic. Once again, a "solution" was enacted that completely ignored the problem.

Rep. Jackson introduced a competing bill to prevent the United States from applying sanctions on South Africa and other sub-Saharan nations that are attempting to make AIDS drugs widely available. "It is the better bill," Rep. Tony Hall (D-Ohio) told me at the time, adding that the African Growth and Opportunity Act "put[s] trade above all other humanitarian concerns." But in the end, the Clinton Administration's pressure was too much to overcome, and ninety-eight Democrats supported the Act, proving once again that in Congress—and America— money speaks louder than the muffled cries of the poor. After all, many of them won't live to see the next election cycle.

But the protesters persisted, and threatened to pursue Gore all the way to the convention. The long-overdue change in the Administration's position is directly traceable to them, and to all the activists who dramatized the consequences of an inhumane trade policy. In September, the U.S. reached an agreement that allowed South Africa to implement its Medicines Act in order "to pursue its much-needed health reforms in the interest of its people." But how many people had to die first?

The power of protest made a difference in the AIDS drug war. Will it make a difference in the war on drugs and the drug industry's war on us?

7

THE QUEST FOR LEADERS

America is a country ready to be taken—in fact, *longing* to be taken—by political leaders who can restore democracy and trust to the political process. We are eager to find a leader to tackle our long-standing problems, even if it means accepting some sacrifices. But for the last few decades too many politicians have seemed afraid of the L-word—"leadership"—because they fear that trying to exercise any might result in that other L-word—"losing."

We need politicians whose campaigns are not cobbled together out of a ragtag assortment of focus group–tested sound bites, but driven by a vision for the future. As a melting pot of diverse religions, traditions, and cultures, America is more dependent than most countries on a common "creed"—composed not only of its founding documents, but also of the great speeches of its leaders: Abraham Lincoln at Gettysburg, Martin Luther King's "I have a dream," Franklin Roosevelt assuring us that "the only thing we have to fear is fear itself," John F. Kennedy challenging Americans to "ask not what your country can do for you—ask what you can do for your country."

But there hasn't been much to add lately to that common creed. As election strategies and techniques have grown more sophisticated, leadership styles have grown more base and degraded. Nevertheless, our need for the kind of inspiring rhetoric that can pull us together and lead us into the future has remained constant, especially after eight years when the most memorable presidential line was "the era of big government is over"—at least until those immortal words, "It depends on what your definition of 'is' is."

Though we're not at war, and economists tell us we're enveloped in prosperity, we stand in a moment of crisis all the same—a crisis of persistent social problems that demand new solutions. To those on Wall Street this may seem like a brilliant hour in our national life. But the truth is very different. And in such moments, just as in times of more obvious crisis, what we need is a leader who can galvanize the American imagination. So instead of electing a chief executive officer to oversee the surging economy that has become our country's sole measure of success, we should be looking for leaders who can mobilize, educate, and inspire us to solve the problems that seethe beneath the high-flying Dow.

Clearly, the majority of voters, who didn't even bother to vote in the last election, aren't happy with leaders as mere managers. The real Clinton fatigue is a reaction not to scandal but to eight years of the kind of leadership Clinton has provided. He has approached the presidency as if he were managing a McDonald's franchise: keeping the prosperity griddle well greased, serving up a narrow range of the tried and true, and careful, above all, not to screw up a good thing—until Assistant Manager Gore gets his promotion.

But more and more of the public is longing for someone who can bring the nation together and inspire us to shake off the complacency and indifference brought on by the Great Prosperity, in the same way that FDR helped beat back the fear brought on by the Great Depression.

Sociologist Max Weber, who introduced the term "charisma," wrote of how charismatic leaders are guided by the unexpressed desires of their times. So while our fast-food politicians labor over their nightly batches of polls, Americans wait for a storyteller to give voice to their hidden longings.

Visionary leaders have always understood the importance of the bully pulpit. "I had to prepare the mind of the country and to educate our party," said Benjamin Disraeli in 1867, the year before he became England's prime minister. Through his novels and speeches, he painted a dramatic picture of the divisions between rich and poor and created a sense of urgency that laid the way for real reform. "In every dark hour of our national life," Franklin Roosevelt said in 1933, "a leadership of frankness and vigor has met with that understanding and support of the people themselves which is essential to victory."

If we're to remake America, we'll need leaders who can inspire citizens to do more than get out and vote. We'll need them to tell us what we may not want to hear. And we'll need them to remind us that the social problems we're facing cannot be solved without our participation, and that our responsibility as citizens begins with ourselves—but does not end there.

So how to do it? How to overthrow this tired old government, and reengage the American people in their own future? This is, of course, a dangerous process, with threatening creepy-crawlies lurking in the undergrowth (Buchanan fans, take note). Charismatic leaders, whose main tools are personality and oratory, can bring about the healing of an epoch, but they can also precipitate its destruction. So as long as the good times continue to roll, why not stick with stolid but solid insiders with unassailable résumés, like Al Gore? Why take the risk?

To answer these questions, I decided to mount my own listening tour—of presidential historians and assorted wise men and women.

"The people are so tired of contrivance and fabrication and hokum," said David McCullough, Harry S Truman's biographer. "They really want to be stirred in their spirit. That's when we are at our best. . . . The great presidents are people who caused those who follow them to do more than they thought they were capable of."

"The American people," said Cornel West, author of the influential *Race Matters*, "want a statesman who will tell the truth about our collective life together, good and bad, up and down, vices and virtues. That is the ultimate act of respect for the American people."

"We want different things from our leaders at different times," said historian Arthur Schlesinger Jr. "There is a latent reserve of idealism in the American people, which presidents like Teddy Roosevelt, Wilson, and Kennedy tapped. I think it's waiting to be tapped again, despite the anesthesia of prosperity."

"What a successful president does," William F. Buckley Jr. agreed, "is transcend the usual marketplace collisions. FDR accomplished that, and so did Teddy Roosevelt and Woodrow Wilson. A successful president isn't necessarily one who takes us in a direction I applaud. But he is somebody who does get the country excited about a political purpose."

Add presidential historian Doris Kearns Goodwin to the mix, and one begins to see a consensus. "We need to get away from a political system that is so filled with minute public opinion polls and focus groups and the ability to know what the electorate is thinking at every moment," she said, "that the leader loses his instincts for boldness. The job is not simply to reflect current opinion but to challenge it, move it forward and shape it. The ability to just take a stand and know that you can move the country to that stand is a lost art we need to recapture."

"The great thing about Kennedy," said McCullough, "is that he didn't say, 'I'm going to make it easier for you.' He said, 'It's going to be harder.' And he wasn't pandering to the less noble side of human nature. He was calling on us to give our best. I was one of those people—and there were thousands of us—who threw aside our jobs, whatever we were doing, to answer the call."

It is a call that transcends ideology. Sen. John McCain (R-Ariz.) identified "the ability to inspire Americans" as the quality most needed at this moment. And he, too, reached back to that defining moment in our history— JFK's speech proposing the Peace Corps: "Young people were willing to live in a village hut in Africa for years and dig irrigation ditches. Why were they willing to do that? Why were they in fact eager to do that? It's because he inspired them to do it." Sen. Paul Wellstone (D-Minn.), who himself nearly ran for president this season, echoed the same feeling: "A great president is one who successfully calls on all Americans to be their own best selves."

"There are very few voices that speak with moral authority today," Bill Galston, who spearheaded the National Commission on Civic Renewal, told me. And he was not just referring to the political world. "Once university presidents could speak with such authority. Now they're administrators and fund-raisers. The law was a profession concerned with civic responsibility. Now it's a business. There used to be a measure of moral seriousness in the media. That's virtually gone."

And it doesn't help that fewer and fewer of our best and brightest are choosing to enter politics. One of the reasons is the way we continue to blur the line between the public and the private realms. We must remember that character does not mean flawlessness, nor does it mean sexual purity. "You have a right to know if I'm a crook," says Bill Bradley. "But you don't have the right to know if I'm a sinner, since we all are."

When Wang Dan, the Chinese dissident, was finally freed in 1998, he spoke about "moral responsibility" and "moral guilt." Morality to him was a matter of life or death, not bedroom politics. So if our national discussion about leadership is to center on character and values, let us be guided by the moral sense of Wang Dan, rather than that of politicians who boast—sometimes without even being asked—that they've never committed adultery.

It's a matter of remembering what the goal is. Abraham Lincoln, for instance, knew better than to look for perfection in his military leaders. He famously responded to a complaint about General Grant's drunkenness by suggesting that the complainer find out what brand of liquor Grant drank and send a case to every one of the Union Army's generals. Grant knew how to win battles, and that was the essential quality of generalship.

The essential qualities of political leadership are not as easy to detect. Political victories are rarely as clear-cut as those on the battlefield. George W. Bush lost a great opportunity to exercise leadership when he was confronted with allegations of past cocaine use. While admitting that he'd "made some mistakes," Bush failed to recognize his biggest mistake of all: fumbling his chance to be the first politician in the post-bimbo-eruption era to take the principled position that his private life is just that— and mean it.

More important, the governor missed a larger opportunity—a chance to transform the dynamic of Campaign 2000 by turning a personal negative into a positive act of political courage and moral leadership. The important drug question was not, What did George sniff and when did he sniff it? It was, How do we handle the legion of nonviolent drug offenders who are now crowding our prisons? This long-overdue discussion is a perfect example of what happens in the absence of leadership. Subjects become "third rails," with neither party willing to touch them for fear of being incinerated on contact. Bush could have changed that by redirecting the media spotlight from the question of his past substance abuse to an issue of actual substance, namely, the racial and economic injustice of a drug policy that has created a two-tiered sentencing system.

By signing legislation in 1997 that made it possible for judges to send to jail even first-time nonviolent offenders carrying less than one gram of cocaine, Bush opened himself to charges of a double standard—if, that is, he should end up admitting that the youthful mistakes he has alluded to include being in possession of less than one gram of cocaine.

It would be a true act of leadership if Bush were to use any personal confession he might one day have to make not only to express his regret, but to decry our present drug policy that makes second chances and learning from one's mistakes nearly impossible. Bush needs to keep demonstrating his compassionate conservatism. The word "compassion" is derived from the Latin root *"compati,"* meaning "to suffer with." This would be Bush's opportunity to show that he has suffered with the 70 million Americans who drug czar Barry McCaffrey says have tried illegal drugs—and that he believes in the ability to turn their lives around, just as he clearly has. Something considerably more difficult if, thanks to Bush, they're in jail.

This would also be a chance to remind us of the power of leadership to change realities. During the war over Kosovo, Rev. Jesse Jackson and Rep. Tom Campbell (R-Calif.) did just that.

When Jackson announced he would be leading a humanitarian delegation to Belgrade last June to secure the release of the three Americans taken prisoner of war by Serbian troops, the Clinton administration tried to stop his mission. National Security Advisor Sandy Berger even claimed the visit could end up prolonging the war. When Jackson's mission succeeded, and the news surged through Washington, it was hard to find any administration official willing to celebrate.

Indeed, acts of leadership such as Jackson's are rarely embraced by the establishment, which resents being forced to rethink hardened positions, and is jealous of those bold enough to take risks. Jackson defined the success of his trip not just in terms of the soldiers' release, but in terms of beginning to rebuild "the bridge of diplomacy, trust and communication," which he called "the biggest bridge blown up" by the war.

Campbell also altered the equation of the war debate by committing a random act of leadership. Despite pressure from Senate Majority Leader Trent Lott and Speaker Dennis Hastert, he insisted on bringing to the House floor two resolutions, one declaring a state of war to exist between the United States and Yugoslavia, the other requiring an end to U.S. military involvement in Kosovo. The Democratic leadership then promptly introduced a counterresolution supporting the air campaign. Its completely unexpected defeat may not have had the finality of Congress cutting off funding for the Vietnam War after Watergate, but it was a dramatic vote of no-confidence in the administration's conduct of an ongoing war. If Campbell hadn't disturbed the congressional torpor, the Democratic leadership would never have been forced to introduce its own defensive motion—and the no-confidence signal might never have been sent.

Campbell's move was reminiscent of another unpopular act of leadership, Egyptian President Anwar Sadat's trip to Israel in 1977. Despite fierce opposition even from within his own cabinet, Sadat took the first steps down the road to peace. His courageous act did not end the ancient hatreds that have scarred the Middle East, but it did lead, ten months later, to the Camp David peace accords, and the opening of a new era of constructive diplomacy.

The ripple effects of real leadership are powerful. No wonder such courageous acts are out of favor in Washington, falling as they do outside what the Pentagon calls the acceptable "threat envelope." As Jackson and Campbell demonstrated, leadership can be unpredictable and uncontrollable—anathema to those for whom not rocking the boat is the highest form of statesmanship.

It was courage, after all, that Pericles identified in his Funeral Oration as the first quality that made Athens great. Right now, it is courage that America's leaders most conspicuously lack. Most of our politicians today zealously follow the notorious advice that Cabinet Minister Iain Macleod gave his colleagues in the Tory Party in England: "Don't stick your necks out unnecessarily, don't take up too many unpopular causes all at once; wait for the climate of opinion to change—as change it will."

One politician who has yet to take Macleod's advice is John McCain. In the first Republican presidential campaign debate last October, he firmly established himself as Campaign 2000's most powerful advocate of reform.

"I will fight to the last breath I draw," he said, "to eliminate the influence of special interests on the tax code and every other part of America. I will not rest until I give the government back to you."

Such is the seismic nature of the political realignment we're going through that of all the candidates from both parties, the only one offering a radical critique of our political system is a conservative Republican member of the world's most exclusive club. There he was, returning again and again to this simple truth: So many of the roads of our political discontent lead back to the corrupting hold big money has on Washington.

It was an impassioned declaration that put to shame Bill Bradley's somnambulant performance in the Democratic debate the night before. When lobbed a softball question about campaign finance abuses in the Clinton-Gore administration, instead of jumping on it and knocking it out of the park, Bradley watched it pass by: "There were some irregularities that were addressed. I'm not going to get into the details at this stage of the game." It was a lifeless response to an issue that should provoke outrage, calling to mind Michael Dukakis's all-brains-no-heart answer to the infamous question about what he would have done if his wife had been raped and murdered.

If Bradley can't muster any outrage in himself, how can he expect to engender it among the electorate? It wasn't that long ago that Bradley was positioning himself as the unabashed populist, the truth-telling pied piper who abandoned the Senate because, as he put it, "politics is broken." His words at the time were unequivocal: "Too much money from too many sources affecting too many decisions and creating enormous conflicts of interest. That's the problem." But when asked in the debate about leaving the Senate, he offered a heap of pallid platitudes; he wanted, he declared wanly, to engage "in a dialogue with the American people." Bradley put the cherry on his wishy-washy sundae when he declared, "You need a president that's going to make campaign fund-raising reform one of the top three or four or five issues." Or six, or seven . . . or eighty or ninety. Why stick your neck out unnecessarily?

We already have a president and plenty of candidates who comfortably place campaign finance reform somewhere between fifth and tenth on their priorities list. But as we've seen, if it's not number one, it's none.

Passionate commitment to a cause is a mark of leadership. Another mark of leadership is what, in a more inspired moment, Bradley isolated as "the ability to see around the corners, to see the future before it's here." But today's leaders are fixated on the immediate—in particular, their immediate reelection, and the voting blocs that will help them win it.

At a time when more than 11 million children in America are living not just without prescription drug benefits but without any health insurance at all, our politicians are spending their time extending benefits to elderly citizens, two-thirds of whom already have some prescription drug coverage. "I don't intend to give up the battle until it is won," President Clinton vowed righteously about his plan to provide a new, $118 billion prescription drug benefit for all Medicare recipients. And this at a time when, despite a thriving economy, the battle for our children is being lost. The percentage of uninsured children rose to 15.4 percent last year. And among poor children under age six, nearly one in four has no insurance.

But unlike the elderly, four out of four children have no vote to throw to the candidate who nods in their direction. If you wonder why we've done so much more for our senior citizens than for our children, the answer is provided by the Committee for the Study of the American Electorate: Voting by those sixty-five and older is actually going up, while turnout at the other end of the age scale continues to plummet. "Democrats lost senior men in '94 and '96," said Democratic pollster Celinda Lake. "Even more important, 1998 was the first time that Democrats have lost senior women. We have to get that constituency back." In other words, Clinton's brave battle was more about filling ballot boxes than filling prescriptions. It's no wonder that Bradley and Gore have been vying for this prized voting bloc with their own competing proposals for the most unlimited prescription drug coverage.

"The moral test of government," said Hubert Humphrey, who helped establish Medicare thirty-four years ago, "is how that government treats those who are in the dawn of life, the children; those who are in the twilight of life, the elderly; and those in the shadows of life, the sick, the needy and the unemployed." If that's the case, our health priorities are stuck in the Twilight Zone. Maybe the answer is for poor, uninsured kids to organize and create a junior version of the AARP—the FVA (Future Voters of America) or perhaps the FTA (Future Thugs of America). Their motto could be, "Help us now—or we'll make your retirement very uncomfortable."

Not only is the focus on more prescription drugs for the elderly a misguided priority, but it also overlooks the fact that, according to a study by the *Journal of the American Medical Association*, 6.6 million elderly Americans were actually being overdrugged—prescribed too many drugs or inappropriate ones "which placed them at risk of such adverse side effects as memory loss, the inability to think clearly, and sedation, leading to falls and serious injuries."

But the president and most politicians dealing with health care are living in the past, not visualizing the future. In his speech announcing the first federal survey of prescription drug prices, the president cited as an example "one of the most popular drugs for lowering cholesterol," which costs $44 for 60 tablets in Canada, but $102 in the States. "Today," he said, "prescription drugs can accomplish what once could be done only through surgery, at far less pain and far less cost." What the president failed to mention is that there are alternatives to cholesterol drugs. Just a couple of days earlier, Dr. Dean Ornish, founder and director of the nonprofit Preventive Medicine Research Institute, had conducted a bipartisan retreat with congressional leaders to introduce them to his revolution-ary—and clinically proven—concept that a program of diet, exercise, and lifestyle changes can often accomplish what is now being done through surgery and drugs.

It's the first program of its kind to demonstrate a reversal of severe heart disease, the number one killer of Americans. For five years Ornish has fought to make his program avail-able to Medicare recipients as an alternative to more expen-sive and dangerous medical treatments. The good news is that the Health Care Financing Administration—with the president's support in this case—has finally agreed to fund a demonstration project for up to 1,800 Medicare patients with coronary artery disease.

"We must focus on health care, not just disease care," Ornish told me. "Drugs frequently can be avoided if peo-ple make changes in lifestyle. We need to teach the elderly how to do this. It would be more compassionate, more competent and more cost-effective."

Rep. Charles Rangel (D-N.Y.), who convened the con-gressional retreat together with his political archenemy Rep. Dan Burton (R-Ind.), is enthusiastic. "Clearly, the tens of billions of dollars that we spend on health care is after the fact, after the disease," he told me. "Dean Ornish's demon-stration project actually makes surgery unnecessary. But it's going to take a long time to educate this country and turn it around to take a serious look at preventive care."

After all, that would require leadership—the ability to embrace new solutions instead of peddling the same old answers. The need for this kind of leadership is particu-larly acute on the issue of race.

Nearly a third of young African Americans are opting not to identify themselves with either party. To understand the growing disaffection, you only have to listen to the presidential candidates, who sound as if they're building a bridge not to the twenty-first century but to the 1950s. "When I was a rookie in the NBA," recalls Bill Bradley, "I got a lot of offers to do advertisements, even though I wasn't the best player on the team. My black teammates, some of whom were better, got none. Thus, white skin privilege." All very noble, but in the era of Michael Jordan and Tiger Woods, not exactly the most timely of appeals.

While Bradley is channeling race relations through his NBA experience, Al Gore is drawing on his inheritance. "When my father saw that thousands of his fellow Tennesseans were forced to obey Jim Crow laws," the vice president said in announcing his candidacy, "he knew America could do better. He saw a horizon in which his black and white constituents shared the same hopes in the same world. . . . Come with me toward America's new horizon."

The destination sounds great, but where's the map? Is acknowledging the existence of open racism in the past enough to exorcise the more complex and hidden variety in the present?

Speaking at a forum in Harlem last summer hosted by Rev. Al Sharpton, Bradley said that racial unity "is not for me a political position. It's who I am. It's what I believe, it's what I care most about, it's one of the main motivations for me to get into politics in the first place." But as Rev. Reginald Jackson of the Black Ministers Council of New

Jersey put it, "People would rather see a sermon than hear a sermon."

In the last election, turnout among eligible black voters fell to 29 percent. By all indications, African Americans are tired of listening to sermons and waiting for a miracle. So in November 2000, their vote may not automatically go to the candidate who merely expresses the noblest sentiments, but to the one who puts them in practice and leads other Americans to do the same.

This can only be accomplished by breaking ranks with the blind partisans in either party. Sticking to your team, no matter what the cost to principle and to the country, is often accompanied by blindness both to new answers and to current corrupt realities. One of the few who has proven willing to step outside the official party line is Sen. Joseph Lieberman of Connecticut. He emerged as the Howard Baker of the campaign finance hearings; out of the millions of words spoken during the Lewinsky scandal, his was the only speech that brought the nation together. Lieberman's eloquent condemnation of the president spoke of the "larger, graver sense of loss for our country," and of his concern "that our society's standards are sinking, that our common moral life is deteriorating and that our public life is coarsening."

Lieberman has long been a thorn in the side of pointless partisanship and insipid political correctness. As the first Orthodox Jew in the Senate, he regularly commits political heresy by refusing to campaign on the Sabbath. In the election of 1994, due to the Jewish holidays, the devout Lieberman missed seventeen days of campaigning during the critical fall months. And in 1988 he even declined to appear at the Connecticut Democratic Convention on a Saturday to accept his own nomination. A political leader who prays twice a day, without making God another cudgel with which to bash his enemies, is a welcome departure for our time.

William Gladstone, the nineteenth-century British prime minister, remarked that he prayed every day for one hour—except when he was very busy, and then he prayed for two. Lieberman brings to mind such a time, when there was nobility to politics and leaders were more than the sum of their polls and focus groups.

Another modern example of true leadership can be found in the Czech Republic. The hallmark of Vaclav Havel's leadership has always been his moral authority. He is a truth teller who speaks powerfully about the "terrible danger" of political power—"that, while pretending to confirm our existence and our identity, it will in fact rob us of them." In a speech he gave in Salzburg in July 1990, Havel painted a portrait of the political leader corrupted by power: "In short, he believes that he has something like an unconditional free pass to anywhere, even to heaven. Anyone who dares to scrutinize his pass is an enemy who does him wrong."

In another of his presidential addresses, Havel issued a warning about the way we live—"a quiet life on the peak of a volcano." He described the need for a moral, even a spiritual, underpinning to an efficient economy, and for citizens whose sense of responsibility goes beyond their own well-feathered little corner offices.

A shining example of a politician with this sense of responsibility is former President Jimmy Carter. Carter has spent his time since leaving office building homes for the poor and using his authority to promote peace abroad. Compare this with his political contemporary Gerald Ford. While Carter has been responsible for the release of fifty thousand conscientious objectors overseas and the building of dozens of Habitat for Humanity homes in the U.S., Ford has spent much of his retirement presiding over the Jerry Ford Invitational Golf Tournament. (To grasp the distance between the two men, try wrapping your tongue around the words "Jimmy Carter Invitational Golf Tournament.")

"More than any other president in memory," wrote Douglas Brinkley, Carter's biographer, "Carter turned his back on money lenders and influence peddlers." But influence peddling has been the blood coursing through most political leaders' veins. Once they leave office, it's as if they've never met a corporate board of directors they didn't want to sit on, or a product—Viagra, anyone?—they weren't willing to push.

So the question arises: What can we do to help produce more politicians of courage and conviction? Unfortunately, there's not much we can do with our current crop of poll-watching pols—and we can't manufacture such leaders in a lab. But we *can* take steps to make it more likely that reform-minded candidates will emerge in the future.

Many of the nuts-and-bolts ways we can open up the system—same-day voter registration, greater candidate access to debates, term limits, ballot access reforms, and

most important, some form of public financing of campaigns—would encourage leaders to take on the establishment and bring about a new kind of politics.

But there's another weapon that might help crack the
exclusionary walls of our political system—and that, as
unlikely as it may seem, is celebrity.

The idea of celebrities as leaders raises as many questions as
it does eyebrows. But the fact is, we live in a celebrity culture.
The battle of ideas is no longer being played out on the bat-
tleground of politics. It's being contested over the airwaves. It
is imperative that, as consumer-citizens, we learn to make distinctions between those alternative candidates whose message
is improving the national dialogue, those whose message is
polluting the national dialogue, and those who have no message at all.

One telltale sign of any insurgent candidacy worth its
salt is that at its heart there is a cause the establishment
candidates are ignoring. Of course there will always be
joke candidates posing as insurgent leaders, and it will all
be good comic relief unless the media spoils the fun by
adding gravitas where a laugh track should be—as they
most spectacularly did in the case of Donald Trump.

Given TV journalists' addiction to the rush of high ratings, it will be up to the viewers/voters to declare that
when it comes to politics, all celebrity is not created equal.
As long as we remember that celebrity can be a useful way
to capture the media's attention and reach the public, then
the famous should be welcome to spend some of their
popularity capital for the common good. After all, we have
no shortage of observers calling attention to the corrup-

tion of our political system and the division of America into two nations, but they are not getting through.

Renown in a nonpolitical arena has always been a leg up for those seeking office—whether it was John Glenn or Ronald Reagan or Bill Bradley. It might now take a celebrity committed to challenging our garrisoned system before the door opens wide enough for less well known, reform-minded candidates to succeed in the future.

If we're going to seize control of our government, we will need leaders able to dramatize the ideas that will change politics in the new century—leaders who can speak truth to power and can rally people who want to fundamentally change the country.

After too many years of pandering, divisive campaigns that appealed only to our narrowest self-interest, isn't it time we recognize that our search for a great president is also a search for our better selves? So finally, a litmus test that matters: Who can lead us to do more good than we believe we can?

8

OUR BODY POLITIC, OURSELVES: RESTORING CIVIL SOCIETY

America has been dedicated from the beginning to "Life, Liberty, and the Pursuit of Happiness." Why didn't the founding fathers instead declare themselves for life, liberty, and the pursuit of virtue? What the signers of the Declaration of Independence assumed is that some truths didn't have to be proven—they were self-evident. One such truth was that by pursuing good, man would achieve happiness—because, as the founders recognized, doing good brings joy to him who does it. So man should be free to pursue happiness—by pursuing justice and mercy. Happiness, for them, wasn't a giggle; it was the happiness of the Book of Proverbs: "Happy is he that has mercy on the poor."

So the inspiration for the merciful aims of the New Deal and the Great Society lay in America's founding. The flaw was not in how much the government programs cost, but in the fact that the cure for poverty eluded them. Thirty-four years ago, Lyndon Johnson signed the Great Society legislation, declaring a "War on Poverty." "The days of the dole are numbered," he said, and *The New York Times* concurred, predicting "the restoration of individual dignity and the long-run reduction of the need for government help." These high-minded pronouncements show how different were the expectations at the dawn of the Great Society.

The missing element that kept them from being realized was one that Arthur Schlesinger had long ago isolated as a necessary ingredient of success. "The social welfare state," he wrote in his seminal 1948 book *The Vital Center,* "is not enough. The sense of duty must be expressed specifically and passionately in the hearts and will of men, in their daily decisions and their daily existence."

What happened was sad but simple: The difficult job of galvanizing individual citizens to help those in need gave way to the much easier task of calling on the government to get the job done. So compassion came to be equated with government action, and moral righteousness with how vociferously one sounded the call.

Welfare reform was supposed to correct the flaws of the Great Society. But it too has failed to mobilize citizens in sufficient numbers. Reform, we were told, would be judged not by how many Americans got off the rolls, but by how many were able to build productive lives—and by how many citizens responded to the challenge to stop delegating compassion to government and get directly involved themselves.

Even ardent supporters of the welfare reform bill spoke of it as only "a first step." But no second step was taken at the national level, and there was no call for stepped-up citizen involvement to help rebuild lives. Peter Edelman, a committed liberal Democrat who resigned from the Clinton administration over the bill, believes that Americans have forgotten the importance of civic action: "Since the '60s, we got into a mind-set of passing a lot of government programs. We lost the emphasis on that part of poverty-fighting that has to involve civic engagement."

In 1996, Reps. J. C. Watts (R-Okla.) and Jim Talent (R-Mo.) introduced the American Community Renewal Act, a bill that would have enabled communities to fight their own war on poverty. Through tax incentives, public housing reforms, and regulatory relief, it aimed to revitalize one hundred neighborhoods torn by drugs, broken families, and failed public schools. And it was just the start.

The charitable tax credit was another important piece of legislation. Sponsored by Rep. John Kasich (R-Ohio) and Sen. Dan Coats (R-Ind.), it would have allowed families to give up to $1,000 of what they owe in taxes to a poverty-fighting charity of their choice. In one fell swoop it would have achieved three crucial objectives: First, it would have provided billions of dollars for effective grassroots groups that at the moment are operating hand-to-mouth. Second, it would have established a much-needed hierarchy of charitable priorities by targeting only those charities that serve the poor. Since less than 10 percent of charitable contributions actually make it to the poor, this shift would have had a real impact. And third, it would have strengthened the frail bonds of community. In the course of deciding which poverty-fighting group to support, citizens would have had the opportunity to become more personally involved in the lives of those in need. Most people who volunteer do so close to home and within their own communities—often in the suburbs, far away from those most at risk.

On the surface, it seems a long way from a thousand-dollar tax credit to rebuilding our moral muscles. But just as we become generous through the practice of generosity, we become compassionate through the practice of compassion.

Yet, just three years later, this hearty stew of solutions has been watered down to a thin gruel. The American Community Renewal Act of 1999 would have targeted only twenty urban and rural "renewal communities." Not only was the act diluted, but its defeat was assured when it was locked into the Taxpayer Refund and Relief Act of 1999, which Republicans knew had no chance of passing.

The debate over how best to help the poor was once agin reduced to two competing caricatures—the entitlement philosophy that places the responsibility for the huddled masses squarely at the government's feet; and the bootstraps philosophy that places the responsibility for getting into poverty, and getting out of it, squarely with the poor. And so the debate about the role of civil society, civic action, and citizen participation was banished to think tanks and conference panels.

"The old energizing myths have lost their power," says Gary Hart, "and the leaders who will be our mythmakers, our storytellers, our visionaries have not emerged yet. Both the Democratic myth of the ability of government to provide a social safety net and the Republican myth that the rising tide will lift all boats have atrophied. Neither offers a compelling vision of a greater future beyond consumption."

So the emerging tension of Campaign 2000 is between candidates from both parties vying for the title of Guardian of the Good Times and the dawning recognition—which has already shaken up the Gore campaign and transformed its rhetoric—that small-caliber issuettes, which worked in 1992 and 1996, just aren't enough this time.

"What America needs now," Jesse Jackson says, "is a president who can define our national interest in terms broad enough to include the interests of all Americans."

Will the emphasis on the public good finally supersede the message of the '90s: "It's the Booming Economy, Stupid"? "All three front-runners in the presidential race have a sense that the American people want something beyond narrow individualism and crude materialism," says Cornel West. "The question is, who's gonna be real about it?" So far, no politician from either party has dared challenge citizens in these complacent times to ask what they can do for their country. Yet in a survey conducted by Mark Penn, the president's pollster, 71 percent of Americans consider contributing to help the less fortunate a "very important obligation." And 91 percent believe that "it is the responsibility of citizens to give back to society through participation in the community." But Colin Powell is the only national figure who is making it his top priority to turn this theoretical consensus into action.

The Republican Revolution of 1994 may have been fueled by the Contract With America, but it was Newt Gingrich's rhetorical emphasis on engaging citizens to volunteer and contribute to poverty-fighting that provided its moral ballast. It turned out to be nothing but hot air, but here's what Gingrich said during his first speech as Speaker:

"The balanced budget is the right thing to do. But it doesn't, in my mind, have the moral urgency of coming to grips with what's happening to the poorest Americans. . . . To those Republicans who believe in total privatization, you can't believe in the Good Samaritan and explain that as long as business is making money we can walk by a fellow American who's hurt and not do something. And I would say to my friends on the Left who believe that there's never been a government program that wasn't worth keeping, you can't look at some of the results we now have and not want to reach out to the humans and forget the bureaucracy. And if we could build that attitude on both sides of this aisle, we would be an amazingly different place, and the country would begin to be a different place." This was supposed to be the philosophical underpinning of welfare reform, which would lead to personal rather than impersonal help, effective rather than ineffective compassion.

I remember how impressed I was when I met Gingrich's scheduler, Hardy Lott. She was spending most of her free time taking care of ten adopted children—from one mother and ten different fathers. Sometimes she would even sneak them into the Speaker's office. Or Brandy McKinney of Rep. Peter Hoekstra's (R-Mich.) office, who organized a group of fellow Hill staffers to mentor children during their lunch hours. I really believed that Hardy and Brandy exemplified what could happen to the nation if citizens were mobilized—as during a natural disaster—to roll up their sleeves and take on poverty, abuse, the crisis of neglected children.

But less than a year after the Speaker's first speech holding the gavel, I felt deceived. "The Republican Compassion Deficit," read the title of a column I wrote in November 1995 on the budget. "Republicans are betraying those core American values of compassion and caring for those most vulnerable. Less government is only half the equation. To get to real solutions, we must meet less government with more of ourselves." But we never did. And soon it was clear that, for Gingrich, the revolution was an accounting exercise of balancing the budget—and, far more cynically, a rhetorical exercise for amassing power.

Then, a couple of short months later in his 1996 State of the Union Address, President Clinton proclaimed that the era of big government was over. Or, as the president said in his second Inaugural: "We, the American people, are the solution." But this, too, proved to be just another nugget of meaningless rhetoric—focus group–tested and poll-approved, no doubt, and served up as if you could solve a problem by simply mentioning it. Such a strategy amounts to a kind of political exorcism; politicians have become expert at ritualistic incantations, and the poll results reward them. If Bill Bradley talks about race, then he's assumed to be good at solving problems of race. If Al Gore says he's on "the side of overworked parents," then we assume he'll fight for them and that it actually means something.

So when President Clinton told the Democratic Leadership Council in December 1996 that "bringing the underclass into the American mainstream" was one of the "great goals" of his administration, we assumed it would be so. In fact, the underclass never became a "great goal"; it didn't even become a footnote. Indeed, such is the prevailing mind-set that there's hardly a politician even asking what will happen to the five million people who have left the welfare rolls since 1996 as they face declining prospects for work. They don't even get lip-service anymore.

For his part, Gingrich had called for a "moral revival" of the kind that fueled the Civil War and the civil rights movement. "I don't believe that there is a single American who can see a news report of a four-year-old thrown off of a public housing project in Chicago by other children and killed and not feel that a part of your heart went. . . . How can any American read about an eleven-year-old buried with his teddy bear because he killed a fourteen-year-old and then another fourteen-year-old killed him and not have some sense of, 'My God, where has this country gone?' How can we not decide that this is a moral crisis equal to segregation, equal to slavery, and how can we not insist that every day we take steps to do something?" Apparently, he later found the answer to his question.

I remember a dinner of assorted conservatives at which Gingrich admonished us that until we pledge ourselves to save the poorest children from drugs, violence, and hopelessness, "we will not save this country and we will not earn the right to lead all Americans of all ethnic backgrounds." Then he talked about the thousands of children within half a mile of his Capitol Hill audience who have been "abandoned, betrayed and left behind." He urged every conservative think tank to come up with a plan to save Washington, and by extension, the nation's crumbling inner cities.

The strange thing was that the Speaker himself had laid out such a plan at a town hall meeting in Washington ten months earlier. It included nine strategies, and burned with a sense of urgency, signaled by Gingrich's reference to Winston Churchill's wartime rubber stamp, "ACTION THIS DAY," designed to "break through the red tape and bureaucracy and force people to get the job done." Before long the sense of urgency fell by the wayside—and soon even the rhetoric was abandoned. And as for action, there was none to be seen from Washington this day, that day, or any day.

But there has been action—sometimes heroic, always transforming—happening all across America, without any help from Washington. "The one thing more tragic than an incurable disease is knowing effective treatment and failing to ensure its widespread use," said Billy Shore, author of *The Cathedral Within*, a compelling manifesto for ending poverty. Coming from a background in Democratic politics—he was political director for Gary Hart and chief of staff for Bob Kerrey—Shore walked out of the corridors of power and founded Share Our Strength to support anti-hunger and anti-poverty efforts. "We want to shine a spotlight on the pockets of poverty that remain in America," the president said as he embarked on his poverty tour last summer. But, as Shore told me, "unless the administration is willing to change its focus to make poverty-fighting its new ethic, the poverty tour will lead to no change."

The challenge of the first decade of the next century will be to identify those private-sector, nonprofit programs that work, and with the dedication of the cathedral-builders of old, use government funding to replicate them, sustain them, and "bring them to market." The fact that poverty has persisted in this country does not mean there are no solutions. It simply means we haven't shown the national will to take the solutions that do exist and implement them on a large scale.

One essential element of every effective treatment—most difficult to address in legislation—was captured by Bill Milliken, the president of Communities in Schools, who has spent his life in the trenches: "No life has ever been turned around without a loving relationship." Which is why even though the task of ending poverty is monumental, it also has to be wrenchingly up close and personal—and to involve our most up close and personal institution, the family.

On Saturday, November 20, America saw its first National Family Volunteer Day. Launched by the Points of Light Foundation, it brought together grassroots organizations, corporate volunteer centers, and Fortune 100 companies with a single goal: getting children to join with their parents, grandparents, aunts, uncles, and siblings to make a difference in their communities.

Family volunteering is not some feel-good act of noblesse oblige, a camera-ready photo op timed for the annual pre-Thanksgiving pity parade ("Oh, look, Bob—it's that heart-tugging soup kitchen float, followed by the giant Homeless Guy balloon. The kids just love him!"). It is an effective answer to the pervasive narcissism of our consumption-crazy culture. Children brought up to feel that their lives have a larger purpose beyond themselves are more likely to keep their own troubles in perspective—and less likely to open fire on their classmates.

In the wake of tragedies like the one in Columbine, TV bookers race to their Rolodexes to line up the usual suspects to explain how something like this could occur. So for the umpteenth time we get the gun-control advocate debating the NRA mouthpiece, and talking heads from the Christian Coalition and the ACLU locking horns over the value of posting the Ten Commandments on the school cafeteria wall.

Now, I'm certainly in favor of all the gun control we can get—but if we want to rebuild our frayed civil society, we'd better reload young people's hearts and spirits at the same time. And while reading the Ten Commandments is great, living them is even better—particularly the biblical admonition about tending to the least among us. The TV bookers need to program their speed dials to include people around the country who are using family volunteering to keep kids connected to their own families as well as their communities.

Modern America is plagued with disconnections—blacks from whites, rich from poor, and perhaps most troubling, parents from children. One of the greatest ways to bridge these divides is teaching children from an early age the importance of making service an integral part of their lives. It helps them see beyond the importance of being popular to the value of being useful.

"My goal," said Julie Abrams, who volunteered at a nursing home with her two children, ages seven and four, "is to let them know that not everyone in the world is rich, white, straight, and healthy. I don't think you can teach them that without showing it to them firsthand." Kimberli Meadows and her three children—ages twelve, five, and one—volunteered at a farm in Maryland that provides fresh produce for families in urban areas: "When we come back home after an event such as this, it's usually our best day together."

National Family Volunteer Day was designed to be not a twenty-four-hour symbolic splash, but a first step toward making family volunteering an essential part of the American culture. When families gather around to decide what they're going to do this weekend—go to the mall? see a movie? hit the beach?—volunteering should be among the regular options. As Al Franken put it in a public service announcement, "Too busy watching TV to help someone else? Are your children listless and irritating? Maybe it's time for your family to get off your duffs and do a little community volunteering."

And in these multitasking times, overworked parents should happily note that family volunteering allows them to kill two birds with one stone: serving their community while spending quality time with their kids. "Finding ways to stay involved with both your children and your community is important," says Beth Lovain, who brings her children along when she delivers food to homebound people with AIDS. "Parenting is such an arduous task that it's easy to lose touch with the larger community."

Family volunteering is also a powerful way to bring another dimension to your relationship with your children. For my own kids, volunteering together has been a profound educational experience—they've absorbed lessons they could easily have rejected if I had just preached them.

We are all born with an instinct for altruism and giving as surely as we are born with instincts for survival, sex, and power. But like muscles that need to be exercised, our children's generosity and compassion can only be developed through regular workouts. Think of family volunteering as aerobics for the soul.

As we drive fancier cars, live in bigger houses, and work longer hours to pay for them, we increasingly recognize that something is missing. Stephen Covey, the bestselling author of *The Seven Habits of Highly Effective People* and a family-volunteering champion, describes it as a win-win-win situation: "Communities win as the recipients of the services that families give. Parents win because they have an organized, workable program for teaching values and bringing their families together. And our children win because they learn the values that are so hard to come by in today's world."

If families are the bricks that make up a strong community, then family volunteering can be the mortar that holds it together. And there are so many places crying out for such help. A Place Called Home in the middle of South Central Los Angeles is one of them. It was founded twelve years ago by Deborah Constance, a successful real estate agent who wanted her life to be about something larger than herself.

She went on to create a zone of caring and love for children and teenagers in the middle of the violence and drugs that surround them. In a precinct that reported 134 robberies, 11 homicides, 134 felony assaults, and 10 attempted murders in one month, A Place Called Home has provided a safe haven for two thousand children, with the help of dedicated citizens giving of their time and money. And central to it all is Deborah herself. Walking with her the first day I met her, through the maze of bustling rooms, I could clearly see that she had found her mission. Every few steps, she would stop to listen to Charley's latest poem, or point proudly at the dolls some children were making, or praise a budding athlete's jump shot in the gym.

Here was someone saving her corner of the country.

On the other coast, right under the nose of our nation's lawmakers, Marsh Ward runs Clean and Sober Streets. This Capitol Hill shelter provides what is often the last chance for drug addicts on the Washington streets. Some of them will wait in line for the whole night to get an admittance form. The next step is to return in a week with the form filled out to prove that they have attended at least three Alcoholics Anonymous meetings. If they skip even one, they will not be admitted.

"Half of them will come back with their sheets filled," Ward told me on Saturday morning as we were eating pancakes with the residents after their weekly community meeting. The pancakes were made by James Roe, who until he discovered Clean and Sober Streets had been a "fire-barrel drunk" his whole adult life. He would build a fire with his other street friends, and they would pass the bottle around.

Now he is working for his high school degree and makes a mean pancake. Everyone has a chore at the shelter, and recovering addicts act as mentors to new arrivals.

One new arrival had recently celebrated her forty-second birthday. "When was the last time," Marsh asked her as she was handing him a piece of cake, "that you had a sober birthday?" "I've never had a sober birthday," she replied. "My parents drugged me ever since I was a baby, and I started drinking or drugging myself as soon as I could." Tears rolled down Marsh's face. This is what makes all he goes through to keep the place open worth it.

When Clean and Sober Streets ran out of money a few years back, Marsh stopped taking a salary, and unable to pay his rent, moved into the shelter himself until things turned around. "We make sure," he said, "that the residents don't even notice that we are scraping to make ends meet."

Two and a half miles away, in Anacostia, Hannah Hawkins runs the Children of Mine Center. She takes in sixty to seventy children and offers them hot meals, help with their homework, Bible studies, and above all proof in everything she does that someone cares for them.

Marsh Ward and Hannah Hawkins run programs too small to be on any national radar screen. But every day, thanks to them, lives are being turned around. They share three powerful tools: a personal one-on-one connection with the people they serve; spiritual nourishment to fill the void left by drugs, alcohol, and absent parents; and a firm challenge to all those they help.

These projects, however successful, can't match the raw buying power of annual government appropriations. But government dollars, however many billions of them, will never be a substitute for individual engagement in helping turn around broken lives. Bringing the two together is the only way we'll be able to save our impoverished communities. The alternative is to let the suffering fester. "Pain," writes Randall Robinson in his new book, *The Debt*, "is difficult. Unremarked, unacknowledged, unobserved pain is usually lethal to collective psychic health. Social harmony, at least, is an early sure victim."

So what we need is nothing less than a crusade to inspire citizens to solve problems locally. An extraordinary level of citizen participation was always at the heart of the American experiment, as Alexis de Tocqueville famously observed. The Reverend Henry Delaney, who has over the last dozen years transformed a neighborhood of boarded-up crack houses in Savannah, Georgia, summed up the mission: "I want to get people involved with what we are doing. It's like putting a poker in the fire. After a while, the fire gets in the poker, too." In sharp contrast to the feeble bromides of our national leaders, the men and women who are every day taking small, concrete, unglamorous steps to end present-day suffering also have a way with words, born from their experience.

There is increasing evidence that Americans are prepared to take those small steps. At the same time that young people are abandoning politics, they're embracing civic participation through service—in soup kitchens, hospitals, and schools. According to a report by the National Association of Secretaries of State, "when it comes to one-on-one volunteering in homeless shelters or in tutoring programs, young people are volunteering in greater numbers than they were a decade ago. . . . Traditional notions of citizenship, which include being politically interested and involved, are much less salient to this generation."

Idealistic young people, who in earlier times would have found a home in political parties, are now trying to change the world directly, tackling poverty, homelessness, health care, and job training from the bottom up. They have learned to stop waiting for the next five-year plan from Washington to solve our social problems.

There is no question: political leaders, gifted with vision, creativity, and determination, would have the power to take us from where we are to where we need to be—working to save the millions of lives now at risk. But few have made civic engagement a priority.

One who has is Kathleen Kennedy Townsend. The two-term lieutenant governor of Maryland has a sense of mission that was born at a young age. When her uncle John F. Kennedy was assassinated, Townsend's father Robert Kennedy penned a note to his twelve-year-old daughter on White House stationery: "As the oldest of the Kennedy grandchildren you have a particular responsibility now. . . . Be kind to others and work for your country. Love, Daddy." The letter, now hanging in her home, has been a guiding force in her life. And it's clear that his passion for civic engagement courses through her veins.

"The central tenet of our American faith," she told a Halloween gathering of children and adults, "is the belief that we have an obligation to one another and a responsibility to work shoulder-to-shoulder to meet the common challenges of our nation." Turning to the parents, she spoke about the need to reawaken a sense of duty in our nation's citizens: "You must engage your best talents and best passions to rebuild our communities."

It was largely through her efforts that Maryland became the first state to require high school students to perform community service in order to graduate. Ninety-five percent of the students who complete the program say they'll continue to be involved in volunteerism after they graduate. "How can they learn American history and the meaning of democracy," she asks, "without understanding in the most personal and direct manner the spirit of community service, justice, civic participation and freedom?"

One of her signature initiatives, the HotSpot Strategy, is a community policing program that targets Maryland's most dangerous neighborhoods. "In Baltimore," she explains, "we focused on six neighborhoods. In five of the six, crime came down almost immediately. What made the sixth different is that there was no cooperation from the community. The lesson is, we can't see government as something that does something to us, or for us, but with us."

Like her father, Townsend is a storyteller—able to put a human face on her programs. In discussing her creation of the nation's first statewide office of character education, for instance, she relates a visit she made to one inner-city school: "Outside the school wall, students endure chaos and violence. But there is peace within. When a small group of fifth graders was asked, 'Is it hard to tell your friends that you don't like the way they're acting?' one girl, Ashley, didn't hesitate: 'Oh, no. We're leaders, and we have a responsibility to the other students and to our teachers and to our school. And we have the bravery and courage to stand up and tell them when they're acting bad.' Listen to the words coming out of the mouths of eleven-year-old children: leaders, responsibility, bravery, courage."

John McCain is another who has made civic engagement a priority. "They tell me there are no great causes," he says. "And I say wherever there's an elderly person that needs shelter, there's a great cause. Wherever there's a hungry child, there's a great cause. Wherever there are people killing each other like in East Timor today, there is a great cause." But it takes the commitment of cathedral builders, not just drive-through dignitaries, to rise to challenges such as these.

And if we as a nation are going to make such a commitment, one way to start is by redefining what it means to be charitable. It is not just a matter of the wealthy giving away more of their wealth; it's a matter of what they are giving it to. Take *Slate* magazine's list of the sixty largest American personal charitable contributions for the first quarter of 1999. First on the list is Audrey Jones Beck, who gave forty-seven Impressionist and Post-Impressionist paintings, estimated to be worth more than $80 million, to the Museum of Fine Arts in Houston. Now, I'm sure that's very nice for the museum, which will name its new building the Audrey Jones Beck Building. Donating paintings is a great—as the fundraisers call it—"naming opportunity." But it certainly isn't charitable giving in the biblical sense of giving to the least fortunate, nor is it probably what *Slate* had in mind by starting its counterlist to the Forbes 400.

It's time to start deconstructing charitable giving, to stop defining it as any tax-deductible contribution to any old 501(c)3. A look at the top givers on the *Slate* list reveals that most of the major gifts have nothing to do with redressing the huge imbalances between those who are getting richer every year and those who are just getting by or falling behind. In fact, a lot of the gifts only serve to make the world of the super-rich just a little nicer.

Domino's Pizza founder Thomas Monaghan gave $50 million to create a Roman Catholic law school. Investor Henry Tippie gave $30 million to the University of Iowa. Film producer Walter Kline gave his movie and videotape archives, estimated at $25 million, to the North Carolina School of the Arts. Bill Gates gave $20 million to the Massachusetts Institute of Technology. Gates and Tippie will soon be joining Mrs. Beck with their very own buildings.

"Elites," Harvard sociologist Francie Ostrower writes in her book *Why the Wealthy Give*, "take philanthropy and adapt it into an entire way of life that serves as a vehicle for the cultural and social life of their class." To reverse these self-referential patterns of giving is going to take some heavy lifting. It's going to take political leaders dropping the pretense that all is well, and stressing, as Housing and Urban Development Secretary Andrew Cuomo did last June, that "the good news is getting better, and the bad news is getting worse." It's going to take political courage to reverse this trend. And it's going to take creative giving that addresses society's pressing needs, rather than the giver's personal interests.

Compare, for example, two gifts listed on the *Slate* 60 as though they exemplified equal public virtue. Robert G.

Mondavi, chairman of the Robert Mondavi winery, gave $20 million to create the American Center for Wine, Food and the Arts in his hometown of Napa, California. Meanwhile, Ron Burkle, Ted Forstmann, and John Walton gave $30 million to the Children's Scholarship Fund for low-income children trapped in dysfunctional schools. I'm sorry, but these two gifts do not even belong in the same category. Yet *Slate*—and the IRS—treat them as equivalent.

If we can't encourage the wealthy to give to the poor out of the goodness of their hearts or their concern for a stable democracy, we'll just have to shame them into doing the right thing. What if corporations and individuals who can afford it were expected as a matter of course to tithe— to give 10 percent of their income to those most in need? (In 1998, corporations gave 1 percent of pretax earnings.)

And what if political campaigns led the way? Bill Bradley says that his "focus is on 15 million children who are poor in America." George W. Bush says he's running to make sure "no one is left behind." So let them ask everyone who contributes to their campaigns to donate 10 percent to a poverty-fighting group of their choice. If they don't, the campaigns should just take 10 percent off the top and give it to those Bush has termed "the armies of compassion."

Which of our Bible-quoting presidential candidates and which of our Forbes 400 millionaires will start putting in practice the Bible's admonition, "From whom much is given, from him that much more shall be expected"?

There are times for building monuments and there are times for building lives. Ours is undoubtedly a time when we should be building lives. Instead we keep building monuments. It's our modern edifice complex. It's another indicator of how out of touch our political leaders are that Bob Dole launched a lavish fund-raising drive to raise $100 million in government and private funds for a World War II memorial at a time when we have at least 270,000 homeless veterans. Close to $70 million has been raised so far. I defer to no one in my gratitude for the sacrifice of those who gave their lives for our freedom. But surely we dishonor the dead when we do not honor the living.

Every time we do something, we forgo doing something else. Economists call it "opportunity cost." Has anyone stopped to consider what $100 million could do for at-risk children? Or for that matter, what $100 million could do for homeless veterans? A $100 million revolving loan fund would make possible five thousand units of self-sustaining, long-term transitional housing, according to the organization LA Vets. And here's a short list of other things we won't be doing with the $100 million that will go to add another monument to a capital city crowded with them:

- $100 million would make it possible for 110,000 people to receive drug rehabilitation treatment, be taught life skills, be placed in a job, and be reunited with their families—according to the Bowery Mission in New York.
- $100 million would feed one million people through six new neighborhood centers and a fleet of vans—according to Love Is Feeding Everyone in Los Angeles.

- $100 million would fund a thousand literacy programs serving 130,000 children—according to the Harlem Educational Activities Fund.
- $100 million would allow 100,000 more children to receive mentoring for one year—according to Big Brothers and Big Sisters.
- $100 million would activate 166 new sites to feed 18,000 children for a year—according to Kid Care in Houston.

And any of the above could be done in the name of World War II heroes.

Across the river from where the World War II monument will stand, in the forgotten city of Anacostia, there are children whose voices are silenced by stray bullets, children who have to be evacuated from their school because water is pouring in from a leaky roof, children who go without books, pencils, and even teachers. How can we be deaf to the voices of fear, the voices that end in a moment—not in a place far from home but in a place ten minutes from where the monument is supposed to be built?

In *The Decline and Fall of the Roman Empire*, Edward Gibbon painted a dramatic picture of what happens when civic virtue and civic engagement atrophy. "Prosperity," he wrote of Rome, "ripened the principle of decay. . . . As soon as time or accident had removed the artificial supports, the stupendous fabric yielded to the pressure of its own weight."

Unless we build a critical mass of men and women engaged in saving our communities, we risk repeating history.

9

THE LONG MARCH OF CAMPAIGN FINANCE REFORM

The strongest signal that we need campaign finance reform is the fact that our leaders refuse to enact any. This is despite the public's overwhelming support for the issue. If the will of the people doesn't matter to them, what does—the will of the big-bucks contributors?

Now, for some, the topic of campaign finance reform—the nuts and bolts of how we fund elections—may seem like inside politics. But that's just the problem: Corruption has crawled inside our political system, like a virus that burrows into a healthy body and cripples its host. "This democracy cannot survive without the confidence of the people in the legislative and electoral process," Sen. Russ Feingold (D-Wisc.) told his colleagues. "The prevalence—no, the dominance—of money in our system of elections and our legislature will in the end cause them to crumble. If we don't take steps to clean up this system it ultimately will consume us along with our finest American ideals."

Doris Haddock—"Granny D," the eighty-nine-year-old great-grandmother who walked from the Pacific to the Atlantic to call attention to the way big money corrupts politics—agrees. "It is my belief," she told the 1999 Reform Party Convention, "that a worthy American ought to be able to run for a public office without having to sell his or her soul to the corporations or the unions. . . . Fund-raising muscle should not be the measure of a candidate. Ideas, character, track record, leadership skills—those ought to be the measures of our leaders."

Granny D has a clear vision of democracy, and that is what motivates her drive to sweep big money out of politics. "It is said that democracy is not something we have, but something we do," she told the convention delegates. "But right now, we cannot do it because we cannot speak. We are shouted down by the bullhorns of big money. It is money with no manners for democracy, and it must be escorted from the room. If money is speech, then those with more money have more speech, and that idea is antithetical to democracy."

She modeled her cross-country trek on that of Mildred Norman, known as the "Peace Pilgrim," who walked across the country seven times between 1948 and 1958 to promote world peace. Each day, the Peace Pilgrim walked until she was offered a place to rest, and fasted until she was handed food. So did Granny D. She trained for her pilgrimage by hiking ten miles a day with a twenty-five-pound knapsack. Her cell phone kept her in regular contact with radio stations around the country.

Haddock was born in Dublin, New Hampshire, the village where she still serves on the town council and is a deacon of the Episcopal Church. Campaign finance reform was a frequent topic of discussion in the Tuesday Morning Academy, which Granny D describes as "a group of old women like me." The issue kept gnawing at her until January 1998, when she saw an old man walking along the highway, "miles and miles from any town or house."

"This old man mesmerized me," she wrote in her diary. "His image resonated with something deep in me. I had been worrying for months about how . . . I might use my time—what I have left of it. As we drove further there seemed to be some connection with this man on the road and that simmering question. I had been on the road myself a long time ago with my husband Jim, and for a high political purpose. This old man was perhaps some ghost of those days, still out there like a part of me. He was calling to me, as might my late husband be calling.

"Something else had been eating at me, too. In the 1960s my husband and I . . . had indeed helped to achieve an impressive political victory to prevent nuclear detonations near an Alaskan village. Part of our success was made possible because we were able to appeal to the sense of fair play of U.S. Senators and Representatives. When they knew what we knew, they gladly and forcefully helped us stop a bad program.

"But things have changed. During my husband's final years I worked hard, and successfully, to bring additional modest services to our town for people with Alzheimer's Disease and dementia. These people needed services, and their family caregivers needed support. The logic and necessity of these programs was obvious, yet our only way of getting funding was to raise money privately, which we did . . . it was no longer possible to just call our Congressperson and get some help. Congresspersons, I discovered, were no longer interested in what someone might have to suggest if they were not big-money contributors, regardless of the merits of their idea or the necessity of a program. I could never fully accept this new fact.

"For the first time in my life I felt politically powerless—which is something no American should ever feel. It was like not living in one's own country. There were solutions to the campaign finance mess, but the best ideas kept getting voted down in Congress. My own senator would not respond to my requests for action—ignoring a stack of petitions I had gathered on the subject. It all sickened me—an old Yankee who was used to calling up my Rep and getting things moving. To not have a Senator or Congressman! My God; one might as well be in China. It was deeply disturbing. A few minutes after seeing the old man on the highway, it occurred to me that I should go on the road, too. I should do it for campaign finance reform."

When Bill Clinton and Al Gore arrived in Little Rock to launch Gore's presidential bid, Haddock held a silent vigil in front of the Statehouse Convention Center to protest Gore's refusal to reject soft money.

"The future," political theorist John Schaar wrote, "is not a result of choices among alternative paths offered by the present, but a place that is created—created first in mind and will, created next in activity." That's a fair summation of Granny D's words and deeds.

Meanwhile, back in Congress, Senator Mitch McConnell and his friends are thumbing their noses at the future. Like drunks on a bender, they know we're on the road to political ruin, but don't have the will to admit they need help. ("Hi, my name is Trent, and I'm a fund-raise-aholic.")

If they ever decide to get clean they won't have to look far for a sponsor. Sen. John McCain knows well the perils of demon money, its powers of addiction. To increase the chances of his bill passing the Senate, McCain and his cosponsor Sen. Russ Feingold even stripped of it a key controversial provision, the ban on issue ads sixty days before an election. What they kept intact is the crown jewel of McCain-Feingold: a complete ban on soft money, the unregulated, unlimited contributions to political parties that have become the lifeblood of our corrupt politics.

The strategy deprived opponents of their favorite hifalutin' argument: that reform is an assault on the First Amendment (with which many of them recently began a passionate and suspicious affair). Soft money corporate contributions—often equally dispersed to both parties— can be looked at as a business investment, or as legalized bribery. But they are certainly not expressions of free speech. Indeed, the ban on corporate campaign contributions was shepherded into law by Teddy Roosevelt in 1907. That ban is still in place; the concept of soft money, far from endangering free speech, is a giant loophole that has effectively abrogated the law.

Granny D was in Washington to lend support as the bill was debated. "I walked with McCain and Feingold from their offices to the Capitol," she told me. (After 2,200 miles, what's a few more blocks for reform?) "I wanted them to know that the people out in the hinterlands are worried, frustrated and feel that their most basic freedom—to be a self-governing people—has been taken from them by big-money politics."

Yet campaign finance foes and presidential candidates continue to propagate the nonsense that contributors are just average Americans participating in the political process. It's the "just folks" spin, used to explain away the millions of dollars raised by Bush, Gore, and Bradley.

The ruse is particularly laughable as a defense of soft money. Nevertheless, it is used again and again, as are any number of unsustainable arguments. There was McConnell during the debate last fall, lashing out at McCain, soft money plumage in full glory, grandiloquently asking, "How can it be corruption if no one is corrupt?" He was clearly counting on McCain's reluctance to name names on the Senate floor. Then two supposed supporters of reform tried to kill it. Sen. Bob Torricelli (D-N.J.)—who, as chairman of the Democratic Senatorial Campaign Committee, was credited with a 130 percent increase in soft money contributed to its coffers—joined Minority Leader Sen. Tom Daschle (D-S.D.) in offering a substitute to the bill that would also regulate "issues advertising." In the name of more perfect reform, the amendment would have ensured that no reform at all got passed by reintroducing a ban on specific-issue ads that is a poison pill to conservatives. It's not surprising that

Torricelli's move came immediately after conservative Kansas Sen. Sam Brownback signed on with McCain. It's a congressional favorite: Don't like a bill? Stick an unpopular amendment to it and watch them both go down.

When the Democratic National Committee announced last summer that it planned to raise $200 million of soft money in time for the presidential race, former Carter pollster Pat Caddell concluded that "to get that kind of money there will have to be a fire sale of the government. This time they won't be renting the Lincoln bedroom, they'll be selling whole wings and entire Cabinet departments." Republicans are just as deeply engaged in the public policy sell-off, having already raised $31 million in soft money, nearly double the amount raised in the same period four years ago. Even more important, they will also have the potential to raise hundreds of millions in soft money through Bush's Pioneers.

What we're watching here is the market system—supply and demand—applied in the one place it doesn't belong: the pursuit of the common good. Just look at Bush. The corporate world senses that he'll be coming into a pretty good supply of public policy in a short while, and the advance orders are flooding in. Which is key in such a tight market. Show up on Election Day to buy yourself some of the public good and you'll find it's already sold out. Buy early, buy often, and then you can sit back and wait for the loopholes and tax and regulatory exemptions to be delivered ... at least until the midterm campaigns begin, when they'll be glad to start filling orders again.

It's not just reformers and those shut out of the system who are disgusted by what's happening. Even corporate leaders, who are at the heart of the soft money quid pro quo, are beginning to balk at the shakedowns. "The pressure to give soft money can be quite intense," said Edward Kangas of the Committee for Economic Development, a group of business executives that came out last year in favor of banning soft money and curbing issue ads. "And the more a business is impacted by federal regulation, the more it feels it doesn't have a choice." But "extortion" is such an ugly word; "soft money" is so much easier on the ears.

As Charles Kolb, president of the committee and a former Bush administration official, added: "We're tired of being hit up and shaken down. . . . The subtext is, 'If you won't play with me, I won't play with you.'" The subtext became the text when McConnell, the human roadblock standing in the way of campaign finance reform, sent blistering letters to members of the CED urging them to resign because of the committee's "all-out campaign to eviscerate private sector participation in politics." I guess he forgot that other way the private sector can participate in politics—voting.

McConnell also claimed that the reforms would "render the Republican Party powerless to defend pro-business candidates from negative TV attacks by labor unions, trial lawyers and radical environmentalists." How inspiring—finally, someone has stepped forward to defend that poor waif the "pro-business candidate."

Last September, McConnell compared his enemies' return year after year to "Glenn Close in the bathtub in *Fatal Attraction.*" He has gone so far as to cloak himself in the moral cloth of the civil rights movement. "On this issue of whether the money is important to speech and campaigns," he said, summarizing a truly impressive amount of gall, "Thurgood Marshall and I are on the same side." Rep. Chris Shays (R-Conn.), who has co-sponsored companion legislation to McCain-Feingold in the House, sees a different parallel. "This is like the civil rights struggle," he told me. "We have to keep bringing the bill up again and again and again, forcing its opponents to expose themselves by filibustering it."

In fact, this battle has even more in common with the civil rights struggle. Years and years from now, long after this legislation has passed and people are shocked that anyone would ever have considered soft money bribes legal, history will render its stern judgment on those who blocked this reform. Yes, Sen. McConnell, civil rights may be the appropriate metaphor here, but it's not one that bodes well for your legacy. Just ask George Wallace.

So the big-bucks binge continues to intoxicate the Senate. But the time has come for an intervention—even if it means dragging the Republican leadership kicking and screaming off to donor detox. After all, the Progressive Era, the last great era of electoral reform (excluding the outburst after Watergate), was led by a Republican, Teddy Roosevelt. "This sums up my whole attitude in the matter," he said on the role of money in politics. "[It] is, after all, simply the question of treating each man, rich or poor, on his merits, and making him feel that at the White House, which is the nation's property, all reputable citizens of the nation are sure of like treatment."

So anyone who's convinced there's no way to change the system, take note: It's been done before. Primary elections, direct elections (until the Progressive Era, U.S. senators were chosen by state legislatures), the initiative and referendum process—all these came as the result of the turn-of-the-century Progressives' movement for clean and open government. But by far the most profound and lasting influence of the Progressive reforms stemmed from their concern about the unchecked power of monopolies over the economic and political life of the nation—indeed, over the very lives of average Americans. The Progressives' reluctant answer was to furnish the federal government— which presumably through the other electoral reforms would be made more responsive to the public—with the power to meet the plutocrats on an equal footing.

In March 1908, Wisconsin Senator Robert La Follette gave one of the most famous speeches ever delivered in the United States Senate. "He attempted to prove," Richard Hofstadter writes in *The Age of Reform*, "with careful documentation from the interlocking directorates of American corporations that fewer than one hundred men, acting in concert, controlled the great business interests of the country. 'Does anyone doubt,' he asked, 'the community of interest that binds these men together?'"

Political liberty is always linked to economic liberty; that was at the heart of Woodrow Wilson's 1912 campaign for president, in which he embarked on "a crusade against powers that have governed us, that have limited our development, that have determined our lives, that have set us in a straitjacket to do as they please." The Jeffersonian ideal was being wiped out by corporations consuming the entire economy. Wilson's great fear was that "the voice of the ordinary

voter would be as effectively eliminated from political influence as the voice of the ordinary stockholder had been from
the conduct of the giant corporation." The power of economic decision had been stolen from the people, and
Progressives feared that the power of political decision
would follow, if not by directly controlled state legislatures,
then by bought-and-paid-for machine politicians. So they
fought to ensure that a freely and democratically elected
government—with vast new powers to regulate—could
stand firm against the power of the plutocrats. It's a battle
that has to be fought again today.

The 1976 Supreme Court decision—*Buckley* v. *Valeo*—
that equated campaign contributions with free speech, has
become the ace in the hole of opponents of electoral
reform. But as A. J. Liebling famously put it, there is only
"freedom of the press for those who can afford to own
one." The same holds true in modern political life: The
democratic process is open only to those who can afford to
own a politician.

Among the forces trying to change this is Public
Campaign, founded by Ellen Miller to bring about a campaign finance strategy known as "Clean Money." "How do
you get to the average citizen?" asks Miller. "Through state-
based organizations and initiatives. We use the states to
organize people around the idea. So the political viability of
Clean Money arises in the states, and then after building
grassroots support, we hope to proceed to federal reforms."

The Clean Money agenda seeks to address the "four
fundamentals" of campaign finance reform: the rising
costs of campaigns, the conflict of interest inherent in pri-

vate donations, the lack of competition for incumbent candidates, and the never-ending money chase.

In order to qualify for Clean Money funding, candidates must pass an eligibility threshold by gathering signatures and raising a prescribed number of contributions, following a strict set of guidelines. Once a candidate has requested Clean Money funding, he agrees to accept no more private contributions during the election cycle. Federal candidates get free and discounted TV and radio airtime. And if a non-participating candidate outspends a Clean Money candidate, or "issues ads" are run against him, the participating candidate is given a limited amount of matching funds.

So far, clean elections laws have been passed via the initiative process in Arizona, Massachusetts, and Maine. On November 5, U.S. District Judge D. Brock Hornby ruled that Maine's law was constitutional, its public financing system not a violation of free speech. In Vermont in June 1997, Gov. Howard Dean signed a comprehensive campaign finance law. "Vermont's law does what everyone wants," Miller says. "[It] caps the cost of campaigns for statewide office, cuts out special interest funders, eliminates raising big money as the test of a candidate's viability, and stops the money chase."

The law also includes a direct challenge to *Buckley* v. *Valeo*. Mandatory limits are imposed on candidates who don't accept the Clean Money public financing, and choose instead to raise private money. This portion of the measure is "severable," and is designed to force a court challenge to Buckley. If it loses in court, the rest of the measure stays intact.

Passed by the legislature (quite a surprise to all those who thought the only way to get reform is via a ballot measure), the law goes into effect in 2000. It calls for the basic Clean Money trade-off: To get public funding, candidates must eschew private donations and agree to spending caps. Candidates for governor must raise $35,000 in contributions of no more than $50 from at least 1,500 registered voters between February and July of the election year; lieutenant governor candidates have to raise half that amount from half the number of registered voters. Candidates for governor get $40,000 for the primary; those who make it to the general receive another $250,000. The public money will come from annual "report fees" paid by domestic and foreign business corporations, a tax on lobbyists' expenditures, and a "Vermont campaign fund add-on"—a pool of voluntary contributions from citizens through a check-off on tax returns.

The way Vermont eliminates soft money is by defining it out of existence, calling it a "direct" contribution and thereby making it subject to stringent limits. "Issues" expenditures made with a candidate's approval or cooperation are also limited, and full disclosure is part of the package.

The stage was set for reform in Vermont after the governor admitted what we know to be true for all candidates: that those who contributed to his campaign had "bought access." Vermonters were especially concerned that money from outside the state, which is relatively poor, was pouring in to buy elections.

As a consequence, a reform coalition was born. Republican state senate leaders, environmentalists, the Vermont Public

Interest Research Group, the League of Women Voters, and the American Association of University Women met every week in the State House cafeteria to develop ways—including phone banks and a letter-writing campaign—to sway uncommitted lawmakers on both sides of the aisle. In the end, their bill was passed 121 to 17 in the Vermont House, and 20 to 9 in the Senate. Miller calls the "Vermont Campaign Option" "the camel's nose under the tent": It won't single-handedly reform American politics, but it's hard to ignore and shows reform can be accomplished.

In California, the Oaks Project—described by chief organizer Bill Gallagher as "a Marine Corps for citizens who want to be the best"—is collecting signatures for a Taxpayer Protection Amendment which would ban public officials from accepting contributions for five years from any private interest they took action to benefit through legislation.

At the federal level, beyond the Shays-Meehan bill in the House and McCain-Feingold in the Senate, other proposed reforms include a pair of so-called "Clean Money, Clean Elections" bills introduced in the Senate by Paul Wellstone (D-Minn.) and John Kerry (D-Mass.) and in the House by Rep. John Tierney (D-Mass.). These bills offer financing from a federal clean-elections fund to candidates who voluntarily forgo private contributions and agree to strict spending limits. They also ban soft money, rein in issues ads, and provide free TV and radio. While no one thinks Wellstone-Kerry has a chance of passing, it is a "marker bill" or a "vision bill"—a look at what could be possible someday and a direction to move in.

Opponents of campaign finance reform who dare not defend the current system argue that "full disclosure" would do the trick. One bill, offered by Rep. John Doolittle (R-Calif.), would completely deregulate the campaign financing system—allowing unlimited contributions to candidates and parties in exchange for full, prompt disclosure through the Federal Elections Commission. Euphemistically called the "Citizen Legislature and Political Freedom Act," it is rightly nicknamed the "Do Little Bill." The bill's defenders, such as Roger Pilon, director of the CATO Institute's Center for Constitutional Studies, argue unconvincingly that "money buys access, it does not buy votes. It is through access that information is imparted and interests made known, which is precisely what political speech is about." But when the only people with access are the ones with money, you know what happens: "Money talks, everyone else walks."

Which brings us back to Granny D, who argues that "businesses are not people," and that to extend First Amendment protections to corporations is to misunderstand and undermine the true meaning of freedom of speech. She's right—but the Supreme Court disagrees, and as a result our political life is drowning in corporate money. Clean Money legislation is specifically calibrated to avoid the First Amendment objection to reform by making most of its provisions voluntary.

An intriguing alternative for reforming campaigns has been put forward by Ian Ayres, a law professor at Yale, and Jeremy Bulow, an economics professor at Stanford. It's the "donor booth," which seeks to correct the rampant buying and selling of influence in the political process by arguing not for complete and instant donor disclosure, as championed by Doolittle and McConnell, but for complete and total donor anonymity.

It is a simple idea—and a radical one. But, as Professor Ayres reminded me, the radical idea on which it's modeled—the secret ballot—is only about a century old, though we take it for granted today. The secret ballot was invented in the late nineteenth century, an era when party bosses would herd voters to the polls where ballots for opposing candidates were printed on different color paper. Voters were expected to wave the ballots over their heads so the bosses could be sure they were getting what they paid for. The secret ballot put a halt to vote buying, and professors Ayres and Bulow found in that development the inspiration for their proposal.

"The voting booth," Ayres says, "made it harder for candidates to buy votes. The 'donor booth' would make it harder for candidates to sell influence." If a candidate can't be sure who votes for him, he is not likely to engage in outright vote-buying. Likewise, contributors who (in the immortal words of Roger Tamraz) consider the buying of influence the "only reason" for giving would lose their main incentive.

Would it really work? In some states, it already has. Louisiana, Tennessee, Washington, and North Dakota have experimented with keeping donors to judicial campaigns anonymous; after all, you wouldn't want to stand before a judge who had just pocketed a few hundred thousand from your opponent. Yet something similar happens in Congress every day.

The reason for the donor booth is the same as the one for the voting booth: to reduce the potential for corruption. In the political arena, the danger is not merely quid pro quo corruption, but the possibility of politicians no longer being open to honest deliberations because they have, in a sense, already sold their position. It is this threat to deliberative democracy the professors are hoping to check with anonymity.

In the last election cycle, less than one-quarter of one percent of Americans contributed $200 or more to a federal candidate. Yet this tiny group generated 80 percent of all donations. McConnell likes to say that in 1996, campaigns overall "spent per eligible voter $3.89, about the price of a McDonald's value meal." It'd be closer to the truth to say that a few thousand people bought up several million value meals—while the rest of America went hungry.

"Under the current system," wrote Ayres and Bulow in their 1998 article for the *Stanford Law Review*, "small donors have virtually no impact on the electoral process. . . . Mandated anonymity, by reducing the importance of large donations, makes small donors relatively more important and thus might induce less affluent donors to give more."

The system would work by having campaign contributions funneled through blind trusts administered by known, reputable financial firms. Anyone who wanted to give money to a particular candidate would mail it to the trust, which would then pass it on to the candidate—without revealing the donor's name. Like any reform, this would create its own set of problems. What's to stop a donor, for instance, from telling the candidate that he just made an "anonymous" donation? Nothing, obviously. But talk is cheap. And what's to stop someone who hasn't made a donation from bragging that he did?

But at this stage, even cynics are ready to exchange a new set of problems for the old ones. The breathing space made possible by the donor booth would—at least until clever lawyers nosed out all the loopholes—provide precious oxygen for our political system.

Sunlight may be the best of disinfectants, and electric light the most efficient policeman, but when it comes to the money-access-policy nexus, no disclosure is better than full disclosure, and less information is better than more. "Imagine what a world with anonymous donations would look like," Ayres and Bulow write. "No more selling nights in the Lincoln bedroom. No more ambassadorships . . . or trade missions for successful fund-raisers. Put simply, it will be more difficult for candidates to sell access or influence if they are unsure whether a donor has paid the price."

With the donor booth, PAC money would dry up— because knowing who's giving is exactly why PACs exist. Donor anonymity would prove—as if more proof were needed—just how many contributions have nothing to do with the donor's political ideas and everything to do with the donor's policy desires—which politicians can satisfy by selling off billions of dollars in contracts, tax write-offs, corporate welfare, government posts, and subsidies. And while the protectors of the status quo keep trying to use constitutional arguments to protect soft money, this proposal is as constitutionally unassailable as the secret ballot.

"Just as there is no constitutional right," the professors wrote, "to be able to prove that you voted for Clinton, there is no constitutional right to be able to prove that you gave Clinton money. The voting booth also burdens political expression: No matter how much a conservative wants, she can never prove that she did not vote for McGovern (or a liberal can't prove he didn't vote for Reagan). Since voting is the quintessential act of political expression, surely denying citizens the right to prove for whom they voted is more burdensome than denying citizens the right to prove they gave a candidate more than $200."

Donor anonymity calls everyone's bluff, and public funding of campaigns cuts the Gordian knot of contributions and public policy. For the moment, there are at least individual citizens who are taking a stand. There are CEOs pledging not to give soft money to either political party; there are candidates who voluntarily choose not to accept money from political action committees. So even if the donation booth never becomes as commonplace as the voting booth, candidates can always take the vow of donor anonymity. All they need to say is, "I won't ask, you don't tell."

But of course they won't. The real reforms, the ones that will change the system forever, will come only when Americans become outraged enough to force their leaders to change—or force them out of business. Indeed, when political elites cling to power even at the expense of the people's expressed will, perhaps it is time to take a lesson from the revolutionaries who founded this country, and in the spirit of that other reform—the Boston Tea Party— toss them all overboard.

10

Waking Up the Media Watchdogs

It's no accident that freedom of the press was guaranteed in Amendment Number One.

Systems of government, even in free, democratic countries, are prone to corruption. And when the corruption becomes entrenched, a dogged, independent press can be a nation's saving grace.

Alexis de Tocqueville stressed the vital part newspapers play in sustaining democracy. "Every day," he wrote, "voters need some intelligence of the state of their public weal. . . . A newspaper can drop the same thought into a thousand minds at the same time. . . . We would underrate their importance if we thought they just guaranteed liberty. They maintain civilization." The expansion of both population and technology has only served to increase the crucial role of the media in what is, after all, the Information Age. Or, as a more contemporary critic, Edward Fouhy of the Pew Center for Civic Journalism, puts it, "News is the

WD-40 of democracy, the lubricant that keeps the system running."

For generations, American reporters have reveled in the role of muckraker—defined by Webster as "one who exposes real or apparent misconduct or vice or corruption on the part of prominent individuals and public officials." From Ida Tarbell's groundbreaking turn-of-the-century series on the misdeeds of Standard Oil to Charles Moore's searing photographs of the civil rights struggle to Seymour Hersh's exposure of the horrors perpetrated at My Lai to Woodward and Bernstein's unraveling of the Watergate scandal, the best of American journalism has taken as its rallying cry Jonathan Swift's admonition to "afflict the comfortable and comfort the afflicted."

Unfortunately, this kind of rigorous and spirited reporting is rapidly disappearing—another victim of corporate pressure to build the bottom line, and of journalists who would rather party with the comfortable than afflict them.

As we've seen, muckraking has been replaced by smutraking—with the media hunting down case studies of human frailty instead of exposing crimes against humanity. When the U.S. dropped its Tomahawk cruise missiles on the Sudan in September 1998, only a handful of journalists questioned the official line. Seymour Hersh wrote a chilling story, based on more than one hundred interviews with intelligence and military sources, that exposed the lies told to the American people long before the administration had to 'fess up that it had blown up a pharmaceutical factory. It's that kind of persistent reporting that we need more than ever, as politicians become increasingly adept at deceiving the public, and we become increasingly inured to it.

Another scandal that made it to the front page of the *New York Times*—above the fold—but which the TV punditocracy couldn't be bothered to take notice of was the guilty verdict in September 1998 against three executives of food giant Archer Daniels Midland.

It's not surprising, just dispiriting, that most of the media had no comment on the ADM scandal; David Brinkley, ADM's official spokesdrone, even continued uninterrupted on TV after his official Sunday-program duties ended, shilling for the giant in TV commercials that drew vague and disingenuous connections between the "Supermarket to the World" and ending world hunger.

We have grown to expect critical issues—like poverty and blighted neighborhoods—to be overshadowed by thong underwear and Larry Flynt's latest revelations. But what the 1998 coverage of sex scandals made clear is that scandals of substance that directly affect our trust in our political leaders continue to die on the vine, unable to compete with the private lives of public figures. In the exposé hierarchy, what is left that can trump celebrity sex? Celebrity incest?

Americans must be aware by now that the big questions facing the nation have nothing to do with politicians' sex lives. But expecting restraint from the ratings-obsessed media is foolhardy. If we're going to put an end to the spectacle, the first thing that must happen is for our leaders to refuse to dignify questions about their sex lives or drug histories with an answer—whether they are asked by

Bob Woodward, Diane Sawyer, Matt Drudge, *Hard Copy*, *Salon* magazine, or some perky coed on MTV.

To do otherwise is to invite debacles like the media firestorm created by George W. Bush's woeful mishandling of "the cocaine question" this past summer. It proved an absolute truth about public disclosures of private lives: Nothing you can say will ever be enough. If one soul-baring admission is good, two is better, three will be the new minimum to be considered nonevasive, and four would be much appreciated by the Nielsen people.

In Bush's case, he started by constructing an impenetrable Maginot Line in front of rumors about his drug use—what he resolutely called his "stake in the ground." But it didn't take too much press persistence before he sounded retreat faster than Corporal Agarn on *F Troop*, lobbing lame, Clintonesque evasions as he scrambled for cover. He swore he'd not used drugs for seven, no fifteen . . . no make that twenty-four years—but wouldn't go farther than that (man, that must have been some twenty-eighth birthday party!). He admitted he'd "made some mistakes," and then assured us he'd learned from mistakes he "may or may not have made."

Apart from the novel idea of learning from mistakes he did not make, instead of standing firm—and looking presidential—Bush came across as just another in the long line of quick-sprouting dissemblers our political landscape is overgrown with. After eight years of watching Clinton the Contortionist twist the truth into linguistic knots, the last thing we need is another master hairsplitter, who did or didn't use drugs depending on what your definition of "snort" is or isn't.

Bush's troubles really began last winter when he decided to play the morality card, triumphantly announcing that he'd been faithful to his wife for twenty-two years, as though he were a three-year-old who had just gone potty by himself and expected a big hug. Then he wanted a pat on the back for not having touched a drop of booze since he was forty. But after parading in front of the press the parts of his private life that made him look good, he suddenly got all shy and demure and tried to yank the curtain shut when reporters pressed him on rumors of drug use during those same years for which he wanted a gold star. If you open up certain parts of your private life, you cannot claim the moral high ground of fighting "gotcha politics" when the press encroaches on other parts. Especially since the area Bush chose to show off—marital fidelity—has no legal consequences. Drug use, on the other hand, does.

While politicians ponder the futility of their attempting to spin the truth about their past, the media had better cop to their own nasty habit—an insatiable addiction to dishy questions about the private sins of our political leaders, no matter how long ago they occurred. The media's disingenuous theory—that these answers are necessary to give the voters a full portrait of the candidate—would be easier to believe if the press showed any evidence of caring as much about the part of the portrait made up of, say, policy positions.

From here on out, we must demand a "Don't Ask, Don't Answer" policy for our media and our leaders, with the added proviso, "And Even If They Do Ask, Don't

Answer!" Whether candidates have a spotless marriage or a wandering eye, have never inhaled or were voted Bong King of their frat house, they should meet all questions about their personal lives with the answer Bill Clinton finally gave—albeit eight months too late: This is between me, my spouse, our family, and God.

In fact, unless a politician has broken the law, and the statute of limitations has not expired, "It's none of your business" is the only legitimate answer to the illegitimate probing of private lives. (If a politician is really popular in his home district, a firm "Go to hell!" would also work.)

Since politicians are busy people—what with running the country, taking money from the Chinese, firming up their soft money, and clocking all those extramarital hours—I've collected some variations on this theme from which they can choose their answer, culled from four kings of the quick comeback—and a queen:

Al Franken suggests: "This is between me, my wife, my daughter and, to a lesser extent, my son."

Harry Shearer offers: "My sex life is my own business. By that I don't mean to leave the impression that it's not my pleasure, but that, too, is my business. By that I don't mean to imply that money changes hands necessarily. Or not, as the case may be."

Bill Maher generously gave three possible answers: "That's for me to know and Larry Flynt to find out." "Yes, Lisa Marie and I have sex. What was the question again?" "Look, I'd love to tell you, but I'm on the phone with Larry Flynt and he wants to know if I have any dirt on reporters."

Craig Kilborn, the host of CBS's *The Late Late Show*, prefers: "Hey—if you want to know about my sex life, I'll gladly show you the videotapes—just as soon as I get them back from Denny Hastert."

And Roseanne feels that you can't improve on perfection. Politicians, she says, should simply echo that presidential classic: When asked if his private life is a disgrace, it is proper for a candidate to answer, "That would depend on what the definition of 'is' is."

And here is one from the annals of history: "If I were to try to read, much less answer, all the attacks made on me," Abraham Lincoln wisely demurred, "this shop might as well be closed for any other business."

By narrowing our definition of morality to sexual morality, we are guilty of ignoring the real moral issues of modern politics: the immoral disregard of those the Bible calls "the least among us," the corrupt selling of public policy to the highest donor, the surrender of principles to polls. Where a politician stands on these matters is infinitely more significant than whom he lies with after hours. The latter, while profoundly important in the private realm, has no place in the domain of politics.

My solution is gloriously simple. Let's apply to the political world the statutes of limitations that govern the legal world. Such statutes exist under law precisely because the passage of time makes it impossible to prove or forever disprove certain charges. If this is true in the legal system, with all its powers to subpoena witnesses and physical evidence, how much truer must it be in the political universe, where one has to search far and wide to find twelve men and women not already partial to one side or the other?

If we don't do something as dramatic as this, our national political debate threatens to become nothing more than a Beltway version of *The Jerry Springer Show*, featuring an endless parade of scorned women stepping forward with their "Sexy Confessions and Angry Accusations." And every time they do, there will be people eager to believe their every claim, no matter how outrageous. Because in the political world, what determines an accuser's credibility is not the evidence—almost always circumstantial—but whether or not the politician in question is someone you like or dislike.

"I believe Anita" read the buttons worn proudly by Clarence Thomas's liberal foes in 1991. "I believe Juanita" read a bumper sticker I saw after Juanita Broaddrick's scandalous accusations hit the airwaves eight years later. Soon thereafter a parade of Clinton opponents hit the talk shows, claiming Broaddrick was "so compelling, so credible, so convincing"—an eerie echo of the parade of Thomas opponents who had found Anita Hill so compelling, so credible, so convincing. Broaddrick cried, Hill did not; the former was hailed by her champions for sharing her pain, the latter for maintaining her dignity. Girlfriends came forward in both cases to recount corroborating conversations from long ago. Such evidence was dismissed by Thomas's defenders, many of whom are now beating the drums for Broaddrick.

Accusations deemed irresolvable in the legal realm are all the more impossible to resolve in the political realm, where allegiances and enmities trump everything. When Sen. Barbara Boxer threatened an amendment to force the

Senate to investigate Sen. Bob Packwood, Sen. Mitch McConnell retaliated by proposing a floor vote to force an investigation into Sen. Ted Kennedy's 1969 Chappaquiddick incident. Driving a woman over a bridge is not morally equivalent to pawing a staffer, just as accusations of rape do not equal accusations of dirty talk in the office. But does anyone expect to bring finality to these charges through a retaliatory political process?

Instead, we must create new ground rules that will save the nation from the scourge of years-old, unprovable allegations. Let us make them, by consensus, as inadmissible in politics as they are in court. For a fundamental problem facing modern American journalism is its tendency to allow unpleasant revelations about public figures to eclipse everything else, ensuring that anything good about them shrinks to nothing.

Then again, maybe there's another way to look at it. In the hype-overdrive of a serious media scandal, it can be difficult to judge just how damaging a set of charges will be once the dust settles—difficult, that is, for all but one person: the obituary writer. After all, who is it that closes the book on a public figure's reputation? Who chooses the headline and the one-line lead? It is the obit writers who get the final word on whether the transgressions will overshadow the achievements.

Our punditocracy is so riddled with expert consultants, why not add a few obituary writers to vet each new scandal for obit-worthiness as soon as it breaks? If it's not worth a mention after they die, chances are it's not worth it while they're living. After all, a statesman is just a dead politician, as the saying goes—a lesson fully demonstrated in the case of the late Commerce Secretary Ron Brown.

Only months before he died, the *New York Times* had called on the president "to ease the Commerce Secretary back into the private sector." Al Hunt had pronounced him in *The Wall Street Journal* "unable to distinguish between public service and private gain." Eleanor Clift had predicted his imminent resignation on *The McLaughlin Group*. And Michael Duffy had ominously proclaimed in *Time* that "Brown's days are beginning to feel numbered."

And these were friends and neutral observers in the press. As for his enemies, they fully expected his indictment before the year's end for a host of conflicts of interest and ethical violations, following a Justice Department investigation into allegations of financial misconduct.

Then, in a blinding flash on the Dubrovnik mountainside, sinner turned into saint and denunciations into hosannas. In the days following his tragic death in a plane crash, Brown was extolled by friend and foe alike as "a magnificent life force," "an inspirational leader," "a Renaissance man of politics," a man who "could accomplish anything because he didn't believe he couldn't do it." But then, even Richard Nixon got a warm eulogy from President Clinton.

Would it not transform our public discourse and the coverage of public figures while they are alive if, even as we raise legitimate questions about their conduct, we also acknowledge their qualities and contributions? Could we not praise what is praiseworthy at the same time we investigate what needs to be investigated and condemn what should be condemned?

This may be too much to ask of political opponents. But what about those covering our leaders? *The Wall Street Journal*, which had been scathing in successive editorials about Ron Brown, acknowledged after his death that "one had to admire his evident, steady success." The man the *Journal* had scorned as a "Beltway wheeler-dealer" was now being lauded as "skilled, articulate . . . a personal force . . . a player." Wasn't he all those things even as he was a Beltway wheeler-dealer?

The effect of every media feeding frenzy is to magnify the transgression until it dwarfs all else. I found the perfect description of this tendency not in the *Columbia Journalism Review* but in Hans Christian Andersen's story "The Snow Queen," which I once discovered as I was reading my children to sleep.

"Once upon a time there was a very bad goblin—so bad, in fact, that he was a demon. One day this bad goblin created a huge mirror that had magic powers. Anything beautiful that was reflected in it shrank to almost nothing. Everything that was worthless or ugly became large and looked worse than ever. When seen in this mirror, the loveliest landscapes looked like boiled spinach, and the warmest people became cold and unfriendly.

"'How very amusing,' the demon said, laughing at his own invention. Those who studied at his goblin school (for he ran a goblin school) declared the mirror wondrous. But student goblins are showoffs. Not wanting to leave well enough alone, these goblins decided to fly up to heaven with the mirror, and to sneer and scoff at the angels there. But the higher they flew, the harder it became to hold on to the mirror, until suddenly it dropped from their hands to the earth, where it shattered into a hundred million pieces. Some of the fragments were nearly invisible, and the wind carried these specks all over the world. Each little fragment had the same power as the whole mirror. Whenever one flew into somebody's eye, it would stick there, and from then on that person would see only the bad side of life."

One of the consequences of this relentless negativism is that the public's opinion of the media has never been lower. According to a national poll by the Roper Center, only 10 percent of Americans have a "great deal of confidence" in the media—a far cry from the balmy days in 1979 when a Gallup poll found that 51 percent of us rated them as trustworthy. In the even balmier days of 1971, the media's most visible paragon, Walter Cronkite, was voted the most trusted man in America. Our reverence for him at that time was something like the reverence tribal people must have once felt for the village explainers—wise men who made plain the world and its wonders. But twenty years on, the village explainers have turned into the village haranguers, and the endless debunking has exhausted our collective patience.

Americans have always had a special reverence and affection for the explainers in our culture. But as they turned first hot and heavy, then loud and shrill, a sort of sacred trust was breached. We began to feel betrayed. What is it that we feel toward the village debunker? We still listen, but we're compelled to guard our most precious valuables: our hopes, our dreams, our values, and ideals. For, to the village debunker, they are no more than ignoble ambitions, full of hot air.

"The men with the muckrakes," Teddy Roosevelt said, "are often indispensable to the well-being of society, but only if they know when to stop raking the mud, and to look upward to the celestial crown above them. . . . If they gradually grow to feel that the whole world is nothing but muck their power of usefulness is gone."

In 1997, a *Times-Mirror* study found that 71 percent of us believe the media actually get in the way of our nation solving its problems. "To many American citizens, the mass media have become the massive media—intrusive, sensational, uncaring, and flawed by bias and inaccuracy," admits Robert Giles, president of the American Society of Newspaper Editors. "To many Americans, we lack intro-spection, discipline, restraint, and a capacity for self-scrutiny."

Consequently, every few months journalists hold con-ferences with soul-searching names like "Why Everyone Hates the Media." Despite much hand-wringing and brow-furrowing, the real causes of the public's eroding trust—cynicism, scandalmongering, a focus on trouble-makers rather than problem-solvers—go largely unex-plored.

The depth of the media's cynicism and their failure to go beneath the surface of our country's problems are matched only by their indifference to any possible solutions. In 1995, when Colin Powell announced he was not running for pres-ident, hundreds of members of the media showed up to report it. In 1997, when Powell announced he would be

chairing the Presidents' Summit for America's Future—
devoting the next three years of his life to seeing that the
thousands of corporate and personal commitments made as
part of the effort were fulfilled and multiplied—they disap-
peared. Barbara Walters, who interviewed Powell on both
occasions, commented on the difference: "This time,
Reuters called but nobody really picked it up," she told me.
"It was ho-hum."

Joe Rutledge, a former NBC executive who was coordinating the media for the Summit, put it another way: "'The
cat sat on the mat' is not news. 'The cat sat on the dog's mat'
is news." In other words, conflict sells. Bringing people
together to improve the lives of 15 million American children who are growing up at risk just doesn't sell the way one
of them opening fire does.

Perhaps one of the reasons reporters ignore solutions is
that they fail to see the problems. "The economy is booming; no news there," wrote the *New York Times*'s Michael
Wines in 1997. "High-profile domestic problems like
crime are, for the moment, in abeyance." Not as much as
news judgment, unfortunately.

Such insulated complacency—because crime is down in
Wines's neighborhood, all is well?—has contributed to a
middle class indifference so blatant that it borders on the
obscene. Three million children are abused every year, an
unprecedented 664,000 belong to gangs, and one in four
black men is in prison, on parole, or on probation. But
fashionable journalists complain there is no news.
Meanwhile, Americans believe in record numbers that
problems like poverty, crime, and homelessness have been

solved simply because they have dropped below the media radar.

A movement is afoot to redress that. Civic, or public, journalism is an attempt to explore most Americans' profound disaffection with public life—to focus a little less on our pathologies and a little more on our potential. Inspired by the belief that journalism has an obligation to our communities that goes well beyond reporting the news, civic journalism seeks to reconnect citizens to their news outlets, their communities, and the political process.

"Readers want us to look for solutions, not just problems," says ASNE President Giles. "They want us to provide news and information to help local communities deal with problems." But, as *Charlotte Observer* editor Jennifer Rae Buckner points out, "All too often, we print stories that move our readers to call us and say, 'What can we do?' And our response is, 'It's not our problem.'"

More and more newspapers and TV news shows are ending their stories with phone numbers and organizations the public can contact if they want to help. For example, in conjunction with a 1998 four-part series about hunger, the *Charlotte Observer* told its readers what they could do to help local organizations feed the hungry.

In San Diego, the *Union-Tribune* has a regular feature called "Solutions," which focuses on individuals and projects that have successfully tackled a community problem. Those profiled have included: Project Genesis, started by the North County Interfaith Council to help homeless families piece their lives back together; Operation Samahan, a community clinic that provides affordable health care to the poor and uninsured; and Streetlights, a local organization that trains the disadvantaged to become production assistants in the film/TV industry. Each story provides contact information so that readers can get involved or start similar programs.

"Solutions" editor Karen Lin Clark says that the stories aren't necessarily ones the paper wouldn't have covered in the past, but they would have been put on the back burner or given no prominence. Now when the "Solutions" stories run, they are teased on the front page—a way of saying that what's important to the community is what's important to the paper.

Although it's hard to measure the impact such stories have, one follow-up report found that they generate interest, community support, and volunteers. And in many cases a story allowed the group profiled to move to the next level—gaining access to foundations and a way to fund-raise that is less hand-to-mouth.

We need to be flooded with stories like these—and like one recent report in the Peoria, Illinois, *Journal Star*. After a survey on attitudes toward local leadership and civic involvement revealed dismal results, the *Journal Star*'s editors convened a community roundtable to discuss why people weren't getting involved. Then they searched for ways to increase participation. A "Neighborhood College" was set up to train would-be local leaders in working with budgets, handling meetings, dealing with the media, and acquiring consensus-building skills. The result was an unusually large field of candidates for mayor—and the winner credited the *Journal Star* leadership series for persuading him to run.

To deal with the problem of underreporting important stories, the Center for Living Democracy launched the American News Service, a wire service that since 1995 has been reporting on stories the mainstream media have largely ignored. Such was the case in the summer of 1999, when ANS ran a remarkable story on a study done by researchers at Cornell and Washington universities that revealed that poverty is not confined to the underclass—that it is, in fact, a "mainstream problem." The study found that for at least one year of their lives, nearly 60 percent of all Americans will live below the poverty line. And that figure climbs to 91 percent for African Americans who reach age seventy-five. Despite the disturbing finding that virtually every black person living in America will experience poverty at some point during his or her life, this story was run by only one major media outlet, the *Washington Post*, before ANS put it on its wire.

Yet another glaring indication that, by and large, the media are still a bigger part of the problem than of the solution, their sins of omission adding up to a deficit of civic journalism that leaves us all the poorer.

Something must also be done about their sins of commission. We must make false speech costly speech. Think of it as an economic intifada. We should also send a message—by boycotting their products and reaching for the remote—to the book publishers, newspapers, and TV shows that use such sordid stories to boost sales and ratings. And I suggest the "O.J. treatment"—being shunned in public, refused service at restaurants, asked to leave country clubs—for the character assassins who plant these literary car bombs.

The alternative is rendering the already fetid air of our political life completely unbreathable, and having our best and our brightest abandon the idea of public service forever.

11

NEW VOTERS' RIGHTS

Citizen participation has become a talking point for practically every presidential hopeful. But the only candidates who aren't just paying lip service to the need for greater involvement in our democracy are Republican John McCain and Democrat Bill Bradley. And their solutions are as different as their histories.

McCain proposes to heal the "cynicism and pessimism, particularly among young people ... by calling them to causes." "Wherever there's a hungry child, there's a cause," he says, echoing Tom Joad's words in *The Grapes of Wrath:* "Wherever they's a fight so hungry people can eat, I'll be there." Of course he is right: there is nothing like a great cause to stir civic involvement. "The problems of American democracy and participation," says Curtis Gans, director of the Committee for the Study of the American Electorate, "don't lie with procedure, but with motivation. Given the opportunity to choose what to do with their weekends, most voters would prefer to go fishing." Only a catalytic leader or cataclysmic event can move the people to action.

But since we can't create those circumstances in the lab, we can in the meantime go along with Bradley, who proposes to address the plummeting voter turnout—a 26 percent drop since 1966—by easing the voting rules with measures like same-day registration and vote-by-mail. It's a series of modest proposals, but they are only the first steps in a new voters' rights movement which this country needs both to make voting easier and to open up the political process to those outside the entrenched two-party system. Consider that a staggering 98.5 percent of House incumbents were reelected in 1998. The dirty little secret of our democracy is just how undemocratic it's become.

Despite a surge in voter registration in the '90s fueled by the Motor Voter law—there was a net increase of 5.5 million Americans registered to vote from 1994 to 1998—voter turnout continues to decline. In 1998, 72.4 million citizens voted and 115.5 million eligible voters sat the election out. It was the lowest turnout since 1942, when millions of Americans were overseas fighting in World War II.

History shows that after the Civil War, when many of the social barriers to African Americans were torn down, black men began participating in the electoral system in large numbers. To counteract this trend, many Southern states erected hurdles aimed at disenfranchising black and poor white voters. Georgia implemented a poll tax, requiring voters to pay a fee to vote. South Carolina and

Florida imposed an "eight-box" law, requiring voters to deposit separate ballots in each of the different candidates' boxes—an impossible task for illiterate voters. And Mississippi forced would-be voters both to pay a poll tax and to pass a literacy test.

These insidious measures, or push factors, proved to be extremely effective. In South Carolina, for example, turnout fell from 83.7 percent in 1880 to 18 percent in 1900.

Clearly, turnout is something that responds to direct action. So, if it can be pushed down, today's reformers hope to introduce *pull* factors that can drive it up. In 1998, when Jesse Ventura's supporters realized that there was a late surge in voter interest in their candidate for governor, they scrambled to find a way to turn that excitement into votes. Luckily for them, Minnesota allows same-day registration, so when "The Body's" candidacy caught fire in the final days, apathetic citizens were able to instantly transform themselves into committed voters.

"It was really good news to discover that many of the procedural roadblocks had been removed," said Bill Hillsman, Ventura's media consultant. "Minnesota is definitely ahead of the game in terms of voters' rights." As a result, turnout in the state went up to 61 percent (the highest in the nation), compared to a pathetically low 36 percent nationwide. Unfortunately, as of now only five other states have same-day voter registration: Idaho, Maine, New Hampshire, Wisconsin, and Wyoming.

But that's just one of a number of new pull-up-the-vote measures. Reformers are also proposing "early voting," which extends the election period from a single day to up to three weeks; "weekend voting," which, like early voting, keeps the polls open longer, and on days that are more convenient; and "vote by mail," an institutionalized form of absentee voting in which an entire election is held by mail.

Of course, once it's easier to vote, the problem becomes finding someone worth voting for. That's where questions of ballot access and debate access come into play.

Ballot access requirements vary dramatically from state to state, many of them involving Byzantine regulations that make it next to impossible for those outside the political mainstream to take on the system. Richard Winger, the editor of *Ballot Access News* and the nation's leading expert on the issue, reports that not since 1920 "has any third party been able to place candidates for the U.S. House of Representatives on the ballot in even half the districts in America."

Want to run for president from a new third party in 2000? Louisiana and Colorado require only a $500 fee. But Oklahoma requires the signatures of nearly 2 percent of the state's registered voters. Until 1996, when the Reform Party won a lawsuit against the rule, petitioners for a third party in Arkansas were forced to collect signatures of 3 percent of the voters in a four-month window in odd-numbered years only. Want to run for president as an independent? North Carolina will ask for almost 100,000 signatures; Iowa, 1,500; and Tennessee, just 25.

In Georgia, no third party has qualified for a congressional seat since 1943, when the state began requiring candidates to gather the signatures of 5 percent of registered voters. West Virginia actually forbids anyone who has signed a petition supporting the placement of a new party on the ballot from voting in the state's next primary election. Those who circulate petitions are required to warn potential signatories of that fact. This requirement is currently facing a court challenge—not surprisingly, the West Virginia Democratic Party argued that it be upheld. So much for giving the voters the right to encourage competition.

The two parties also try to hold on to power by pushing back qualifying deadlines further and further. In Illinois and South Dakota, for example, the legislatures voted to move the petition dates for new parties and independent candidates from August of an election year to June. The most famous third party in American history—the Republican Party—was founded on July 6, 1854, and went on to win a plurality of seats in the U.S. House that fall. If current state laws had been in effect then, the GOP would have failed to get on the ballot in over half the states.

The other way the two parties try to perpetuate their duopoly is by limiting access to debates. The importance of open access was illustrated in 1998 by Ventura's participation in the Minnesota gubernatorial debates. His effective performance helped propel him to victory. Jamin B. Raskin, an attorney for the Reform Party and a professor of constitutional law at American University, believes that one of the main reasons for America's declining voter participation is the lack of open debate. "There is no real democracy," he writes, "without debate, which should be 'uninhibited, robust, and wide-open' in all cases, but above all during elections, when we as democratic citizens reconstitute the official leadership of government."

In fact, our debates have become decidedly less robust and wide-open since the advent of the Commission on Presidential Debates. Formed in 1985, the commission was the brainchild of the then-chairmen of the Democratic and Republican National Committees, Frank Fahrenkopf Jr. and Paul Kirk, who decided that the two parties should work together (some would say conspire) to cosponsor presidential debates. According to an agreement they drafted, they would seek to replace the traditional League of Women Voters–sponsored debates with "nationally televised joint appearances conducted between the presidential and vice-presidential nominees of the two major political parties during general election campaigns," with the format and most other details of these appearances "determined through negotiations between the chairmen and the nominees of the two political parties."

They were successful—by 1996, the system had become closed off. The Clinton and Dole campaigns imposed a set of such stringent and nonnegotiable demands that the League of Women Voters promptly withdrew its sponsorship of the debates. Moreover, it denounced the two parties and their demands, which they believed "would perpetrate a fraud on the American voter." "It has become clear to us," Nancy Newman, the League's president said, "that the candidates' organizations aim to add debate to their list of campaign-trail charades devoid of substance and spontaneity. . . . The League has no intention of becoming an accessory to the hoodwinking of the American public."

The debates that followed—now sponsored by Philip Morris, Sprint, Sara Lee, Dun and Bradstreet, and Lucent Technologies—constituted just the kind of farce the League had predicted. Ross Perot, whose presence in the 1992 debates helped him win 18.7 percent of the vote, was excluded—a major factor in his getting only 8.4 percent of the vote in '96. Which was exactly what Clinton had hoped for. As George Stephanopoulos later put it, "[W]e didn't want [people] to pay attention. The debates were a metaphor for the campaign. We wanted the debates to be a non-event." And indeed, 100 million fewer people tuned in than did in 1992, making it the lowest-watched general-election presidential debate in television history.

Debate access promises to be a particularly thorny problem this election cycle, with the increased interest in third parties. The Commission on Presidential Debates has become the living embodiment of our political duopoly—formed by the two parties, run by former party chairmen, and funded by the same corporate interests that lavishly support the two-party structure. Rep. Ron Paul (R-Tex.), a former third-party member himself, has introduced a bill that would make it possible for any presidential candidate on the ballot in at least forty states to participate in the debates. But the commission is likely once again to try to shut out other voices and turn the first debates of the new millennium into another non-event.

So far, the third-party spotlight has shone only on the Buchanan Brigade and the Trump Circus. But there are other, little-noticed third-party hats in the ring: John Hagelin of the Natural Law Party, Harry Browne of the

Libertarian Party, Brian Saunders of the Internet Party, and Ralph Nader, who in 1996 got nearly 700,000 votes as the nominee of the Green Party. And lest we forget, there is the Pulitzer Prize–winning satirist Dave Barry, this generation's Pat Paulsen, who has decided to make his third run for the Oval Office. The determining factor, he wrote, was Dan Quayle—before he dropped out.

In one form or another, the decision process is the same for any third-party candidate: taking a look at the current field and saying, I can do better. The millions of Americans who will, if trends continue, sit out the 2000 election must also be thinking, We can do better. Indeed, behind all the horse-race fun and games so beloved by the media, something serious is going on: a growing disenchantment with both parties that makes them more vulnerable than ever to a challenge to their hegemony. The public's allegiance to the two parties has never been weaker—perhaps because the two parties' allegiance is no longer to the public. In a survey last September by the Pew Research Center, nearly two-thirds of Americans believed that "large political donors" have "too much" influence on which candidates become presidential nominees, while 62 percent thought "average votors" have "too little."

It's up to us as concerned citizens to change this corrupted system. Third-party advocates, and others looking to shake up the status quo, must begin enlisting disaffected Democrats, Republicans, and others in acts of civil disobedience—protests at campaign events, marches, sit-ins, hanging up on pollsters, and movements like the "None of the Above" initiative in California.

In 1997, Ralph Nader spearheaded a signature drive to
place a similar initiative on the California ballot. His effort
failed, but the ball has been picked up by high-tech businessman Al Shugart, who collected more than 500,000 signatures to place it on the March 2000 ballot as Proposition
23. The Shugart initiative is patterned after Nevada's, for
now the only state in the nation with a "None of the Above"
ballot line. Nevada's law and the proposed California initiative are nonbinding—i.e., the candidate with the highest
vote total still wins.

At the national level, Rep. Peter Hoekstra (R-Mich.)
sponsored legislation in 1997 to place a "None of the
Above" line on the ballots of all federal elections. If NOTA
received more votes than any of the candidates, a new election would have to be held. The bill died for lack of support.
"Many members here," Hoekstra told me, "are threatened
by efforts to engage the disaffected voters. There is a lot of
uncertainty involved because we don't know where these
voters are going to go. As we saw in Ventura's case, they
could go away from the two parties." But Hoekstra is not
giving up. "I am considering re-introducing NOTA in
2000," he said. "This is a movement waiting to happen. But
the American people will have to demand it."

It's hard to imagine a harsher rejection for a politician
than losing to "nobody." What is he to say the day after
the election? That "no one" smeared him, that "nobody"
distorted his record? Another advantage of NOTA is that
there would always be at least one challenger who wasn't
scared off—by an incumbent's fat campaign war chest or
political machine. Nothing, after all, can ever scare off

"nobody." Even better, "None of the Above" is impervious to money and may actually entice nonvoters into the political process. And it will stand that old political adage— "You can't beat something with nothing"—on its head.

The Voting Rights Act, when signed by Lyndon Johnson, marked the culmination of nearly seven decades of civil protest and disobedience. It grew specifically out of the Mississippi Freedom Party—and similar electoral efforts among Southern blacks to push their own candidates and agenda—to find another way of overcoming the Democratic Party's dismal failure to work within the system to address the fundamental rights of black Americans. But the movement dates back at least as far as the era of the suffragettes— led in the nineteenth century by Elizabeth Cady Stanton and Susan B. Anthony—who were finally able to secure the right to vote for women only after more than seventy years of agitation, including publishing their own newspapers and marching on the White House.

Today, civil disobedience can even take place from your favorite easy chair in the comfort of your living room. All you have to do is hang up on pollsters.

Our political leaders have been turned into spineless followers of opinion polls. Since we cannot expect them ever to kick the habit on their own, we must focus on stopping the polls at their source. We the people are the source, and if enough of us stop talking to pollsters, we could force our leaders to think for themselves. In that spirit, along with satirist and all-purpose good guy Harry Shearer, I launched the "Partnership for a Poll-Free America."

Last fall the American Association of Public Opinion Research had its 54th annual convention in St. Louis. The pollsters were there to celebrate their profession and look ahead to a bright future, full of slavish, unthinking politicians. But if you "agree strongly" or "agree somewhat" with me, you want that future to be bleak—so bleak, in fact, that at least 90 percent (plus or minus four points) of them are forced into occupational retraining. I wouldn't even mind if it were government-funded. Maybe it could help them break into something less damaging—like growing tobacco or producing *The Jerry Springer Show*. In fact, if all goes well, by the year 2001, Harry and I—a mere .00000001 percent of Americans 18 or older—will ensure that the 56th convention doesn't take place.

What have pollsters done to deserve extinction, you may ask? Well, besides filling our heads with needless "factoids"—like 59 percent of all Americans think "Ed" is an "okay" name, while 64 percent put on their pants left leg first—they have brought our political system to its knees. Alas, as long as pollsters exist, politicians are going to consult them. So in order to wean our political leaders off their daily numbers habit, what we need to do is contaminate the product—by making the numbers themselves completely unreliable. And that's as easy as hanging up your phone.

That's right. Every time a pollster calls, you can help save our democracy by simply putting the receiver in its cradle. Because of what they call "random-digit dialing," pollsters claim that "every person in America has an equal chance of being selected for one of our polls." Leaving aside for the moment the joke of treating this like some kind of lottery prize, what if more and more—millions more of us—select ourselves right out of the process just by refusing to answer pollsters' questions?

Thanks to the polling response rates, we have a great head start for our civil disobedience campaign. It already takes 7,000 calls to get a 1,000-person sample. Once our crusade sweeps the nation, the pollsters' sample will consist only of very bored, very lonely Americans who want somebody to talk to. As a result, polling data will become so polluted that it will be useless to politicians. Then maybe they'll stop feeding us so much candy—which tends to rot the infrastructure—and put the country on a more healthy diet.

Polling, you may say, is only a symptom of a deeper political crisis. Fair enough, but at least—unlike the crisis of leadership—this is something we can do something about. Starting now. Starting tonight. What if all 270 million of us collectively decided to hang up the next time some stranger from a polling company interrupted our dinner with moronic questions like: "Do you describe yourself as very liberal/somewhat liberal/moderate/somewhat conservative/very conservative?"

For those in politics, yet another form of protest is just a letter away—a resignation letter.

In another time, resignation was viewed as an act of principle and integrity, the ultimate public statement of disapproval of a policy or the last honorable step for a statesman who had lost his honor.

Today, however, the noble act of resignation has been replaced by the ignoble pursuit of power at any price, of hanging on to your political job by your fingertips, at least until your agent calls to inform you the tell-all book has been sold.

Back in 1945, Interior Secretary Harold L. Ickes—father of Clinton's former deputy chief of staff—condemned President Truman's "lack of adherence to the strict truth" and resigned from the Cabinet. "I don't care to stay in an administration," he said, "where I am expected to commit perjury for the sake of the party." The distance we've traveled between Harold Ickes *pere* and Harold Ickes *fils* shows how far down we have defined presidential deviancy.

During the Clinton years, principled resignations have become practically extinct. Wendell Primus, former deputy assistant secretary of the Health and Human Services department, is an exception. He resigned in protest over the president's signing of the welfare reform bill. In his resignation letter to Secretary Donna Shalala, he wrote: "To remain would be to disown all the analysis my office has produced regarding the impact of the bill."

Joining Primus were Peter Edelman, an assistant secretary and head of planning at HHS and husband of Clinton friend Marian Wright Edelman, and Mary Jo Bane, the Clinton administration's top welfare adviser. Three years later Edelman criticized Clinton over his poverty tour, writing in a *New York Times* op-ed piece that it was not "based on the real facts about the state of the poor in America . . . It is not just a matter of pockets of poverty. Persistent poverty is endemic in cities and rural areas and is increasingly present, if less visibly so, in suburbs."

Where was HHS Secretary Donna Shalala's resignation letter? Where was Robert Reich's? Where, for that matter, was Hillary's? Perhaps they all believed that signing the bill was morally the right thing to do by 73 to 12 percent. Primus believed that resigning was the right thing to do by the power of one.

Compare Primus to Attorney General Janet Reno, certainly no stranger to calls for resignation. Those calls intensified across the political spectrum in the wake of the FBI's admission—after six years of denials—that it fired incendiary tear gas canisters at the Branch Davidian compound.

Ironically, Reno offered to resign the day of the raid. "If that's what the president wants, I'm happy to do so," she told *Nightline*. Having delegated too much in the first place, she now delegated her conscience. But her boss, as she knew he would, dismissed her offer: "I was frankly— surprised would be a mild word—that anyone would suggest that the attorney general should resign because some religious fanatics murdered themselves," said Clinton.

In the end, of course, Reno kept her job, emerging unscathed from congressional questioning, even after emphasizing that "I'm accountable. The buck stops with me." Does it really? At the time, she said of the raid, "I don't think it was mishandled and I think the FBI acted very professionally . . . and with great restraint." But in the wake of the new revelations, it was obvious that Reno's offer to resign was only a political message, worth about as much as her opinion of the FBI.

Registration drives, new voting laws, and voter "education" campaigns can go only so far in attracting disaffected Americans to the polls. "Young people and poor people have the lowest rate of participation, and their rates have been declining the most," says Curtis Gans. "It speaks to a lack of hope from the bottom end of the income scale and a lack of vision to inspire the young."

Hope and vision—those are the missing ingredients. How long will it take before Washington gets *our* message, that we're no longer willing to accept the conditions that prevail? Will the voters of East Timor—who risked their lives to flock to the polls to overthrow *their* corrupt government—be our inspiration, or will we be shamed by comparison?

12

THE MACHINE TO BEAT THE MACHINE

So voter turnout is down; apathy is up; well-funded incumbents operate with impunity, and we're drowning in polls. But don't sound the death knell just yet. Help may be just a keystroke away.

A study released last fall revealed "a vast but largely untapped potential for using new technologies to mobilize people for social change." Call it the machine to beat the machine: the Internet is exploding as a revolutionary tool for political change. Consider: Of all the American citizens who can be reached via the Net, half weren't online just two years ago. By Election Day 2000, 70 percent of eligible voters will have Internet access.

Only 15 percent of those currently online surf the Net in search of political news. But of the 11 million who do, many are looking for something beyond the usual horse race election information. They are using the Web as a tool for regaining control of a government that far too frequently ignores their concerns. These wired voters represent a real threat to politics as usual. For one thing, the Net provides a way to get around the two-party lock on information. In fact, a survey by the Democracy Online Project found that Independents are more likely to get their information about candidates from the Internet than either Democrats or Republicans. From the printing press to the TV screen, new information technologies have historically helped loosen the grip of established power—and the Internet is likely to be powerful in ways no other medium has ever been.

To date, the most revolutionary use of the Net in American politics has been Jesse Ventura's campaign. As Steve Clift, chairman of Minnesota's E-Democracy Project put it, "Ventura's was a made-for-the-Net campaign. It's no exaggeration to suggest that Ventura might never have become governor if not for his Web site."

Ventura's Web master, Phil Madsen, who spent a total of $600 on the Web site from beginning to end, used the site as a volunteer recruitment and coordinating center. JesseNet, an army of 3,000 volunteers, helped coordinate Ventura's campaign, including the decisive final three-day drive to victory. A cyber-savvy "Geek Squad" traveled with the candidate, constantly updating his Web page from the road so that potential supporters could participate online practically in real time. The site also functioned as a permanent virtual fund-raiser—with roughly 10 percent of all Ventura campaign funds donated via the Web.

According to one study, over half of the Internet volunteers in the last election cycle had never volunteered for a campaign before; 91 percent signed up without even being recruited. In working on the Ventura site, one of the things Madsen discovered was how easy it was to recruit campaign helpers online. This was especially critical for Ventura, who as a third-party candidate had to make an end-run around the political establishment. "I don't fit into either of the other two parties," said Ventura. "There are thousands of other people like me." And cyberspace was the perfect place to find them.

Other candidates are benefiting from this citizen involvement as well. After launching his high-tech presidential campaign, Steve Forbes managed to enroll nearly 13,000 "cyber-vols" in the site's first six weeks through a system of "E-Precincts," "E-Blocks," and "E-Neighborhoods." "I may not be the first person to invent a political machine," says his Web guru Rick Segal, "but I may be the first to create a political machine that's really a machine."

In his bid for California governor, Dan Lungren signed up 1,500 volunteers online. Gov. Jeb Bush of Florida picked up more than 1,000. "Ventura innovated out of necessity," says Clift. "Now other campaigns are taking advantage of these lessons and using them to raise volunteers and money."

Of the presidential candidates mining the Internet for campaign cash, Bill Bradley is currently the hands-out champ, having raised well over a million dollars. He even asked for—and was granted—Federal Election Commission approval for federal matching funds for Internet credit card donations. In second place is John McCain, with over $260,000. The two front-runners, Al Gore and George W.

Bush, have each raised only about one-tenth of Bradley's total over the Web. But in order to soften the criticism leveled at him for the unprecedented sums of money he has raised through conventional means, Bush has voluntarily listed all of his donors—more than 100,000 of them—on more than 900 pages of his Web site.

But for all the Internet's vast potential, most mainstream politicians have been slow to tap into the new medium. A survey by George Washington University's Democracy Online Project found that only 28 percent of incumbents in the last election had campaign Web sites, compared to 64 percent of challengers. "It's great to see that this is one medium where incumbents don't have the advantage," says George Washington University Professor Michael Cornfield. "Challengers have really jumped at the chance to use the Web to put them over the top."

Richard Perle, Ronald Reagan's former assistant secretary of defense and currently the man in charge of Internet development for the Hollinger publishing group, says it's all about access. "Before too long we'll have continuous video on the Internet," he told me, "and underfunded candidates will be able to get their message out without having to buy TV time—the single greatest expenditure item of modern campaigns."

Not surprisingly, there's a direct correlation between challenger status and the amount of money and effort expended on reaching voters through the Net. Of the presidential candidates' Web sites, Steve Forbes's is by far the most ambitious—and most expensive. He has invested an estimated $500,000 on it, compared to the $15,000 initially spent by George W. Bush—a number exceeded by even his brother Jeb's 1998 Florida gubernatorial campaign site.

Many of these sites are little more than gussied-up cyber-press releases; most campaigns have yet to tap into the Internet's potential to do more than merely inform voters. And the key to unlocking this potential—a feature unique to the Internet—is *interactivity*. A Web site can be beautifully designed and chock full of facts, but any campaign that wants to use it to foster greater political engagement will have to find ways to turn surf potatoes into civic activists.

Take the case of MoveOn.org. Back in 1998, frustrated with the way Congress was being distracted by the Lewinsky scandal, Silicon Valley entrepreneurs Joan Blades and Wes Boyd founded MoveOn as a way to help average Americans get their voices heard inside the Beltway. They were convinced the Internet could enhance democratic participation.

So they shelled out $89.95 for a Web site and sent roughly eighty e-mails to friends asking them to add their names to the e-letter and pass on the information. The e-mail asked Congress to "censure" the president and "move on" with the more important business of governing the country.

Within twenty-four hours, 506 people had signed on— and by the time Congress began to debate the shape of its impeachment inquiry, MoveOn had collected 200,000 responses. In total, the group estimates that it generated 250,000 phone calls and one million e-mails to Congress— all of them coming from disgruntled ciizens Blades calls "five-minute activists."

After the House of Representatives voted to go ahead with impeachment anyway, MoveOn.org e-mailed its 450,000 supporters and urged them to make a "We Will Remember" pledge—a commitment to defeat the incumbents who voted for impeachment. The pledge required a donation of at least $25 to selected campaigns in the upcoming elections. In less than two months, it raised $13 million.

MoveOn's next campaign focused on gun control, "promoting commonsense regulation of firearms." Its online petition garnered 25,000 signatures in the first day.

Such e-mail advocacy is becoming increasingly common. That's what the FDIC discovered when it tried to implement a new "Know Your Customer" rule that would have allowed banks to "monitor" customers' accounts, develop customer "profiles," and report any "unusual" transactions to federal investigators. Upon learning of the agency's plan, the Libertarian Party mounted an all-out "flash-campaign" that sent the FDIC 257,000 comments—205,000 by e-mail. The agency soon withdrew its proposal, with FDIC Chairman Donna Tanoue acknowledging that the electronic blizzard had forced their hand.

Another example of an effective cyber-protest occurred when the computer chip giant Intel announced that its Pentium III microprocessors would contain a new generation of silicon chip that would transmit a unique ID number when users were online. While this "Processor Serial Number" was theoretically designed to protect electronic transactions, critics like the Center for Democracy and Technology, Junkbusters, and the Electronic Privacy

Information Center (EPIC) noted that it would also help marketers track consumers' every click on the Web. Privacy advocates feared the new chips would lead to the permanent loss of anonymity online.

So EPIC, Junkbusters, and Privacy International joined together to launch an "Internet chain letter" campaign. Within a week of Intel's announcement, the company had received such a storm of e-criticism that they decided to e-compromise—promising to distribute software that would enable computer owners to hide their PSNs.

These successes could easily be translated into effective, grassroots politics—turning enraged surfers into engaged citizens. Today, one out of four adults who are involved in social causes are already online. Edward Schwartz, a forty-year organizer of anti-poverty and community groups in Philadelphia, noted that "overwhelmingly, the people who show up are the people on the e-mail list, even though our print mail goes out to a far larger number."

So here's some food for thought: If e-mail is the "killer app" of the political Web, and Internet fund-raising the most potent weapon for bringing new donors into the system, then couldn't online *voting* be a system-shattering way of engaging nonvoters.

Two-thirds of Americans say they would like to vote over the Internet. But for now, it's not even legal to register to vote online (although twenty-three states allow you to download a voter registration form and mail it in). So far, California is the only state that has appointed a task force to study online voting. But trials in digital democracy are beginning. In Arizona, the state Democratic Party is allowing online voting in their March presidential primary. And the Pentagon, through its federal voting assistance program, is developing guidelines for a pilot project to allow military and civilian overseas residents of five states—Florida, Missouri, South Carolina, Texas, and Utah—to vote over the Internet in time for the 2000 elections.

So the future is full of possibilities for bringing in new voters, mobilizing volunteers, leveling the playing field for underfunded challengers, creating a new consensus around issues, and quickly countering the effects of big-money–fed negative campaigning. For instance, during Ventura's campaign, when the media inaccurately reported that he favored legalizing prostitution and marijuana use—thus drawing attacks from his two opponents—his Internet "Geek Squad" put up a correction on his Web site within hours, neutralizing the issue.

The Web is hardly a political panacea, though. Establishment candidates and their consultants are already scrambling to figure out how to combine the new technologies with their tired old campaign tricks—using the Net to manipulate voters, just as they've been doing for years with TV spots and direct mail. Some, like Forbes, have even brought direct-marketing techniques to political cyberspace, tracking the "psychographics" of potential voters by running intricate computer analyses of their personal characteristics.

So another battle is joined—this one between those looking to drag the Internet down into the muddy trenches of old-style political strong-arming, and those eager to use it to bring about reform. "We can do whiz-bang Web sites, but if people think nothing will make a difference, then nothing does make a difference," says California Voter Foundation director Kim Alexander. "My biggest fear is that the manipulators of the political process will win." With the year 2000 upon us, a few hours spent surfing the tepid waters of the presidential candidates' Web sites reveals that, for the moment, Alexander's fear may be justified. So far, it's no more than politics as usual: empty rhetoric and pleas for money.

The good news is, the technology is here. What's missing is the brave new content—but that can only be provided by fresh candidates with bold ideas. And you can't assemble those in Silicon Valley.

Coda

A CALL TO ACTION

At the moment, throughout the nation, it seems as though the reform impulse is being undercut at every level. But make no mistake: Reform *can happen*. And sometimes, despite the best efforts of the political establishment, it does.

In Massachusetts last fall, young activists proved the power of protest—even in the face of overwhelming odds—to lead to reform and a changed political landscape.

A little history: After state lawmakers repeatedly failed to approve campaign finance reform, a group of Massachusetts activists took their case directly to the people. Over six thousand volunteers launched two separate signature-gathering drives to place the Massachusetts Clean Elections Law on the November 1998 ballot. The law sought to shrink the influence of special interests by banning soft money and providing public financing for candidates who agree to limit their campaign spending. The signature drive was backed by the state's entire congressional delegation, many state legislators, some businesses, as well as Common Cause, the League of Women Voters, the AFL-CIO, the AARP, and the Sierra Club.

The initiative won a resounding two-to-one victory at the polls, capturing 67 percent of the vote. But what seemed like democracy in action soon became democracy denied. Voters in Massachusetts have the power to enact laws via the ballot box but can't appropriate the money to fund them, so incumbents set out to nullify the public's vote. After initially vowing to accede to the electorate's wishes—"The voters have approved it, so I will be funding it"—Republican Gov. Paul Cellucci turned around and a mere ten weeks later filed a budget that contained none of the money needed to implement the program.

Then the Democrat-controlled state legislature took a few whacks. Like a playground cheater who cries "Do over!" anytime things don't go his way, the House agreed to fund the measure but only after tacking on an amendment that would require voters to reapprove the same initiative they had just endorsed. Just trying to make sure the people knew what they were doing, I suppose.

The ensuing uproar by activists and opinion-makers ensured that that turkey didn't fly. Undaunted, the legislature then carved a gaping loophole into the Clean Elections Law by allowing incumbents to raise and spend unlimited amounts of money and still qualify for public funding in the last few months of their campaign. In effect, they could have their special interest cake and eat it, too—with a silver taxpayer-funded spoon.

State Senate President Thomas Birmingham, who origi-
nally had hailed Clean Elections as "an idea whose time
has come," defended its evisceration by claiming that
office-holders require more money than the new law
would allow for "expenses that are expected of them and
sometimes needed." But a study released the same week
revealed that the majority of such spending was related to
solidifying incumbency—fund-raising, gift-giving, hospi-
tality, travel, even pricey golf tournaments and lavish
cocktail parties.

With the clean-elections ball back in his court, the governor announced that he would veto the massive loophole—but also the $10 million that the legislature had
reluctantly appropriated to implement it. "The legislature
can't have it both ways," he told me. "They can't have
both special interest money and public funding. At the
same time, it is not clear in the bill how the funding for
district offices would be raised."

It's little wonder, I thought, that voter turnout in
Massachusetts has fallen to its lowest point since the early
1800s. It's as if the political elites are taunting us: "Yeah,
we're making a mockery out of the democratic process—
what are ya gonna do about it?"

What the Clean Elections activists decided to do about
it was simple: protest.

First they held a "Stand by the Voters" rally at the
Statehouse, attended by 150 people. Then the rally leaders
decided to try to speak with Governor Cellucci, marching
to a room in the Statehouse where he was meeting with
Republican lawmakers. At the same time, another group

of 15 protesters staged a sit-in outside the governor's office.

"One of the dangers with all this is that we lose idealism, that everyone becomes so cynical," said David Donnelly, the thirty-year-old director of Mass Voters for Clean Elections. "It's worse than a roller coaster. It's one of those freaky scare rides at the carnival." But the young activists refused to give up, and finally the governor agreed to meet with Donnelly and four others.

By Tuesday afternoon, Cellucci had changed his mind and decided not to veto the necessary funding after all. "To substantially change what the voters have approved would be wrong," Cellucci said—especially when those voters start getting mad.

Once the legislature failed to override the veto, Clean Elections' victory was assured. It was a huge win for reform, and a tribute to both the governor, who showed true leadership in his willingness to listen, and the Clean Elections movement, which demonstrated the power of protest and persistence.

"It's clear that the voters of this state have been heard," said Donnelly. "Through the public pressure that the voters placed on the governor and the legislative leaders, the Clean Elections Law remains intact and is funded for this year."

Let us, then, take the work of the Massachusetts volunteers as an inspiration, and start tackling the challenges before us.

The following pages offer a list of things you can do to help save your country. Activism is not a relic of the 1960s.

It's one of the cornerstones of our democracy. And it's our responsibility.

Help renew our democracy. Help strengthen our civil society. Help speed the pace of reform, and keep America from disintegrating even further into two nations. Here are some ways to get started:

- Demonstrate at political rallies.
- Engage in acts of civil disobedience: protests, marches, sit-ins. They're still happening—and *they work*. Ask the WTO.
- Join a third, fourth, or fifth party. Get active in an independent campaign.
- *Start* a third, fourth, or fifth party. Run yourself as an independent candidate.
- Join former President Jimmy Carter in building a Habitat for Humanity home.
- Push for same-day voter registration, greater candidate access to debates, term limits, ballot access reforms, and public financing of campaigns.
- Support charitable tax credits (giving money directly to poverty-fighting organizations instead of the IRS).
- Become personally involved in the lives of those in need within your communities.
- Support Colin Powell's America's Promise campaign.
- Mentor children during your lunch hour.
- Join Bill Shore's Share Our Strength campaign to support anti-hunger and anti-poverty efforts.
- Get up close and personal by volunteering with organizations like those of Bill Milliken, Jeffrey Canada,

Deborah Constance, Marsh Ward, Hannah Hawkins, and all the other community leaders who help turn lives around every day.

- Join the growing number of our nation's young people who volunteer at soup kitchens, hospitals, and schools.
- Join the Partnership for a Poll-Free America and hang up on pollsters.
- Help convince our nation's best and brightest to return to politics.
- Adopt Dean Ornish's lifestyle-changes regimen; make sure you're able to be part of the solution and not part of our ever-growing health care crisis.
- Petition for laws such as Maryland's that require high school students to perform community service in order to graduate.
- Push for character education in our schools, to help teach our children right from wrong.
- Give to the Children's Scholarship Fund for low-income children trapped in dysfunctional schools.
- Tithe to poverty-fighting groups. Shame rich people and corporations into doing the right thing by donating to those most in need, and boycott those corporations that don't.
- Push "compassionate" candidates to put their money where their mouth is by giving 10 percent of their campaign contributions to the poverty-fighting groups of their choice.
- Direct your donations not to concrete (art museums, World War II monuments) but to concrete solutions

(groups like Do Something in New York, Homeboy Industries in L.A., Teen Challenge in San Antonio, and Clean and Sober Streets in Washington, D.C.).

- Mentor a child through the Big Brothers and Big Sisters programs.
- Write, e-mail, and call your elected representatives to support campaign finance reform.
- Patronize those corporations that refuse to take part in the soft-money quid pro quo.
- Sign Clean Money initiatives—or better yet, volunteer to collect the signatures.
- Demand a "Don't Ask, Don't Tell" policy from our media and candidates when it comes to questions about politicians' personal lives.
- Encourage your local papers, as well as TV and radio stations, to cover community solutions and focus on problem solvers. And look to alternative news sources such as the American News Service and on the Internet.
- Push for ways to make voting easier—such as vote-by-mail, early voting, weekend voting, and Internet voting.
- Support the Oaks Project and other groups trying to open up the voting process.
- Support "None of the Above" ballot initiatives like the upcoming one in California.
- Volunteer with your family—call the Points of Light Foundation to find out where and how.

We cannot wait for leaders to emerge who will do these things for us.

We must act—and act now.

APPENDIX A:

A STATE-BY-STATE ROAD MAP TO REFORM

Limits on contributions from individuals to statewide candidates (per election)

[Primary source: Campaign Finance Law '98, by Edward Feigenbaum and James Palmer, published by the Federal Election Commission; with updates from several state activists]

ALABAMA	unlimited
ALASKA	$1,000
ARIZONA	$608 *
ARKANSAS	$1,000 {X}
CALIFORNIA	$1,000
COLORADO	$500
CONNECTICUT	$2,500 for governor $1,500 other
DELAWARE	$1,200
DC	$2,000
FLORIDA	$500 {X}
GEORGIA	$8,000 total for all statewide offices {X}
HAWAII	$6,000
IDAHO	$5,000 {X}
ILLINOIS	unlimited
INDIANA	unlimited
IOWA	unlimited
KANSAS	$2,000
KENTUCKY	$1,000
LOUISIANA	$5,000
MAINE	$500 *
MARYLAND	$4,000
MASSACHUSETTS	$500 *
MICHIGAN	$3,400 {X}

MINNESOTA	$3,500 {X}
MISSISSIPPI	unlimited
MISSOURI	$1,075 {X}
MONTANA	$400 {X}
NEBRASKA	unlimited
NEVADA	$5,000 {X}
NEW HAMPSHIRE	$5,000
NEW JERSEY	$2,100
NEW MEXICO	unlimited
NEW YORK	$41,400 {X}
NORTH CAROLINA	$4,000 {X}
NORTH DAKOTA	unlimited
OHIO	$2,500
OKLAHOMA	$5,000
OREGON	unlimited
PENNSYLVANIA	unlimited
RHODE ISLAND	$2,000
SOUTH CAROLINA	$3,500 {X}
SOUTH DAKOTA	$4,000
TENNESSEE	$2,500 {X}
TEXAS	unlimited
UTAH	unlimited
VERMONT	$400 *
VIRGINIA	unlimited
WASHINGTON	$1,150 {X}
WEST VIRGINIA	$1,000
WISCONSIN	$10,000
WYOMING	$1,000

{X}—the state allows unlimited individual contributions to parties, which can then easily spend those amounts on behalf of their candidates, making the lower direct contribution limit essentially meaningless

*—lower limits apply to contributions to candidates seeking Clean Elections funding in these four states

Internet disclosure of campaign finance data

(note: every state requires some form of disclosure of campaign financing, but not all make it easy for citizens to find out who has given to whom by providing this data over the Internet)

ALABAMA	not required
ALASKA	going online {*}
ARIZONA	online {*}
ARKANSAS	not required
CALIFORNIA	online {*}
COLORADO	going online {*}
CONNECTICUT	online {*}
DELAWARE	going online
DC	not required
FLORIDA	online {*}
GEORGIA	not required {*}
HAWAII	online
IDAHO	online {*}
ILLINOIS	going online {*}
INDIANA	online {*}
IOWA	going online {*}
KANSAS	online {*}
KENTUCKY	not required {*}
LOUISIANA	online
MAINE	going online {*}
MARYLAND	going online
MASSACHUSETTS	online {*}
MICHIGAN	online {*}
MINNESOTA	going online {*}
MISSISSIPPI	not required
MISSOURI	going online {*}
MONTANA	not required {*}
NEBRASKA	not required

NEVADA	not required {*}
NEW HAMPSHIRE	online {*}
NEW JERSEY	online
NEW MEXICO	not required {*}
NEW YORK	going online
NORTH CAROLINA	online {*}
NORTH DAKOTA	not required
OHIO	online {*}
OKLAHOMA	online
OREGON	online {*}
PENNSYLVANIA	online
RHODE ISLAND	not required {*}
SOUTH CAROLINA	not required
SOUTH DAKOTA	not required
TENNESSEE	going online {*}
TEXAS	not required
UTAH	online {*}
VERMONT	not required {*}
VIRGINIA	going online
WASHINGTON	online {*}
WEST VIRGINIA	going online
WISCONSIN	going online
WYOMING	not required {*}

online—means data are collected and made available online by the relevant state agency (not necessarily for all offices, however)

going online—means the system is in the process of being implemented as of 1999

{*}—state data have been collected and analyzed and are available online from the National Institute on Money in State Politics at www.followthemoney.org

Sources: Center for Responsive Politics, National Institute on Money in Politics, Digital Sunlight (California Voter Foundation), Campaign Finance Information Center

Partial or full public financing for candidates who voluntarily limit spending

ALABAMA	
ALASKA	
ARIZONA	full; to all state offices {*}
ARKANSAS	
CALIFORNIA	
COLORADO	
CONNECTICUT	
DELAWARE	
DC	
FLORIDA	partial; to statewide candidates {*}
GEORGIA	
HAWAII	partial; to all non-federal offices {*}
IDAHO	
ILLINOIS	
INDIANA	
IOWA	
KANSAS	
KENTUCKY	
LOUISIANA	
MAINE	full; to all state offices {*}
MARYLAND	partial; to governor and lt. governor {*}
MASSACHUSETTS	full; to all state offices {*}
MICHIGAN	partial; to governor and lt. governor {*}
MINNESOTA	partial but generous; to all state offices {*}
MISSISSIPPI	
MISSOURI	
MONTANA	
NEBRASKA	partial, only under special circumstances {*}
NEVADA	

NEW HAMPSHIRE	
NEW JERSEY	partial, to governor {*}
NEW MEXICO	
NEW YORK	
NORTH CAROLINA	
NORTH DAKOTA	
OHIO	
OKLAHOMA	
OREGON	
PENNSYLVANIA	
RHODE ISLAND	partial, to statewide candidates {*}
SOUTH CAROLINA	
SOUTH DAKOTA	
TENNESSEE	
TEXAS	
UTAH	
VERMONT	full, to governor and lt. governor {*}
VIRGINIA	
WASHINGTON	
WEST VIRGINIA	
WISCONSIN	partial, to all state offices {*}
WYOMING	

{*}—Third-party candidates can qualify for public financing, sometimes only in amounts proportional to their ballot strength

Individual tax credits or refunds for political contributions to parties and/or candidates

(another source of public financing other than direct grants or matching funds to candidates)

ALABAMA	
ALASKA	
ARIZONA	up to $100 deduction, to a party
ARKANSAS	up to $50 credit, to candidate, small donor PAC or party
CALIFORNIA	
COLORADO	
CONNECTICUT	
DELAWARE	
DC	credit of 50% of up to $50
FLORIDA	
GEORGIA	
HAWAII	deduction of up to $500 given to candidates, $100 to party
IDAHO	
ILLINOIS	
INDIANA	
IOWA	
KANSAS	
KENTUCKY	
LOUISIANA	
MAINE	
MARYLAND	
MASSACHUSETTS	
MICHIGAN	
MINNESOTA	refund of up to $50 given to candidates or a party
MISSISSIPPI	

MISSOURI	
MONTANA	
NEBRASKA	
NEVADA	
NEW HAMPSHIRE	
NEW JERSEY	
NEW MEXICO	
NEW YORK	
NORTH CAROLINA	deduction of up to $25
NORTH DAKOTA	
OHIO	credit of up to $50 given to statewide candidates
OKLAHOMA	deduction of up to $100
OREGON	credit of up to $50
PENNSYLVANIA	
RHODE ISLAND	
SOUTH CAROLINA	
SOUTH DAKOTA	
TENNESSEE	
TEXAS	
UTAH	
VERMONT	
VIRGINIA	
WASHINGTON	
WEST VIRGINIA	
WISCONSIN	
WYOMING	

State voter registration deadlines for general elections

(Source: Federal Elections Commission)

ALABAMA	10 days prior
ALASKA	30
ARIZONA	29
ARKANSAS	30
CALIFORNIA	29
COLORADO	29
CONNECTICUT	14
DELAWARE	20
DC	30
FLORIDA	29
GEORGIA	36
HAWAII	30
IDAHO	same day
ILLINOIS	28
INDIANA	29
IOWA	10
KANSAS	15
KENTUCKY	28
LOUISIANA	24
MAINE	same day
MARYLAND	36
MASSACHUSETTS	20
MICHIGAN	30
MINNESOTA	same day
MISSISSIPPI	30
MISSOURI	28
MONTANA	30
NEBRASKA	11
NEVADA	32

NEW HAMPSHIRE	same day
NEW JERSEY	29
NEW MEXICO	28
NEW YORK	25
NORTH CAROLINA	25
NORTH DAKOTA	no voter registration
OHIO	30
OKLAHOMA	25
OREGON	21
PENNSYLVANIA	30
RHODE ISLAND	30
SOUTH CAROLINA	30
SOUTH DAKOTA	15
TENNESSEE	30
TEXAS	30
UTAH	20
VERMONT	11
VIRGINIA	29
WASHINGTON	15
WEST VIRGINIA	30
WISCONSIN	same day
WYOMING	same day

Ballot access requirements to primaries of already qualified parties for president

(Source: Richard Winger, Ballot Access News; compiled based on state laws as of July 15, 1999)

ALABAMA	500 signatures
ALASKA	no primary
ARIZONA	just request a place
ARKANSAS	pay filing fee set by party
CALIFORNIA	automatic*
COLORADO	5000 signatures or $500 fee
CONNECTICUT	automatic*
DELAWARE	500 signatures, or qualify for federal matching funds
DC	1,000 signatures
FLORIDA	up to state party
GEORGIA	up to state party
HAWAII	no primary
IDAHO	automatic
ILLINOIS	3,000 signatures
INDIANA	5,000 signatures
IOWA	no primary
KANSAS	1000 signatures or $100 fee
KENTUCKY	5,000 signatures or be on ballot in 20 other states
LOUISIANA	8,000 signatures or $750 fee
MAINE	2,000 signatures or $2,500
MARYLAND	automatic*
MASSACHUSETTS	automatic*
MICHIGAN	automatic*
MINNESOTA	no primary
MISSISSIPPI	automatic*
MISSOURI	5,000 signatures or $1,000 fee
MONTANA	500 signatures
NEBRASKA	automatic*

NEVADA	no primary
NEW HAMPSHIRE	$1,000 fee
NEW JERSEY	1,000 signatures
NEW MEXICO	automatic*
NEW YORK	20,000 (est.)[1]
NORTH CAROLINA	10,000 signatures or qualify for federal matching funds
NORTH DAKOTA	no primary
OHIO	1,000 signatures or qualify for federal matching funds
OKLAHOMA	6,000 signatures or $2,500 fee
OREGON	automatic*
PENNSYLVANIA	2,000 signatures
RHODE ISLAND	1,000 signatures
SOUTH CAROLINA	pay filing fee set by party
SOUTH DAKOTA	1,000 signatures (est.) or support of party
TENNESSEE	automatic*
TEXAS	pay filing fee set by party
UTAH	$500 fee
VERMONT	1,000 signatures and $2,000 fee
VIRGINIA	10,000 signatures
WASHINGTON	automatic*
WEST VIRGINIA	pay fee of 1% of salary
WISCONSIN	automatic*
WYOMING	no primary

* If the candidacy has been discussed by the state media, as determined by the secretary of state. In two states, Kentucky and Rhode Island, this standard has been rejected by the courts as too vague

1 In New York, a presidential candidate needs to collect signatures from .5 percent of the number of party members registered in each of the state's congressional districts, plus an additional 5,000 signatures

Ballot access requirements to primaries of already qualified parties for statewide office

(Source: Richard Winger, Ballot Access News; compiled based on state laws as of July 15, 1999)

ALABAMA	Pay filing fee set by party
ALASKA	$100 fee
ARIZONA	5,000 signatures (est.)
ARKANSAS	Pay filing fee set by party
CALIFORNIA	65 party members signatures + pay fee of 2% salary
COLORADO	Automatic if supported at party meeting
CONNECTICUT	Automatic if supported at party meeting
DELAWARE	Pay filing fee set by party
DC	1,000 signatures
FLORIDA	Pay fee of 6% annual salary
GEORGIA	Pay fee of 3% annual salary
HAWAII	25 signatures + $75 fee
IDAHO	1,000 signatures + $250 fee
ILLINOIS	5,000 signatures
INDIANA	5,000 signatures
IOWA	2,500 signatures (est.)
KANSAS	Pay fee of 1% annual salary
KENTUCKY	$500 fee
LOUISIANA	$600 fee
MAINE	2,000 signatures of party members
MARYLAND	$290 fee
MASSACHUSETTS	10,000 signatures
MICHIGAN	17,000 signatures (est.)
MINNESOTA	$400 fee
MISSISSIPPI	$300 fee
MISSOURI	$100 fee
MONTANA	Pay fee of 1% annual salary
NEBRASKA	pay fee of 1% annual salary

NEVADA	$500 fee
NEW HAMPSHIRE	$100 fee
NEW JERSEY	1,000 signatures
NEW MEXICO	5,000 signatures (est.)
NEW YORK	Automatic if supported at party meeting
NORTH CAROLINA	pay fee of 1% annual salary
NORTH DAKOTA	Automatic if supported at party meeting
OHIO	1,000 signatures + $100 fee
OKLAHOMA	$1,000 fee
OREGON	$150 fee
PENNSYLVANIA	2,000 member signatures + $200 fee
RHODE ISLAND	1,000 signatures
SOUTH CAROLINA	pay filing fee set by party
SOUTH DAKOTA	1,600 signatures (est.)
TENNESSEE	25 signatures
TEXAS	$4,000 fee
UTAH	fee of .125% of term salary
VERMONT	500 signatures
VIRGINIA	10,000 signatures + fee of 2% salary
WASHINGTON	fee of 1% annual salary
WEST VIRGINIA	fee of 1% annual salary
WISCONSIN	2,000 signatures
WYOMING	—no primary

* If the candidacy has been discussed by the state media, as determined by the secretary of state. In two states, Kentucky and Rhode Island, this standard has been rejected by the courts as too vague
1 In New York, a presidential candidate needs to collect signatures from .5 percent of the number of party members registered in each of the state's congressional districts, plus an additional 5,000 signatures

Ballot access requirements to primaries of already qualified parties for U.S. House of Representatives

(Source: Richard Winger, Ballot Access News; compiled based on state laws as of July 15, 1999)

ALABAMA	pay filing fee set by party
ALASKA	$100 fee
ARIZONA	900 member signatures (est.)
ARKANSAS	pay filing fee set by party
CALIFORNIA	40 member signatures + pay fee of 1% salary
COLORADO	automatic if supported at party meeting
CONNECTICUT	automatic if supported at party meeting
DELAWARE	pay filing fee set by party
DC	2,000 signatures
FLORIDA	pay fee of 6% annual salary
GEORGIA	pay fee of 3% annual salary
HAWAII	25 signatures + $75 fee
IDAHO	500 signatures + $150 fee
ILLINOIS	475 signatures (est.)
INDIANA	file declaration of candidacy
IOWA	1000 signatures (est.)
KANSAS	pay fee of 1% salary
KENTUCKY	$500 fee
LOUISIANA	$600 fee
MAINE	1,000 members' signatures
MARYLAND	$100 fee
MASSACHUSETTS	2,000 signatures
MICHIGAN	1,000 signatures (est.)
MINNESOTA	$300 fee
MISSISSIPPI	$200 fee
MISSOURI	$100 fee
MONTANA	pay fee of 1% annual salary
NEBRASKA	pay fee of 1% annual salary

NEVADA	$300 fee
NEW HAMPSHIRE	$50 fee
NEW JERSEY	100 signatures
NEW MEXICO	1,700 signatures (est.)
NEW YORK	1,250 members' signatures
NORTH CAROLINA	pay fee of 1% annual salary
NORTH DAKOTA	automatic if supported at party meeting
OHIO	50 signatures + $50 fee
OKLAHOMA	$750 fee
OREGON	$100 fee
PENNSYLVANIA	1000 members' signatures + $150 fee
RHODE ISLAND	500 signatures
SOUTH CAROLINA	pay filing fee set by party
SOUTH DAKOTA	1,700 signatures (est.)
TENNESSEE	25 signatures
TEXAS	$2500 fee
UTAH	fee of .125% of term salary
VERMONT	500 signatures
VIRGINIA	1,000 signatures + fee of 2% salary
WASHINGTON	fee of 1% annual salary
WEST VIRGINIA	fee of 1% annual salary
WISCONSIN	1,000 signatures
WYOMING	$200 fee

* If the candidacy has been discussed by the state media, as determined by the secretary of state. In two states, Kentucky and Rhode Island, this standard has been rejected by the courts as too vague

1 In New York, a presidential candidate needs to collect signatures from .5 percent of the number of party members registered in each of the state's congressional districts, plus an additional 5,000 signatures

Ballot access requirements for candidates to the State House

	Signatures required for an independent candidate[2]	% of registered voters[3]	Signatures required for a candidate of a new party	% of registered voters
ALABAMA	377	1.61	377	1.61
ALASKA	55	.49	55	.49
ARIZONA	133 (est.)	.35	133 (est.)	.35
ARKANSAS	212	1.44	no procedure #	
CALIFORNIA	5,613	3.00	no procedure	
COLORADO	400	1.01	400	1.01
CONNECTICUT	57	.44	57	.44
DELAWARE	115 (est.)	1.00	no procedure	
DC	not applicable			
FLORIDA	just pay filing fee	.00	just pay filing fee	.00
GEORGIA	1,086	5.00	1,086	5.00
HAWAII	25*	.00+	no procedure	
IDAHO	50	.53	no procedure	
ILLINOIS	2,589	4.56	1,295	2.28
INDIANA	307	.83	307	.83
IOWA	191	1.08	191	1.08
KANSAS	484 (est.)	4.00	no procedure	
KENTUCKY	100	.39	100	.39
LOUISIANA	just pay filing fee	.00	no procedure	
MAINE	50	.80	50	.80
MARYLAND	182 (est.)	3.00	no procedure	
MASSACHUSETTS	150	.65	150	.65
MICHIGAN	550	.88	no procedure	
MINNESOTA	500	1.92	500	.96
MISSISSIPPI	50	.35	no procedure	
MISSOURI	263	1.18	263	1.18
MONTANA	98	1.54	98	1.55
NEBRASKA	leg is nonpartisan			
NEVADA	97	.46	no procedure	
NEW HAMPSHIRE	150	8.03	150	8.03
NEW JERSEY	100	.18	100	.09
NEW MEXICO	214	1.64	no procedure	
NEW YORK	1,500	2.13	1,500	2.13

NORTH CAROLINA	1,588 (est.)	4.00	no procedure	
NORTH DAKOTA	300	6.18	no procedure	
OHIO	339	.53	no procedure	
OKLAHOMA	just pay filing fee	.00	no procedure	
OREGON	229	.72	270	.85
PENNSYLVANIA	198	.55	198	.55
RHODE ISLAND	50	.79	50	.79
SOUTH CAROLINA	815	5.00	no procedure	
SOUTH DAKOTA	37	.57	37	.57
TENNESSEE	25	.08	no procedure	
TEXAS	500	.65	no procedure	
UTAH	300	2.01	300	2.01
VERMONT	100	6.21	100	6.21
VIRGINIA	149 (est.)	.46	186 (est.)	.50
WASHINGTON	25*	.04	25	.04
WEST VIRGINIA	112	.66	70	.70
WISCONSIN	200	.55	200	.51
WYOMING	164	4.19	no procedure	

2 To get on the November 2000 ballot, or, for those states which don't elect state legislators in 2000, to get on the 1999 or 1998 ballot

3 As of fall 1998

* In Hawaii and Washington, an independent candidate must poll a certain number of votes in the primary to be on the November ballot. In Hawaii, the candidate has to get more votes than the weakest party nominee. To be on the primary ballot, 25 signatures are needed in both states

In states listed as having "no procedure," the candidate of a new party cannot get on the ballot (with the party label, that is) unless that new party has qualified itself for the statewide ballot

Ballot access requirements for statewide candidates (i.e., senator, governor, etc., but not president)

	Signatures required for an independent candidate	% of registered voters [5]	Signatures required for a candidate of a new party [6]	% of registered voters
ALABAMA	39,536	1.61	39,536	1.61
ALASKA	2,217	.49	2,217	.49
ARIZONA	8,000 (est.)	.35	8,000 (est.)	.35
ARKANSAS	10,000	.68	21,181	1.44
CALIFORNIA	149,692	1.00	86,027*	.57
COLORADO	1,000	.04	1,000	.04
CONNECTICUT	7,500	.38	7,500	.38
DELAWARE	4,700 (est.)	1.00	235 (est.)*	.05
DC	3,000	.85	3,000	.85
FLORIDA	pay fee	.00	pay fee	.00
GEORGIA	39,094	1.00	39,094	1.00
HAWAII	25 [7]	.00+	602	.10
IDAHO	1,000	.15	9,835	1.49
ILLINOIS	25,000	.37	25,000	.37
INDIANA	30,717	.83	30,717	.83
IOWA	1,500	.08	1,500	.08
KANSAS	5,000	.33	14,854	.98
KENTUCKY	5,000	.19	5,000	.19
LOUISIANA	pay fee	.00	134,460 (est.)*	5.00
MAINE	4,000	.42	4,000	.42
MARYLAND	26,000 (est.)	1.01	36,000 (est.)	1.39
MASSACHUSETTS	10,000	.27	10,000	.27
MICHIGAN	30,272	.44	30,272	.44
MINNESOTA	2,000	.06	2,000	.06
MISSISSIPPI	1,000	.06	just be organized	.00
MISSOURI	10,000	.28	10,000	.28
MONTANA	5,000	.78	5,000	.78
NEBRASKA	2,000	.19	5,367	.51
NEVADA	4,099	.46	4,099	.46
NEW HAMPSHIRE	3,000	.40	3,000	.40
NEW JERSEY	800	.02	800	.02
NEW MEXICO	14,964	1.64	7,482[8]	.82

NEW YORK	15,000	.14	15,000	.14
NORTH CAROLINA	95,000 (est.)	1.88	51,324	1.08
NORTH DAKOTA	1,000	.21	7,000	1.47
OHIO	5,000	.07	33,543	.47
OKLAHOMA	pay fee	.00	43,680	2.13
OREGON	13,755	.72	16,257	.85
PENNSYLVANIA	22,000 (est.)	.30	22,000 (est.)	.30
RHODE ISLAND	1,000	.16	1,000	.16
SOUTH CAROLINA	10,000	.49	10,000	.49
SOUTH DAKOTA	2,602	.57	2,602	.57
TENNESSEE	25	.00+	23,819	.79
TEXAS	37,385	.32	37,385	.32
UTAH	1,000	.09	1,000	.09
VERMONT	1,000	.25	just be organized	.00
VIRGINIA	10,000	.27	10,000	.27
WASHINGTON	9,000 (est.)	.29	9,000 (est.)	.29
WEST VIRGINIA	11,914	1.18	11,914	1.18
WISCONSIN	2,000	.06	2,000	.06
WYOMING	3,485	1.47	3,485	1.47

4 To get on the November 2000 ballot

5 As of fall 1998

6 Where a state has more than one method to qualify a new party candidate, the number required under the easier method is shown

7 Hawaii requires that an independent candidate collect 25 petition signatures and out-poll any party's nominee in the state's primary

8 New Mexico requires two separate petitions: 2,494 signatures to qualify the party and then 4,000 to qualify a candidate

* In these three states, the new party has to register this number of voters as members in order to qualify their candidate for the ballot

Ballot access requirements for U.S. House candidates

	Signatures required for an independent candidate[8]	% of registered voters[9]	Signatures required for a candidate of a new party	% of registered voters
ALABAMA	5,648	1.61	5,648	1.61
ALASKA	2,217	.49	2,217	.49
ARIZONA	1,333 (est.)	.35	1,333 (est.)	.35
ARKANSAS	2,000	.54	no procedure[10]	
CALIFORNIA	8,636	3.00	no procedure	
COLORADO	800	.19	800	.19
CONNECTICUT	1,591	.49	1,591	.49
DELAWARE	4,700	1.00	235 (est.)[11]	.05
DC	3,000	.85	3,000	.85
FLORIDA	just pay filing fee	.00	just pay filing fee	.00
GEORGIA	17,770	5.00	17,770	5.00
HAWAII	25*		no procedure	
IDAHO	500	.15	no procedure	
ILLINOIS	8,039	2.40	8,039	2.40
INDIANA	3,072	.85	3,072	.85
IOWA	300	.08	300	.08
KANSAS	5,000	1.32	no procedure	
KENTUCKY	400	.09	400	.09
LOUISIANA	just pay filing fee	.00	no procedure	
MAINE	2,000	.42	2,000	.42
MARYLAND	3,250 (est.)	1.00	no procedure	
MASSACHUSETTS	2,000	.54	2,000	.54
MICHIGAN	3,784	.88	no procedure	
MINNESOTA	1,000	.24	1,000	.24
MISSISSIPPI	200	.06	no procedure	
MISSOURI	4,761	1.18	4,761	1.18
MONTANA	5,000	.78	5,000	.78
NEBRASKA	2,000	.57	1,789	.51
NEVADA	2,050	.46	2,050	.46
NEW HAMPSHIRE	1,500	.40	1,500	.40
NEW JERSEY	100	.03	100	.03
NEW MEXICO	4,988	1.64	no procedure	
NEW YORK	3,500	1.03	3,500	1.03

NORTH CAROLINA	15,880	4.00	no procedure	
NORTH DAKOTA	1,000	.21	7,000	1.47
OHIO	1,765	.53	no procedure	
OKLAHOMA	just pay filing fee	.00	no procedure	
OREGON	2,751	.72	3,251	.85
PENNSYLVANIA	1,910	.55	1,910	.55
RHODE ISLAND	500	.16	500	.16
SOUTH CAROLINA	16,848	5.00	no procedure	
SOUTH DAKOTA	2,602	.57	2,602	.57
TENNESSEE	25	.01	no procedure	
TEXAS	500	.13	no procedure	
UTAH	300	.09	300	.09
VERMONT	1,000	.26	1,000	.26
VIRGINIA	1,000	.30	1,000	.30
WASHINGTON	1,100 (est.) *	.32	1,100 (est.) *	.32
WEST VIRGINIA	2,343	.70	2,343	.70
WISCONSIN	1,000	.23	1,000	.23
WYOMING	3,485	1.47	3,485	1.47

8 To get on the November 2000 ballot

9 As of fall 1998

10 In all the states listed as having "no procedure," the candidate of a new party can't get on the ballot for the U.S. House (with the party label, that is) unless that new party has qualified itself for the statewide ballot

11 To qualify its candidate for the ballot, the party has to register this number of voters in the district

* In both Hawaii and Washington, an independent candidate must poll a certain number of votes in the primary to be on the November ballot. In Hawaii, the candidate must get more votes in the primary than the weakest party nominee. In Washington, the candidate must get at least 1% of the total primary vote. To get on the primary ballot, the candidate needs to file 25 petition signatures

Ballot access requirements for presidential candidates

	Signatures required for an independent candidate[12]	% of registered voters[13]	Signatures required for a candidate of a new party	% of registered voters
ALABAMA	5,000	.2	39,536	1.61
ALASKA	no procedure		2,410	.53
ARIZONA	8,000 (est.)[14]	.35	8,000 (est.)	.35
ARKANSAS	1,000	.07	1,000	.07
CALIFORNIA	149,692	1.00	86,027	.57
COLORADO	just pay $500 fee	.00	just pay $500 fee	.00
CONNECTICUT	7,500	.38	7,500	.38
DELAWARE	4,700 (est.)	1.00	235 (est.)	.05
DC	3,500 (est.)	1.00	3,500 (est.)	1.00
FLORIDA	82,203	1.00	—[15]	.00
GEORGIA	39,094	1.00	39,094	1.00
HAWAII	3,703	.62	602	.10
IDAHO	4,918	.74	9,835	1.49
ILLINOIS	25,000	.37	25,000	.37
INDIANA	30,717	.83	30,717	.83
IOWA	1,500	.08	1,500	.08
KANSAS	5,000	.33	14,854	.98
KENTUCKY	5,000	.19	5,000	.19
LOUISIANA	just pay $500 fee	.00	just pay $500 fee	.00
MAINE	4,000	.42	4,000	.42
MARYLAND	26,000 (est.)	1.00	10,000	.39
MASSACHUSETTS	10,000	.27	10,000	.27
MICHIGAN	30,272	.44	30,272	.44
MINNESOTA	2,000	.06	2,000	.06
MISSISSIPPI	1,000	.06	1,000	.06
MISSOURI	10,000	.28	10,000	.28
MONTANA	5,000	.78	5,000	.86
NEBRASKA	2,500	.24	5,367	.51
NEVADA	4,099	.46	4,099	.46
NEW HAMPSHIRE	3,000	.4	3,000	.40
NEW JERSEY	800	.02	800	.02
NEW MEXICO	14,964	1.64	2,494	.27
NEW YORK	15,000	.14	15,000	.14

NORTH CAROLINA	95,000 (est.)	1.98	51,324	1.08
NORTH DAKOTA	4,000	.84	7,000	1.47
OHIO	5,000	.07	33,543	.47
OKLAHOMA	36,202	1.77	36,202	1.77
OREGON	13,755	.72	16,257	.85
PENNSYLVANIA	22,000 (est.)	.30	22,000	.30
RHODE ISLAND	1,000	.16	1,000	.16
SOUTH CAROLINA	10,000	.49	10,000	.49
SOUTH DAKOTA	2,602	.57	2,602	.57
TENNESSEE	25	.00+	23,819	.79
TEXAS	56,117	.49	37,385	.32
UTAH	300	.03	300	.03
VERMONT	1,000	.25	1,000	.25
VIRGINIA	10,000	.27	10,000	.27
WASHINGTON	200	.01	200	.01
WEST VIRGINIA	12,730	1.26	2,730	1.26
WISCONSIN	2,000	.06	2,000	.06
WYOMING	3,485	1.47	3,485	1.47

12 Number of petition signatures needed to get on the November 2000 ballot
13 As of fall 1998
14 Estimates, where noted, are required because state law bases the number on something that has yet to be determined. For example, Arizona law calls for petitioners to collect 3% of the number of independent voters in mid-2000. Delaware calls for 1% of the total number of registered voters in December 1999
15 Florida requires only that a new party file a list of officers and hold a national convention to place its presidential candidate on the ballot- - ·

APPENDIX B

A Call to Action Directory

What follows is a list of groups—some large and national, some small and local. It's a mixture of good government and advocacy groups, foundations, and community service organizations that I have either been personally involved with or whose work I admire. These are the kinds of groups it will take to bring about political reform and strengthen civil society. Go to their websites or call to find out more about them—and get involved.

America's Promise—The Alliance for Youth
909 North Washington Street,
   Suite 400
Alexandria, VA 22314–1556
(703) 684–4500
http://www.americaspromise.org

The Annie E. Casey Foundation
701 St. Paul Street
Baltimore, MD 21202
410–547–6600
http://www.aecf.org

Ashoka: Innovators for the Public
1700 North Moore Street,
   Suite 1920
Arlington, VA 22209
(703) 527–8300
http://www.ashoka.org

Best Friends
4455 Connecticut Ave. NW,
   Suite 310
Washington, DC 20008
(202) 237–8156

Big Brothers Big Sisters of America
230 North 13th Street
Philadelphia, PA 19107
(215) 567–7000
http://www.bbbsa.org

Boys and Girls Clubs of America
1230 W. Peachtree Street, NW
Atlanta, GA 30309
(404) 815–5700
(800) 854-CLUB (2582)
http://www.bcga.org

The Center for Renewal
9525 Katy Freeway
Houston, TX 77024
(713) 984–1343
http://www.centerforrenewal.org

The Center for Responsive Politics
1320 19th Street, NW, Suite 620
Washington, DC 20036
(202) 857–0044
http://www.opensecrets.com

Chicago Children's Choir
Chicago Cultural Center
78 East Washington
Chicago, IL 60602
(312) 849–8300

Children's Health Fund
317 East 64th Street
New York, NY 10021
(212) 535–9400
http://www.childrenshealthfund.org

The Children of Mine Center
2263 Mount View Place, SE
Washington, DC 20020
(202) 610–1055

Children of the Night
PO Box 4343
Hollywood, CA 90078
(818) 908–4470

Chrysalis
516 South Main Street
Los Angeles, CA 90013
(213) 895–7525
http://www.chrysalisworks.org

City Year
285 Columbus Ave.
Boston, MA 02116
(617) 927–2500
http://www.city-year.org

Clean and Sober Streets
425 Second Street NW,
  2nd Floor North
Washington, DC 20001
(202) 783-7343

Communities in Schools
1199 N. Fairfax Street,
  Suite 300
Alexandria, VA 22314–1436
(703) 519–8999
http://www.cis.org

Common Cause
1250 Connecticut Ave., NW
Washington, DC 20036
(202) 833–1200
http://www.commoncause.org

Congressional Hunger Center
229½ Pennsylvania Ave., SE
Washington, DC 20003
(202) 547–7022
http://www.hungercenter.org

Darrell Green Learning Center
1713 Benning Road, NE, Suite 45
Washington, DC 20002
(202) 398–7902
http://www.darrellgreen.com

Delancy Street Foundation
600 Embarcadero
San Francisco, CA 94107
(415) 957–9800

Do Something
423 W. 55th Street, 8th Floor
New York, NY 10019
(212) 523–1175
http://www.dosomething.org

Echoing Green
198 Madison Ave., 8th Floor
New York, NY 10016
(212) 689–1165
http://www.echoinggreen.org

The Enterprise Foundation
American City Building
10227 Wincopin Circle, Suite 500
Columbia, MD 21044
(410) 964–1230
http://enterprisefoundation.org

The Faith & Politics Institute
110 Maryland Ave., NE,
  Suite 304
Washington, DC 20002
(202) 546–1299
http://www.faith-and-politics.org

Father Flanagan's Boys Town
Boys Town, NE 68010
(402) 498–1111
http://www.boystown.org

Gospel Rescue Ministries
810 Fifth Street, NW
Washington, DC 20001
(202) 842–1731
http://www.gospelrescue.org

**Government Accountability
  Project**
1402 Third Ave., Suite 1215
Seattle, WA 98101
(206) 292–2850 Seattle Office
(202) 408–0034 Wash., DC Office
http://www.whistleblower.org

The Greyston Foundation
21 Park Ave.
Yonkers, NY 10703
(914) 376–3900

Habitat for Humanity
121 Habitat Street
Americus, GA 31709–3498
(912) 924–6935
http://www.habitat.org

The Harvard Mentoring Project
Harvard School of Public Health
677 Huntington Ave.
Boston, MA 02115–6096
(617) 432–1038
http://www.hsph.harvard.edu/chc/

Haven House, Inc.
PO Box 50007
Pasadena, CA 91115–0007
(213) 681–2626

Homeboy Industries
1848 East First Street
Los Angeles, CA 90033
(800) 526–1254
http://homeboyindustries.org

Independent Sector
1200 Eighteenth Street NW,
  Suite 200
Washington, DC 20036
(202) 467–6100
http://www.independentsector.org

Institute for Justice
1717 Pennsylvania Ave. NW,
  Suite 200 South
Washington, DC 20004–2505
(202) 955–1300
http://www.ij.org

International Youth Foundation
32 South Street, Suite 500
Baltimore, MD 21202
(410) 347–1500
http://www.iyfnet.org

Kid Care Houston
PO Box 10441
Houston, TX 77206
(713) 695–5437
http://www.kid-care.org

Kids Hope USA
17011 Hickory Street
Spring Lake, MI 49456
(616) 846–7490
http://www.internationalaid.org

LA's Best
200 N. Main Street, Suite 700
Los Angeles, CA 90012
(213) 847–3681
http://www.lasbest.org

Liberty Hill Foundation
2121 Cloverfield Blvd.,
  Suite 113
Santa Monica, CA 90404
(310) 453–3611
http://www.libertyhill.org

Martha's Table
2114 14th Street, NW
Washington, DC 20009
(202) 328–6608
http://marthastable.org

**The National Center for
  Social Entrepreneurs**
5801 Duluth Street, Suite 310
Minneapolis, MN 55422
(612) 595–0890
http://www.socialentrepreneurs. org

**The National Mentoring
  Partnership**
1400 I Street NW, Suite 850
Washington, DC 20005
(202) 729–4340
http://www.mentoring.org

The Oaks Project
1750 Ocean Park Blvd.,
  Suite 200
Santa Monica, CA 90405
(310) 392–0522
http://www.consumerwatchdog. org

Pioneer Human Services
2200 Rainier Avenue South
Seattle, WA 98144
(206) 322–6645

A Place Called Home
2830 South Central Ave.
Los Angeles, CA 90011
(323) 232–7653
http://www.apch.org

**The Points of Light
  Foundation**
1400 I Street NW, Suite 800
Washington, DC 20005
(202) 729–8000
http://www.pointsoflight.org

The Preamble Center
1737 21st Street, NW
Washington, DC 20009
(202) 265–3263
http://www.preamble.org

Public Campaign
1320 19th Street NW, Suite M–1
Washington, DC 20036
(202) 293–0222
http://www.publicampaign.org

Public Citizen
1600 20th Street, NW
Washington, D.C. 20009
(202) 588–1000
http://www.publiccitizen.org

**The Right Alternative Family
  Center**
4455 Congress Street
Milwaukee, WI 53218
(414) 444–6100

Second Harvest
116 S. Michigan Ave., Suite 4
Chicago, IL 60603
(312) 263–2303
http://www.secondharvest.org

Share Our Strength
733 15th Street NW, Suite 640
Washington, DC 20005
(202) 393–2925
http://strength.com

Shepherd's Gate
1639 Portola Ave.
PO Box 894
Livermore, CA 94550
(925) 443–4283
http://shepgate@.com

Teach for America
20 Exchange Place
New York, NY 10005
(212) 425–9039
http://teachforamerica.org

Teen Challenge USA
3850 South West Loop, #1
San Antonio, TX 78264
(210) 624–2075
http://www.teenchallenge.com

United for a Fair Economy
37 Temple Place, 2nd Floor
Boston, MA 02111
(617) 423–2148
http://www.stw.org

United Way of America
701 N. Fairfax Street
Alexandria, VA 22314–2045
(703) 836–7100
(800) UWA–2757
http://www.unitedway.org

Venice Family Clinic
604 Rose Ave.
Venice, CA 90291
(310) 664–7631

Voice of Calvary Health Center
1065 Tecan Park Circle
Jackson, MS 39209
(601) 355–0241

Voice of Hope
Mailing Address: PO Box 224845
Dallas, TX 75222–4845
Location: 4116 Gentry Street
Dallas, TX 75212
http://www.voiceofhope.org

Youth Service America
1101 15th Street, Suite 200
Washington, DC 20005
(202) 296–2992
http://www.servenet.org

ACKNOWLEDGMENTS

More than any other book I've written, this one changed me—and radicalized me. It's hard to spend months researching and documenting the corruption of American politics and all the myriad ways in which it undermines the public good and increases suffering without wanting to overthrow the government and change the system from its roots.

In the process I lost friends, and I made new ones—William Bradley, Pat Caddell, Marc Cooper, and Ellen Miller among them. They helped in many different ways, including steering me to activists in the field who are struggling every day to bring about reform, and to others like Barbara Osborn and Greg Goldin, who helped with the research. My thanks go to them, as well as to Micah Sifry who, with the help of Richard Winger of *Ballot Access News*, was instrumental in putting together the state-by-state guide to conditions that make reform more likely or more difficult. I'm also thankful to Ethan Nadelmann for his many useful comments on the chapter on the drug war and the drug industry's war on us.

I am grateful to Roy Sekoff, not only for his creativity and editorial input but for the fervor he brought to the subject, and for all the great anecdotes about Zack—his four-year-old son—that he brought to our book conversations.

Many thanks also go to Stephen Sherrill, for all the ways in which he improved the manuscript, and to Claire Fredrick, Adam Daifallah, Kellee McDonald, Andrew Breitbart, Bruce Wilmot, and Jacob Yunker, who helped me meet each succeeding deadline, either by working on the book, or by working on the rest of my life to free me up for the book.

John Herr worked on the book from the first outline to the final draft, bringing to the research task a dedication and insightfulness that were invaluable. We fed each other's compulsiveness, editing and rechecking facts even as the final manuscript was being carted away at 4 A.M. to make an early morning flight to New York.

I also would like to thank those who joined with me in the different crusades featured in the book, especially Harry Shearer, who founded with me the Partnership for a Poll-Free America, and Rep. Dennis Kucinich, without whose help I would not have been able to pursue the truth about the drug industry, anti-depressants, children, and the FDA.

I will always be grateful to Judith Regan not only for setting me on this remarkable and surprising journey, but also for believing in the book from the beginning, and coming up with the title and the idea of launching it with Boston Tea Parties around the country.

I could not have wished for a more superb editor than Cal Morgan, who brought to the book skills ranging from his deep knowledge of American politics to his thesis at Yale on John Steinbeck.

My deep thanks also go to Charles Woods for his imaginative design of the cover, to Maggie McMahon for the unflagging enthusiasm she brought to the book's promotion, and to Vanessa Stich and Andrew Yamato for the many ways they helped the book see the light of day.

As always, I'm grateful to my agent, Richard Pine, on whose judgment I'm so lucky to be able to rely.

No amount of gratitude can adequately honor the debt I owe my mother, Elli. When she was hospitalized for two weeks during the writing of this, the vacuum was felt not just by me but by everyone in my office who missed her endless supply of food—and love.

This book is dedicated to my older daughter, Christina, still eight years away from voting—who, together with her younger sister, Isabella, will always be the most important thing in my life. Let's hope that by the time they are old enough to vote, the act will lift their hearts, not turn their stomachs.